# COINS AND THEIR CITIES

# COINS AND THEIR CITIES

Architecture on the ancient coins of Greece, Rome,
and Palestine

by

## MARTIN JESSOP PRICE

and

## BLUMA L. TRELL

V. C. Vecchi and Sons,
23 Great Smith Street,
London SW1

Wayne State University Press,
Detroit,
Michigan 48202

1977

# ACKNOWLEDGEMENTS

Most of the coins were photographed by M. Price. A few, from the British Museum, were the work of Ray Gardner; those from New York were by Toni Di Biase; those from Athens by J. Kroll; and those from Vienna are courtesy of G. Dembski. Acknowledgements for other photographs are noted in the text.

To the following we are indebted for practical help and encouragement:

Maria Cruz Perez Acorta - A. Adams - Howard L. Adelson - Ekrem Akurgal - Yucel Akyurek - American Council of Learned Societies - C.H. Anscombe - Marion M. Archibald - Vahit Armagan - Ceuziye Artuk - Ibrahim Artuk - Bernard Ashmole - M. Avi-Yonah - K. Ayling - Jean Babelon - Roger S. Bagnall - Donald M. Bailey - Anton Bammer - Richard D. Barnett - P. Bastien - Gabriella Battaglia - Alfred R. Bellinger - L. Belova - Rose Belsky - Seth Benardete - Anna Benjamin - Adolf Berger - Peter Berghaus - Elie J. Bickerman - Margarete Bieber - Albert Billheimer - Ann Birchall - Sylvia Bird - George Blake - Harry Bober - Phyllis Pray Bober — Larissa Bonfante - Annemarie Boning - Lore Borner - E. Bosch - Bernard V. Bothmer - Angie Bowlin - Jean Bram - Richard Breaden - Otto Brendel - Franklin Brill - Blanche R. Brown - Donald F. Brown - Mary Kathleen Brown - Milton Brown - Guido Bruck - Theodore V. Buttrey Jr. - H. Butzmann - Herbert A. Cahn - Francis D. Campbell, Jr. - Marie Cantion - Vincenzo Cappelletti - Jennifer Cargill Thompson - Robert A. G. Carson - Judy Casson - Lionel Casson - S.A. Castle - Betty Chagaris - Mohamed Chaieb - M. Chapoutot-Remadi - Peter Clayton - Robert J. Clements - Howard Comfort - Mary Bryce Comstock - Brian F. Cook - Walter W.S. Cook - H.S.A. Copinger - Peter E. Corbett - Persy Coronis - Eliana Covacich - J.E. Cribb - Paul E. Culley - Raoul Curiel - Stephen Daitz - Ellen Davis - Gunter Dembski - Sylvie de Roquefeuil - Michael DiBiase - Mervin R. Dilts - R.H.M. Dolley - Necati Dolunay - Francoise Dumas - Charles W. Dunmore - Jean Duplessy - Elisbeth Dusenbery - John Dusenbery - Leslie A. Elam - Ellen Epstein - Halek Ergulec - Kenan T. Erim - E. Erxleben - Joan M. Fagerlie - Beatrice Farwell - Otto Feld - David H. Filipek - M.I. Finley - Nezih Firatli - Joan Fisher - Louis Foucher - Peter F. Franke - Ray Gardner - Georg Gaster - Theodor H. Gaster - Theodore Gerassimov - Jean-Baptiste Giard - J. Frank Gilliam - Einar Gjerstad - Theresa Goell - Tuncay Goynu - Bernard Goldman - Norma Goldman - Cyrus H. Gordon - Isabel S. Gordon - Ralph Gordon - Claireve Grandjouan - Michael Grant - Beatrice Green - Tamara Green - Philip Grierson - Konrad Gries - Henry Grunthal - Hans. G. Guterbock - Tony Hackens - George M.A. Hanfmann - Jacob Hammer - Susan Handler - William Owen Hassell - Walter Havernick - Denys E.L. Haynes - Sybil Haynes - Richard M. Haywood - Rex Heaton-Sessions — Fritz M. Heichelheim - Adelheid Heimann - Charles A. Hersh - Ernest L. Hettich - R.A. Higgins - Abraham Holtz - Eduard Holzmair - L. Hooley - K.A. Howes - Harald Ingholt - H.W. Janson - Josephe Jaquiot - G. Kenneth Jenkins - Nina Jidejian - Jotham Johnson - F. Elmore Jones - Hans Jucker Leo Kadman - Baruch Kanael - Balogs Kapossy - Vassos Karageorghis - Phyllis Katz - Ranon Katzoff - Jean Keith - John P.C. Kent - J. Alexander Kerns - Arie Kindler - Fred S. Kleiner - Ernst W. Klimowsky - Bernard Koch - Guenter H. Kopcke - Marie Kozakiewicz - Dya Kozaman - Colin M. Kraay - Aleksandra Krzyzanowska - Casper J. Kraemer, Jr. - John H. Kroll - George L. Kustas — Harald Kuthmann - H. Kwaku - Merrill Lake - Paul Lampl - Robin Laurence - Marcel LeGlay - Karl Lehmann - Phyllis W. Lehmann - Georges Le Rider - Annalina Levi - Mario Levi - Harry Levy - Helen Lewis - Naphtali Lewis - Samuel Lieberman - Stephen Liberman - Katherine Linnet - Kenneth Linser - Elaine Loeffler - Pamela Long - Stanislaw Lorentz - Iris Love - Nicholas M. Lowick - Denit Lowry - Heath W. Lowry - David W. Macdowall - James R. McCredie - Raymond E. Main - Monique Mainjonet - Lawrence J. Majewski - Rose Mangini - Joan S. Martin - Philip Mayerson - R. Medden - Gloria S. Merker - Erwin Merker - Y. Meshorer - David M. Metcalf - William E. Metcalf - Henri Metzger - Maria Angeles Mezquiriz - Melanie Mihalink - George C. Miles - Helen Mitchell Brown - David Gordon Mitten - Otto Morkholm - Sawyer McA. Mosser - Wolfgang Mueller - Oscar White Muscarella - Ernest Nash - Paul M.F. Naster - Rudolf Naumann - L. Nemeskal - Edward T. Newell - New York University Graduate School of Arts & Science Research Fund — Helene Nicolet - Sidney P. Noe - Emanuela Nohejlova-Pratova - Geoffrey H. North - Edward L. Ochsenschlager - Mando Oeconomidou - Nekriman Olcay - Saadet Onat-Taner - David R. Owen - Francis Paar - Gaetano Panazza - Erwin Panofsky - Klaus Parlasca - Andre Parrot - Efrem Pegan — Francis E. Peters - Charles Picard - Karl Pink - Hugh Plommer - A. Poljakov - J. Graham Pollard - Enrica Pozzi - S.H. Prescott - James B. Pritchard - U. Pschlow - Zelko Rahkic - Franklin Ray - Gisela M.A. Richter - Anne S. Robertson - Jerry M. Robinson - Elisabeth Rohde - Claire Rosen - Edward Rosen - Lucy F. Sanlder - Nada Saporiti - Serge Sauneron - Gert Schiff - A. Arthur Schiller - Ursula Schoenheim - Alan Schulman - Sabine Schultz - H.D. Schultz - Willy Schwabacher - Nora E. Scott - Henri Seyrig — Stuart Shaw - Theresa Shirer - Beulah P. Shonnard - Stephen Skouronek - Morton Smith - William H. Stahl - Jarmila Stepkova - Donald E. Strong - Meriwether Stuart - Arthur Suhle - Mate Suic - Richard G. Summers - C.H.V. Sutherland - Geroge F. Taylor - Abdelgelil Temimi - Raci Temizer - Margaret Thompson - Mary Lee Thompson - Ibrahim Tozen - Joseph B. Trapp - Franz Unterkirche - Edibe Uzunoglu - Cornelius C. Vermeule III - Irene Varoucha-Christodoulopoulos - Hans von Aulock - Peter von Blanckenhagen - Paul von Khrum - Nancy M. Waggoner - Charles Walker - J.B. Ward-Perkins - Hans Weber - Gladys D. Weinberg - Saul Weinberg - Bartlett Wells - C. Bradford Welles - Edna Williamson - Jordanka Youroukova - Jacques Yvon - Fritz Zink - A.N. Zadocks-Jitta

# To the two M's

ISBN 0—8143—1586—0.

Printed in England by the Friary Press Ltd., Dorchester and London

# CONTENTS

# LIST OF COLOUR PLATES

# PREFACE

Ancient coins illustrate more than a thousand different buildings most of which are now lost without trace. We tend to forget that a line of foundation stones is all that remains of the human effort of planning and labour which goes into the erection of an architectural monument; and it is therefore salutary to begin this study by comparing extracts from letters sent by a provincial governor to the emperor at Rome, dealing with the construction of just such buildings as appear on the coins. The letters come from the interesting correspondence of Pliny the Younger, while he was governor of the province of Bithynia and Pontus in Asia Minor, about A.D. 110, and they show the important part that such large building projects played in the day to day life of the Roman governors; and they show equally the age-old incompetence and self-seeking of local administrators.

### Pliny to the Emperor Trajan (Book X, letter 37):

"Sire, the people of Nicomedeia have spent 3,318,000 sestertii on an aqueduct which they abandoned before it was completed, and it has now been demolished. They then voted another 200,000 sestertii towards another aqueduct; but this too has been abandoned; and so even after such large amounts have been squandered to no effect, there is still need for a great outlay if they are to have a water supply...."

### Trajan to Pliny (Book X, 38):

"You must make sure that the citizens of Nicomedeia have a water supply; I am sure that you will apply yourself diligently to providing for what has to be done. But equally you should set up an enquiry to find who is responsible for such waste of public funds to date, in case certain individuals are profiting from starting and abandoning aqueducts. Let me know the findings of the enquiry."

### Pliny to the Emperor Trajan (Book X, 39):

"Sire, the theatre at Nicaea, although still unfinished, is now well advanced; but I am told that the cost has been ten million sestertii (I have not been able to examine the accounts), and I am afraid that this has been wasted. The building is sinking, and cracks have appeared, either because the subsoil is too soft, or because the stone itself is too poor and friable....A number of additions have also been promised by private individuals, such as colonnades around the theatre and an arcade above the auditorium; and now all these are delayed until work can be completed on the main structure.

Also at Nicaea, the citizens have begun to rebuild the gymnasium which was destroyed by fire before my arrival; but they plan it on a much larger and more extensive scale that before, and have already spent a large sum. Yet there is a danger that it may be to no avail, since it has been poorly and too openly planned.....

The citizens of Claudiopolis are also excavating rather than building a huge bath complex in a natural hollow at the foot of a mountain...

I must therefore request you to send an architect to inspect both the theatre and the bath..."

**Trajan to Pliny (Book X, 40):**

"You are in the best position to make the decision about what must happen to the unfinished theatre at Nicaea. It will be sufficient for me to know your decision.... These Greeks are very lavish on their gymnasia, and perhaps the Nicaeans were too ambitious in their building scheme. They must be content with one which suits their needs. Again it is you who must decide on the future of the bath at Claudiopolis, which you state in your letter to have been started on an unsuitable site. You can have no lack of architects. Every province has a number of skilled and experienced men; and you should not think that they can be sent out more quickly from Rome, when they usually come to us anyway from Greek lands."

Such were some of the building schemes with which Pliny had to deal during his governorship in Bithynia. The main gymnasium and a large theatre, possibly those of which Pliny was writing, are still to be seen at Nicaea. Yet the literary and archaeological evidence, although of paramount importance is in some ways more limited than that of the miniature buildings found on the coins, and it is to these that we must turn for a general view of many of the most important pieces of architecture in the Roman empire.

This book is mainly concerned with the coins of the provincial cities of the Roman empire which have never previously been collected in this way. The coins of Rome herself, on the other hand, are readily available for study in the general books on Rome listed in the bibliography; and we have therefore selected but a few examples to show their fine contribution to the study of the architecture of that city. We make no apology for this, since the number and variety of the provincial issues have never been recognized, whereas the coins of Rome, though much fewer in number, are better known.

Each building represented in the list at the back of this book could itself be the subject for a study with comparative archaeological and literary material. We have selected only a few cities to demonstrate how the coins may be studied, limiting ourselves to the problems of architectural details; but it will be clear that these in turn lead to questions of function and ritual which would require a separate study.

Fig. 285

Fig. 277

*Fig. 277 SIDON: The sanctuary of Astarte/Europe. BM.*
*Fig. 285 CAPITOLIAS: Gateway to the sanctuary of Zeus. BM.*

Fig. 26

Fig. 71

Fig. 86

Fig. 182

Fig. 26 NICOPOLIS AD ISTRUM: City gate with temple visible within, and above, a large public building. BM.

Fig. 71 NEOCAESAREA, Pontus : Portico with city goddess. BM.

Fig. 86 AUGUSTA TRAIANA : Military gateway. Berlin

Fig. 182 NICAEA: Gate. BM.

# ON THE IMPORTANCE OF COINS FOR THE HISTORY
# OF ANCIENT ARCHITECTURE

"Hundreds of thousands of coins.... have revealed to us not only the external appearance of many ancient cities but also the main feature of every aspect of their life — their walls, streets, gates, and public and private buildings...."
M. Rostovtzeff

This is the first attempt to collect in one place the buildings which appear on ancient coins. T.L. Donaldson's pioneering *Architectura Numismatica*, the only other such work in this field, published in 1859 and reprinted in 1966, was written before scientific archaeology became an important discipline for the study of the ancient world. It gives little idea of the amazing variety and detail presented by the coins. With the increasing specialization of modern times, coins have become the province of the numismatist, whose interests, often inward looking, have tended to stray away from other disciplines such as epigraphy, sculpture, and architecture. On the other hand the archaeologist for his part has tended to ignore or misuse such evidence as is offered by the coins, so that text books on architecture are produced without even a reference to the coins. This book is dedicated to healing this breach, and to showing the contribution which can be made to our knowledge of ancient architecture by studying the contemporary views of buildings as they are found on the coins. A glance at the illustrations will show the enormous variety of buildings for the very existence of which the coins are now the only evidence. Even when a building has been excavated the coins are often the only evidence for the superstructure, the part most vulnerable to act of God and man.

In the past bronze coins have often been neglected. Their utilitarian function may not have been thought worthy of a place in the history of art: They become more worn, and they corrode more easily than coins of precious metals. Yet architectural types are usually found on bronzes, and they exist today in thousands of examples. Indeed most of the 800 different buildings found on Greek coins occur on bronze issues of the cities of the Roman empire. Such coins are not only overlooked by many collectors, but are normally published only in academic works. They are to be found scattered throughout a labyrinth of books, articles, and catalogues which would daunt all but the most courageous reader. But when, as in this book, a single theme is pursued, and salient information is extracted, the importance and fascination of the coins become at once apparent. Each coin die was hand-cut by an engraver; each engraver was an artist (even if sometimes a bad artist!); and each artist had a different view of the three-dimensional building which he was transferring to the two-dimensional plane of a miniature relief sculpture. Since the buildings illustrated on

15

*Fig. 1 CYNAETHA, Peloponnese: View of the main buildings in the city (Caracalla A.D. 198–211) Berlin.*

*Fig. 2 BURA, Peloponnese: View of the city with the oracle of Heracles below (Geta A.D. 198–211) Athens.*

*Fig. 3 PERGAMUM, Asia: Temple of Zeus Philios and Trajan (Trajan A.D. 98–117) Paris.*

*Fig. 5 ODESSUS, Moesia: Temple of Fortuna (Gordian III A.D. 238–244) BM. See colour plate p.32.*

*Fig. 4. GYTHEION, Peloponnese: Temple of Asclepius (Septimius Severus A.D. 193–211) BM.*

16

ancient coins are usually no longer extant, each variation becomes of the utmost Fig.
importance. One artist will emphasize the general appearance of the facade of the
building; another will put it in its natural setting, on top of a mountain or in a wooded
grove; another will give details of the superstructure, or of the column capitals, or of
the cult image. In each case the artist was concerned to identify for those who were to
handle the coins, the particular building in the city depicted; and to achieve this, he
was bound to use certain forms of shorthand. Only with the full recognition of
commonly used 'conventions' can we compare the coins with such literary or
archaeological information as may exist, and so build up a picture of any particular
building.

In the second century A.D. Pausanias travelled throughout southern Greece and he
has left us his famous descriptive itinerary, for which the coins make a poignant
commentary. When he arrived in Arcadia, he visited the town of Cynaetha of which   1
nothing now remains, and saw there among other things a stoa, sanctuary, and tree.
The very stoa, sanctuary, and tree are depicted on the only known coin of the city. At
neighbouring Bura, in Achaea, he also visited the oracle of Heracles, situated in the   2
cave which may today contain the monastery of Mega Spilion; and this too is recorded
on a coin, on the hillside below the town.

*Fig. 6 AMASEIA, Pontus: Temple of Tyche with the facade removed to emphasize the cult image (Caracalla A.D. 209) BM.*

*Fig. 7 HERACLEA PONTICA, Bithynia: Temple of Roma with the facade opened to reveal the inner shrine (Philip I A.D. 244–249) BM.*

*Fig. 8– 9 SEBASTOPOLIS– HERACLEOPOLIS, Pontus:*
*Sanctuary of Heracles. Two projecting wings flank a courtyard*
*to which access is restricted by a prominent barrier.*
*8 (Caracalla A.D. 198– 211) Paris.*
*9 Detail. (Julia Domna A.D. 193– 211) Berlin.*

18

## Artists' conventions

There are those who condemn the coins as stylized representations of buildings with Fig.
little use in the study of architecture; but the illustrations of this book provide a
sufficient reply. Carefully delineated architectural details should particularly be
noticed, such as the sculptured drums at the base of the columns of the temple of 221
Artemis at Ephesus, the parotids flanking the steps in front of the temple of Trajan at 3
Pergamum, and the great stairway in front of the temple of Jupiter at Baalbek. All 278
these can be checked against the existing remains of the buildings to witness to the
accuracy of the impressions, however sketchy, given by the coins; and in the many
cases where nothing now remains, such details, even on worn or badly preserved coins,
as half fluted or spiral fluted columns, windows in the pediment, stairways, and
colonnades around the sanctuary, may be all important in allowing an accurate
reconstruction of the architecture. It should however be stressed that variations in
detail at different times need not imply a change in the architecture of the actual
building.

At the same time, the die-maker could show in a manner that would baffle the 4—7
modern photographer, parts both of the interior and of the exterior of a building. It
was not necessary for purposes of identification to show the exact number of columns
on the facade of a temple; it sufficed merely to indicate that there was a columned
portico. The columns could be reduced so that the engraver could place in the facade
the cult image, which actually stood in the interior of the temple. Equally commonly,
the space between the central columns was widened to accomodate the image which
usually identifies the shrine with no possible ambiguity; and the artist achieves this
identification in a way that would suggest the age-old custom of epiphany, a god
appearing in person before his worshippers. On the other hand the careful artist would
never show more than the actual number of columns; and so with a long series of coins,
we can usually deduce how many columns a building had. On some coins the architrave
of the facade was completely omitted by the die engraver, the better to show on the
facade the cult image. Furthermore many coins show the architrave of the temple
arched to present an architectural form known as an arcuated lintel. Although this is 361—
commonly found on coins of Syria and Anatolia, in the remains of actual buildings it is 377
extremely rare. The one example on coins which can be paralleled with existing
remains is the famous gate to the sanctuary of Jupiter at Baalbek. It seems therefore 284
impossible that all the coins with arcuated lintel illustrate buildings with that actual
architectural form — indeed sometimes the same building is shown with and without
the arch. It may be supposed that the engraver was normally using this as a device to
reflect the domed baldachino or arched shell-in-niche which covered the cult image
within the temple. This could be brought to the facade for the same reason that the
architrave was sometimes omitted — the better to show the cult image. Much more
rarely three 'interior' arches are also brought out to the facade with the cult images to 116
show that a triad of deities was worshipped, and that the cella was divided into three
chapels. Three niches, sometimes abbreviated to one, appear on the 'stoa' of 8—9
Sebastopolis, Pontus. Heracles, who alone is shown, was here worshipped in a
sanctuary of most unusual form, divided into three separate parts. As a result of the

Fig. 10 CAESAREA PANIAS, Syria: Sanctuary of Pan (Julia Maesa A.D. 218–225) Berlin.

Fig. 11 CAESAREA PANIAS, Syria: Grotto and sanctuary of Pan (Elagabalus A.D. 218–222) BM.

Fig. 12 CAESAREA PANIAS, Syria: Grotto of Pan (Elagabalus A.D. 218–222) Berlin.

Fig. 13 CYME, Asia: Aedicula of Artemis, the architrave supported by Caryatids (Nerva A.D. 96–98) BM.

Fig. 14 CAESAREA AD LIBANUM, Syria: Aedicula of Artemis, the arch supported by Caryatids (Elagabalus A.D. 218–222) Paris.

*Fig. 16 ALEXANDRIA, Egypt:*
*Combined view of gate and altar*
*(Hadrian A.D. 117–138) Paris.*

*Fig. 15 HADRIANOPOLIS, Asia: Gate to an altar court*
*(Hadrian A.D.117–138) Berlin*

different coin types of Caesarea Panias in Palestine, we can restore the sacred precinct $^{Fig.}$ of Pan. In one type the statue of the god appears in a circular courtyard, clearly a $_{10-12}$ bird's eye view of his sanctuary; in another he appears in a grotto above the sacred temenos; and in the third, the grotto alone is shown so that Pan may be better seen within his mountain home.

While a baldachino or aedicula is often brought out to the facade of a temple, it also $_{13-14}$ appears alone to represent the whole building. The artist allows the essential part, the holy of holies, to stand for the whole, so that in some cases the aedicula may even be an abbreviated view of the temple building itself. The recognition that interior details were deliberately brought to the exterior has facilitated our interpretation of many monuments.

In some cases, as at Amaseia and at Emisa, an altar stands for the cult image, $_{163}$ suggesting that the altar itself was the focal point of the worship and this in turn $_{301}$ implies that it stood in an open altar court. Elsewhere, we must peer, as it were, through the facade of a gate to understand the arrangement of the court behind. The altar of the great court at Pergamum, which is known to have been open to the skies, is $_{217}$ placed by the die-engraver between the columns of the monumental entrance. The gate to the court at Neocaesarea is shown with a variety of statues and sacred objects, in $_{165-}$ addition to the altar, within the facade. Hadrianopolis offers an example similar to that $_{172}$ of Pergamum. The stepped altar, while it may have stood at a considerable distance $_{15}$ from the gate, is shown between the centre columns. Most unusual is the combination of gate and altar at Alexandria in which the flaming altar appears to form the top part $_{16}$ of a columned portico. In fact, the figure of Tyche stands between the columns to identify the cult of the sanctuary, and the architrave of the 'gate' forms the top of a near eastern 'horned' altar.

21

Fig. 17 APERLAE, Lycia: Gate to an altar court (Gordian III A.D. 238– 244) Berlin.

Fig. 18 APERLAE, Lycia: Bird's eye view of the altar court (Gordian III A.D. 238– 244) Berlin.

Fig. 18A Detail of fig. 18.

22

*Fig. 19 PHILOMELIUM, Asia: Temple of Dionysus and hexagonal court (Otacilia Severa A.D. 244–249) Trell collection.*

*Fig. 20 CYME, Asia: The gymnasium (Gordian III A.D. 238–244) BM.*

*Fig. 21 CNOSSUS, Crete: The labyrinth (3rd Cent. B.C.) BM.*

*Fig. 22 ZEUGMA, Commagene: Sanctuary of Zeus on the Acropolis (Philip II A.D. 244–249) BM.*

## Perspective

<sup></sup>

17—18 At Aperlae in Lycia we find not only a facade with the altar replacing the cult image, but also another coin which gives a bird's eye view of the court to show the altar in the centre and a columned arcade around. Similarly at Byblos, the walls of the court have been opened to bring out the splendid altar surmounted by its sacred stone. Such use of perspective which makes part of the design almost a ground plan appears in many views of harbours both on Roman and Greek coins. At Philomelium the hexagonal court in which the temple stood is shown merely as a line. The agora at Corinth with the temple arranged at the central point and the gymnasium at Cyme are particularly good examples; and a 'ground plan' is the obvious way to depict the legendary labyrinth at Cnossus.

A different kind of bird's eye view in which the whole of the front is also depicted is even more impressive. At Zeugma, the temple of Zeus certainly stood at the top of the mountain, with a portico at the foot, much as on Mt. Gerizim in Syria; but the colonnades placed on the coins at either side of the mountain, may well represent the courtyard in which the temple actually stood. In this case the artist has combined a perspective view of temple, forecourt, mountain, and portico into a single design. More immediately intelligible are the Colosseum at Rome, which is so open to the skies that one can all but see the performance, and the forum at Laodicea where even the paving stones are visible.

Views of whole cities are shown on some coins, where the most important piece of architecture of the city, as a bastion of the Roman empire, was the wall that protected it against the invading Dacians or Goths. At Bizya and Marcianopolis, for example, the interesting details foreshadow later Byzantine art. The Greek engravers included the exquisite decorations of gates and towers, and placed within the walls stoas, temples, and other buildings.

An extreme variation of this type of view is a convention which had its roots in earliest Mesopotamia. This was to place above what actually stood behind. Just as the mediaeval artist arranged his angels in ranks one above the other, the better to show them, so the die maker placed one monument above the other. Errors of interpretation have often been made as the result of not recognizing the convention. At Sidon, a temple building is shown supported by two colossal columns, which would be inconceivable as an actual architectural structure. The temple naturally stood behind the columns which thus formed the entrance to the forecourt. In the case of Nicopolis ad Istrum, we must assume that the stoa-like building that weighs so heavily on a city gate, actually stood behind it; and through the gate we can see the facade of another building beyond. It is worth noting that the early die engraver at Sidon, who showed a ship immediately in front of the walls, could not give as many details as the later artists. Engravers certainly had difficulties with such multiple planes, but they could be overcome. An examination of the coin of Apollonia in Caria shows that the hands of the deities actually extend in front of the columns, and at Docimeum, a horseman appears from behind a column. There are some further remarkable representations of buildings in three-quarter view which almost seem to anticipate Uccello.

24

*Fig. 23 LAODICEA, Asia: The Roman Forum. A temple, probably of the imperial cult, stands at the head of the forum, and the emperor is seen bestowing honours on the leading citizens (Caracalla A.D. 211–217) Courtesy Museum of Fine Arts, Boston. See colour plate p. 31*

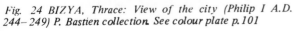

*Fig. 24 BIZYA, Thrace: View of the city (Philip I A.D. 244–249) P. Bastien collection. See colour plate p. 101*

*Fig. 25 MARCIANOPOLIS, Thrace: View of the city (Gordian III A.D. 238–244) Sofia.*

*Fig. 26 NICOPOLIS AD ISTRUM. Moesia: Detail showing city gate with temple visible within, and above, a large public building, probably a sanctuary (Septimius Severus A.D. 192–211) B.M. See colour plate p.49*

*Fig. 27 APOLLONIA SALBACE, Asia: Temple of Apollo (Gallienus A.D. 253–268) Paris.*

*Fig. 28 DOCIMEUM, Asia: Heroon? (early 3rd cent. A.D.) Vienna.*

26

*Topography*

Trees added to the scenes with temples at many towns in Greece emphasize the fact that the temples were placed in sacred groves, and thus reflect Greco-Roman pastoral painting. We should distinguish between the purely topographical elements which underline the position of the building within the city, and sacred trees actually worshipped for themselves, as part of the cult ceremonies, which did not necessarily stand in a pastoral setting. The former, more often found on purely Greek coins, would 29 include mountain scenes such as at Pautalia and Corinth; but trees as sacred objects 135 beside an altar or within an enclosure are also found in many places.

On the other hand the engraver often depicts two or more buildings on a single coin, 30 without any intention of suggesting a geographical relationship within the city. This is 446 done particularly when the "neocorate" temples are depicted, temples dedicated to the 458 imperial cult, or to an important cult shared by the whole province which earned for the city the coveted title "neocoros." Although the architecture of such little representations of two or more buildings is very schematic, every attempt is made to identify each building, sometimes with the name of the emperor worshipped in the pediment, and therefore the coins play an important role in the history of the city.

*Fig. 29 PAUTALIA, Thrace: View of sacred buildings and a cave within the sanctuary of the mountain (Macrinus A.D. 217–218) Vienna.*

27

*Fig. 30 PERGAMUM, Asia: The neocorate temples to Augustus, Caracalla, and Trajan with the names inscribed in the pediments (Caracalla A.D. 211–217) ANS.*

*Fig. 31 SARDIS, Asia: The sanctuary of Aphrodite Paphia, probably a building within the city of Sardis (Hadrian A.D. 117–138) BM.*

*Fig. 32 EUMENEIA, Asia: The temple of Artemis Ephesia. Note the prominent sculptured bases of the columns, and the figures in the pediment. (Hadrian A.D. 117–138) BM. See colour plate p.120*

*Fig. 33 ALEXANDRIA, Egypt: An arch with prominent sculptured figure in relief on one side, copied from a Roman coin of Nero (Trajan A.D. 103) Paris.*

28

*Fig. 34 TYRE, Phoenicia: The Phoenician Queen Dido supervising the building of Carthage (Gordian III 238–244) BM.*

*Fig. 35 AEGEAE, Cilicia: Cadmus, the brother of Europa, in front of the gate of Thebes where he later settled (Macrinus A.D. 217–218) Paris.*

*Fig. 36 ABYDUS, Asia: Leander swimming to Hero's tower at Sestos, leaving his clothes and weapons on the Asian shore of the Hellespont (Commodus c.A.D. 177) BM.*

Fig. 37 ILICI, Spain: Temple with dedication on the architrave to Juno (Augustus 31 B.C.–A.D. 14) BM.

Fig. 38 MAURETANIA: Gate to a sanctuary with three Atlas Caryatids; above three horned altars decorated with figures (Juba I 60–46 B.C.) Paris.

Fig. 39 CHALCIS, Euboea: Shrine of Oriental form with flat roof in which sacred baetyl (1st cent. A.D.) BM.

Fig. 23

*Fig. 23 LAODICEA, Asia : Roman forum. Berlin.*

Fig. 5

Fig. 326

Fig. 238

Fig. 327

Fig. 5 ODESSUS: Temple of Fortune. BM.
Fig. 326 SMYRNA: Octastyle temple with figures decorating the parotids (Domitian A.D.81 – 98) Berlin.
Fig. 238 TRIPOLIS: Phoenicia: The temple of Zeus Hagios with gate. (Caracalla A.D. 212) BM.
Fig. 327 PERGAMUM: Temple of Asclepius (Commodus A.D. 175–177) BM.

If the apparent geographical relationship within the city is illusory, did the artist Fig.
ever represent monuments that were located beyond the limits of the mint city? At
Pergamum and Sardis, shrines of Paphian Aphrodite are shown identical with her shrine 31, 268
at Paphos in Cyprus. Does this mean that such shrines actually stood within the cities, 266
or that in celebrating the cult on the coins the artists chose to depict her well-known 32
shrine hundreds of miles away? Again, at Eumeneia, we find an exact copy of the great
temple of Artemis at Ephesus. Could such a small city afford to build so extravagant a
building, or was this simply a die engraver's reference to the cult itself? Silver
cistophori issued by the provinces illustrate some local buildings, but at least two show 109, 122
buildings at Rome and not within the province — the temple of Mars Ultor and the
temple of the Capitol; and a coin of Alexandria similarly copies a Roman coin type to 33
illustrate the arch of Nero which actually stood at Rome. There are several other such 107
exceptions, but as a general rule it is buildings within the city that are illustrated on
local coins.

There are certain mythological scenes which include buildings historically long
removed from the artists of the Roman world — Dido supervising the walls of Carthage, 34
Cadmus in front of the walls of Thebes, Hero awaiting her Leander in a tower at 35
Sestos. With these we may also link the temple of Jehovah at Jerusalem which appears 36
on coins sixty years after its destruction by the Romans. Furthermore, a recent study 306
by Konrad Kraft of imperial coins of Asia Minor has led to the surprising theory that
many cities did not mint their own coins, and that they even borrowed types, of little
relevance to the city, from a central "mint" often hundreds of miles away! Much more
evidence, however, will be needed before his conclusions become acceptable, but as far
as buildings are concerned, while we may admit that stylized representations could be
the result of such a minting practice, there is generally such close attention to detail,
and so many obvious attempts to identify the building, that we must assume that in
such instances the coins usually depict an actual piece of architecture within the city.

*Eastern influences*

With few exceptions therefore the monuments on the coins must have been, in the
main, buildings situated within the mint city, and they illustrate particularly the
influence of oriental forms in the Greek and Roman world. In the West, local coinage
was suppressed in the mid 1st century A.D. and so there is little to show of the great
cities of Africa and Spain. Excavations in these areas, however, have revealed more
about Phoenician architecture than excavations in Phoenicia itself. In Syria and
Anatolia by contrast, our knowledge of ancient buildings derives less from excavation
than it does from the coins which give us a fascinating picture of oriental architecture
and show its influence in the West. The coins indicate the three part division of the
temple cella, associated with the worship of a triad of deities. This is found in the 115—7,
Capitolium in Rome and in the temple of Aphrodite at Paphos, both with ancient 266
traditions which, it is plausible to assume, had a common origin in the East. Spanish 37
coins emphasize the sacred portal; North African coins have the oriental flat roof with 38
horned altars, caryatids, and narrow stairways. Similarly oriental characteristics are
found on coins attributed to Chalcis in Euboea, Greece, where the cult object is a 39

*Fig.40 TYRE, Phoenicia: Portable shrine fitted with carry bars at its base, a typically oriental style of building (Volusian A.D. 251–253). Paris.*

Fig.
17—8 sacred stone or baetyl and the roof is decorated with crenellations. The appearance of a typically Semitic altar court on the coins of Aperlae in Lycia is also significant for new discoveries in the area. Added to the recent excavation of a shrine divided into three sections and of another that was both a tomb and a sacred building, it is now clear that Lycia was in some significant ways closer to north Syria than to the Greek world.

Some of these architectural conventions have parallels in earliest Mesopotamia and Egypt, such as windows in the upper storey of temple facades, and processional
40 shrines. One class of portable shrine found on coins, with flat roof and unmistakably
459—70 Eastern decorations underlines the oriental origin of such a class of shrines although
41 coins depict it as far west as Megara in Greece. At Antioch, Syria, only the carry bars at
42 the base of the shrine identify it as a portable shrine to be carried in procession through the streets of the city.

Art historians interested in the post-Roman period will be surprised to know that
43 the prototype of Islam's mihrab can be found on the coins of Damascus, the city where one of Islam's first mosques was constructed. The coins actually show the shell-in-arch of the mihrab, a motif which had a wide history in the Graeco-Roman world. On this coin Tyche appears to be seated on the steps of the temple with the river god at her feet; but it must be clear to all that the artist has combined the cult image in its niche with the facade of the temple. Similarly, windows in the pediments of ancient temples
230 were adopted by the Syrian churches of the 5th and 6th centuries A.D. which in turn directly influenced Romanesque architecture. The towers that are found on the
285, 288 temples of Capitolias and Abila had their origin in the ancient East, and their mediaeval descendants in the towers that decorate Notre Dame and Canterbury cathedrals. Again,
44 the delightful convention of a sacred person holding a shrine — whether an ancient deity or a Christian saint — existed in the ancient Near East and the mediaeval West.
416 How true it is that in all art and culture everything derives from the East — omnia ex oriente.

34

*Fig. 41 MEGARA, Greece: Statue of Demeter carried in a processional shrine on a horse-drawn waggon (Septimius Severus A.D. 193–211) ANS.*

*Fig. 42 ANTIOCH, Syria: Shrine of the goddess Tyche (Fortuna) fitted with carry-bars at its base (Trebonianus Gallus A.D. 251–253) Trell collection.*

*Fig. 43 DAMASCUS, Syria: Temple of Tyche with shell decoration in the pediment (Macrinus A.D. 217–218) Paris.*

*Fig. 44 PERINTHUS, Thrace: Tyche holding the two neocorate temples of the city (Alexander Severus A.D. 222–235) Paris.*

*Fig. 47 EPIDAURUS, Peloponnese: Round shrine of Elpis, probably the tholos found in the excavations of the sanctuary of Asclepius (Antoninus Pius A.D. 138–161) Berlin.*

## Round Buildings

Round buildings, although they are rare on coins as well as in excavation sites, appear surprisingly often on coins of mainland Greek cities. The round buildings in the sacred sanctuary of Cyzicus were copies of the 'Arsinoeion' of Greek Samothrace; and no less than three round buildings appear on the coins of the cities of the Argolid Argos, Troezen, and Epidaurus. At Epidaurus the round shrine of Elpis is almost certainly the famous round 'tholos' found in the excavations of the sanctuary, the purpose of which is much disputed. From Nicopolis in Epirus comes a domed 'heroon', a most unusual two storey building which cannot yet be identified with certainty. It is clear that the round building had no place in a truly 'oriental' sanctuary, although by no means all examples are from mainland Greece. At Prusa in Bithynia there is a fine illustration of such a round temple, and others may be discerned at Philomelium and Side.

*Fig.*

*198–202*

*45–47*

*48*

*49*

*19*

*470*

36

*Fig. 45 ARGOS, Peloponnese: Round shrine of Athena on a podium (Antoninus Pius A.D. 238–161) BM.*

*Fig. 46 TROEZEN, Peloponnese: Round temple with colonnade and prominent closed doors (Commodus A.D. 177–192) Berlin.*

47

*Fig. 48 NICOPOLIS, Epirus: Detail of 'Heroon'. The structure is of two stories with elaborate lantern (Faustina I c.A.D. 141) Paris.*

*Fig. 49 PRUSA AD OLYMPUM, Bithynia: Sacrifice at an altar in front of a round shrine on podium, with prominent conical roof (Geta A.D. 211–212) Paris. See colour plate p.102*

37

Fig. 50 PERSIS: Sacred 'fire-temple' (3rd cent. B.C.) BM.

Fig. 51 PERSIS: Sacred Portal to the temple surmounted by three horned altars (3rd cent. B.C.) BM.

Fig. 52 ETENNA, Pisidia: Caduceus monument flanked by two cult statues (Septimius Severus A.D. 193–211) BM.

Fig. 53 EPHESUS, Asia: Isis Pharia and a flaming beacon (Gordian III A.D. 238–244) Paris.

### Tower-altar-shrines

A new class of ancient monument was only recently recognized when the so-called tower-altar was excavated in the sacred court of the temple complex at Baalbek. A similar altar can be seen on the coins of Persis which in turn has been equated with the famous fire "temple" near Persepolis. A more striking equation should be made between the horned altars on the flat roof of the shrine of Persis and the similar details on the coins of Juba I of Mauretania in Africa. Many other altar-shrines should be added to the list — the altars of Bostra, Parium, Selge, the sanctuary at Sagalassus, and the stele monument on the coins of Etenna, and even the flaming towers at Ephesus and Magnesia and the "pyres" of Roman coinage. The relationship between the tower-altar-shrine and a tomb shrine such as the Mausoleum at Halicarnassus is now the subject of fascinating speculation. The coins will play a part in that inquiry.

*Margin notes: Fig. 50—51, 38, 257, 52—53*

38

*Fig. 54 CAESAREA, Cappadocia: Mount Argaeus placed on an altar within the temple (Commodus A.D. 177–192) Paris.*

*Fig. 56 PELLA, Syria: View of the city with the great temple terrace crowning the Acropolis (Commodus A.D. 177–192) Paris. See colour plate p. 172.*

*Fig. 55 NEAPOLIS, Syria: Mount Gerizim in sacred procession with the stone of Elagabal from Emisa on a carriage drawn by four horses (Elagabalus A.D. 218–222) B.M.*

## Sacred Mountain sanctuaries

Eastern cities worshipped many sacred objects, from the simple stone to the highest mountain, and we are shown such objects on the coins. The Bible gives testimony of very early sacred mountains and there is certainly no ambiguity about the testimony of the coins: Mt. Argaeus is placed on an altar between the columns of a temple; Mt. Gerizim is found in a procession with horses. In both cases the mountain itself is the cult object. On other coins, the mountain appears decorated with an altar or a temple at its top in addition to sacred ways and other sacred buildings — at Zela, Zeugma, Baalbek and many other cities. The coins clearly show that the "bamah" of the Old Testament was literally a "High Place" like the ziggurat, which as a mountain substitute was needed to make the temple sacred. Roman architectural forms are naturally combined with the eastern traditions. The substructure of the temples shown on the coins of Zeugma, Pella, and Neapolis is similar to structures actually found, for example, at Pergamum. In contrast to the eastern sacred mountains are those shown on coins of Greek cities, Athens, Corinth, Pautalia, etc. For the ancient Greek, the sacred monument was the temple building, and the mountain, as we have said above, was no more than a setting for the sanctuary. There is no suggestion that the mountain itself, as was the case in the East, was worshipped.

Fig.

54

55

304, 22

282

56

302–3

305

130–1

135

29

Fig. 57 CAESAREA GERMANICA, Bithynia: View of the harbour (Pescennius Niger A.D. 193–194) Paris. See colour plate p. 50.

Fig. 58 Lead token, probably Egyptian: View of a harbour entrance (mid. 2nd. cent. A.D.) Courtesy of Municipal Museum of Ancient Art, Haifa.

## Harbours and Lighthouses

Fig.    Long before underwater archaeology became a popular discipline, harbours and lighthouses were known from the coins. In some cases, harbours are engraved in bird's
57  eye view, with indications wharves and installations. It is interesting to find that in many examples a temple stands at the end of the jetty; actual temples have been found
58  as part of harbour installations. An exceptional view on a lead token shows a harbour entrance seen from within the bay, flanked by towers similar to those at the end of a modern breakwater. Harbour buildings as well as ships are shown in several instances
59  with most interesting details at Aegina, and at Patras. The most unusual is the
60–61  construction, the upper part of which represents the gate to the city at Vienne, which
62  seems to stand on the ship's deck but which actually stood on the shore behind.

313    The Pharos of Alexandria gave its form and name to later 'light-houses', and on the
147,  coins of Corinth, Heracleia, Berytus, and Laodiceia, the characteristic receding stories
63–65  are shown. In some cases, however, unless a ship is present in the design, it is not possible to distinguish a lighthouse from a simple tower. At Aegeae in Cilicia, for
66  example, the lighthouse is such a tower of masonry blocks. To declare that the building
67  on coins of Panormus cannot be a lighthouse because it has no openings, is to misinterpret the evidence. Indeed the function of such buildings is not beyond dispute, as discussed below in connection with the Pharos of Alexandria. It is important to note
485  that at Berytus and Aegeae guards stood on the tower as the ships passed.

40

*Fig. 59 AEGINA, Greece: View of the harbour with steps leading through the colonnades on the shore (Julia Domna c.A.D. 200–210) Berlin.*

*Fig. 60 PATRAS, Peloponnese: View of the harbour from the sea, the city and temples behind (Commodus A.D. 177–192) BM.*

*Fig. 61 PATRAS, Peloponnese: View across the harbour from the jetty (Geta A.D. 198–211) Berlin.*

*Fig. 62 VIENNE, Gaul: Harbour buildings and city gate beyond the prow of a ship (Augustus 31 B.C. – A.D. 14) BM.*

Fig. 63 HERACLEA PONTICA, Bithynia: Lighthouse in three receding stories, with the second story hexagonal, and the top story round (Gallienus A.D. 253–268) Oxford.

Fig. 64 BERYTUS, Phoenicia: Galley rowing past the lighthouse on which a guard is posted (Septimius Severus and Caracalla A.D. 198–211) Paris.

Fig. 67 PANORMUS, Sicily: Tower or lighthouse (early 1st cent. A.D.) BM.

Fig. 65 LAODICEA, Syria: Lighthouse reached by a flight of steps; two stories surmounted by a statue (mid. 2nd cent. A.D.) BM.

Fig. 66 AEGEAE, Cilicia: Galley sailing past the lighthouse, a single crenellated tower (Trajan Decius A.D. 249–251) BM.

Fig. 68 ROME: The nymphaeum (Alexander Severus A.D. 222–235) BM.

Fig. 69 HADRIANOPOLIS, Thrace: The decorated facade of the nymphaeum (Septimius Severus A.D. 193–211) Paris.

Fig. 70 NICOPOLIS AD ISTRUM, Moesia: The nymphaeum (Septimus Severus A.D. 193–211) Berlin. See colour plate p.49.

Fig. 71 NEOCAESAREA, Pontus: Elaborate portico, with the city goddess in the gateway (Alexander Severus A.D. 222–235) BM See colour plate p.14

*Fig. 72 PELLA, Syria: Nymphaeum (Elagabalus 218–222) Paris.*

*Fig. 73 AKE–PTOLEMAIS, Phoenicia: Nymphaeum with pavement in front (Elagabalus A.D. 218–222) Courtesy of Municipal Museum of Ancient Art, Haifa.*

## Fountains

The nymphaeum, a temple of decorative type dedicated to the nymphs often including a watering place, was not found, as far as we know, in every city. Comparatively few examples are known and of many of these little or nothing remains. Five coin buildings have been termed monumental nymphaea, at Rome, Hadrianopolis, Nicopolis, Neocaesarea, and, in Syria, Pella. The last, which is so inscribed, can be identified with certainty, but the building at Neocaesarea resembles a gate more than a fountain and certainly does not have the spouts at the base to indicate the nature of the monument. Another coin building, however, of Ptolemais in Phoenicia, although published as a harbour, appears to have such spouts as well as a court in front. Smaller fountain houses and free-standing fountains are also found on coins. Particularly striking is the one at Patras with water pouring down a series of catchment basins, and that found at Troezen where the water cascades from a lion's mouth. Others equally interesting are found at Rome, the Meta Sudans and its copies in Greek cities, and at Corinth, the fountain house of Peirene. At Alexandria, Heracles is shown using a fountain with gushing water to clean out the Augean stables.

*Fig.*

*68—72*

*73*

*74*

*75*

*112, 76*

*139, 77*

Fig. 74 PATRAS, Peloponnese: Fountain with water cascading from lion head spouts. The statue is that of Heracles (Domitian A.D. 81–96) BM.

Fig. 75 TROEZEN, Peloponnese: The 'fountain of Heracles': water pours from the lion's mouth into an elaborate basin (Septimius Severus A.D. 193–211) Berlin.

Fig. 76 NICOPOLIS, Epirus: The fountain of a 'Meta Sudans' type, possibly a copy of that at Rome (Hadrian A.D. 117–138) Berlin.

Fig. 77 ALEXANDRIA, Egypt: Heracles at a fountain (Antoninus Pius A.D. 138–161) Berlin.

Fig. 78 DORYLAEUM, Asia: Aqueduct above reclining river god (Alexander Severus A.D. 222–235) BM.

Fig. 79 ROME: The Aqueduct of Trajan with the river Tiber reclining below (Trajan A.D. 104–111) BM.

Fig. 80 BUTHROTUM, Epirus: Aqueduct: A rank of huge piers supporting arches above (Nero A.D. 54–68) BM.

Fig. 81 ANAZARBUS, Cilicia: Aqueduct with swimming river god below; the upper structure indicates the presence of a sluice gate or settlement tank (Alexander Severus A.D. 222–235) BM. See colour plate p. 50.

## Aqueducts and Bridges

By one of the strangest literary quirks in history we know more about aqueducts Fig. than about any other ancient monument; for the authority Frontinus, dull as he is, has left us the fullest possible details about the most utilitarian building of the ancient world. In the Greek world, only three aqueducts appear on coins. At Dorylaeum, the 78 representation is identical to that of the Aqua Traiana on Roman coins, and at 79 Buthrotum, the building has normally been regarded as a bridge. The former almost 80 certainly commemorates the erection of an aqueduct in the city; the latter, which lacks the normal characteristics of a bridge, may also do so. The most impressive is that at Anazarbus which can be directly related to the ruins of an aqueduct still standing at the 81 site of the city. The coin shows the bridge-like structure with central tower which may represent a sluice gate, and the relevance to water is provided by the presence, below, of a river god. The examples of bridges at Antioch and Mopsus, and on Roman coins, 82–84 emphasize that great arches usually dominated the end of the bridge. Very few such arches are extant. On a series of Roman denarii celebrating Augustus' repairs of the roads in Italy, bridges are shown with arches at both ends and even in the middle.

## Arches and gates

Several triumphal arches and gates have survived; but for their appearance in ancient times one must again look to the coins. They tell us, as we know from the cuttings in the stones of the preserved structures, that the arch served as a support for an elaborate 85—87 quadriga or other piece of statuary. Many arches, such as the arch of Nero at Rome, are types known only from coins. A provincial issue from Callatis indicates, like the arch 88 of Nero, that sometimes a single heroic and spectacular figure in relief decorated one 107 side of the arch or gate. No such decoration is otherwise known. It is interesting that as early as the 1st century A.D., coins of the eastern provinces show arches with three gateways. Such arches are not found that early at Rome. The only extant example of similar antiquity is in Gaul. The windows and pediment above the arches of an Alexandrian coin are certainly an inheritance from local religious architecture.            89

It will already have become evident that architectural coin types do not at a stroke solve all problems connected with the buildings they depict. As with any other form of evidence, they must be used with care. Where design is extremely complicated or the building of an unusual form, we can only point to the coins as problems which later research or excavations may solve. They do, however, provide a remarkable contemporary guide to the architecture of the Graeco—Roman world. The coins with all their varieties remain as fascinating vignettes for the map of the Roman empire, similar to the vignettes of the Peutinger table, but with far greater reliability and detail. We can determine from the coins details of hundreds of buildings which have been lost beyond hope of recovery by the spade of the archaeologist.

*Fig. 82 ANTIOCH AD MAEANDRUM, Asia: Bridge over the Maeander river (Gallienus A.D. 253–268) BM. See colour plate p.50.*

*Fig. 83 MOPSUS, Cilicia: Bridge over the river Pyramus (Valerian A.D. 253–258) BM.*

*Fig. 84 ROME: The Aelian bridge over the Tiber (Trajan A.D. 104–111) BM.*

Fig. 70

Fig. 169

Fig. 244

Fig. 328

*Fig. 70 NICOPOLIS AD ISTRUM: The nymphaeum. Berlin.*
*Fig. 169 NEOCAESAREA: The gate to the sanctuary. Berlin.*
*Fig. 244 SARDIS: The great altar of Zeus Lydios. Paris*
*Fig. 328 SARDIS: The two neocorate temples (Septimius Severus A.D. 193–211) Paris.*

*Fig. 57 CAESAREA GERMANICA: View of the harbour. Paris.*
*Fig. 82 ANTIOCH AD MAIANDRUM: Bridge. BM.*
*Fig. 81 ANAZARBUS: Aqueduct. BM.*

*Fig. 85 MARCIANOPOLIS, Moesia: Triumphal arch surmounted by four figures on pedestals (Macrinus and Diadumenian A.D. 217–218). Berlin.*

Fig. 86 AUGUSTA TRAIANA, Thrace: Military gateway to the city with three towers, one placed centrally over the door (Caracalla A.D. 211–217) Berlin. See colour plate p.14

Fig. 87 ANCHIALUS, Thrace: City gate with two towers; above, a 'warrior', and beyond a temple facade (Septimius Severus A.D. 193–211) Berlin.

Fig. 88 CALLATIS, Moesia: City gate with male statue on the right hand tower (Geta A.D. 198–211) Berlin.

Fig. 89 ALEXANDRIA, Egypt: Gate or triumphal arch. The decorative elements include windows, Doric entablature and pediment (Trajan A.D. 111) BM.

52

# EARLY ARCHITECTURAL TYPES

With a few exceptions the coins to be discussed in detail in this book are of the Fig. Roman imperial period, issued either by Rome herself, or by the cities of the Roman empire around the Mediterranean basin. The earliest coins to show an awareness of architectural motifs, however, are rare silver pieces of the early 5th century B.C., struck by one of the islands of the Dodecanese, which use a palmette, possibly an 90 antefix from a tiled roof, as a coin type. Later in the same century, we find fountain houses within the sanctuary of a local goddess at Himera; with charming and natural 91 perspective a Silenus wades knee deep in the basin below the lion head spout. The little Silenus can be compared to the long necked bird which sits upon the surface of a fountain pool of a later coin of Terina. It is surprising that of all the religious and 92 secular buildings of a city, fountains should first have been chosen; but they can be paralleled on many Greek vases and reliefs to show their importance for the peoples of the ancient world.

A 4th century B.C. coin of Sidon in Phoenicia represents the walls of the city with a 93 galley drawn up on the slipway in front. The close attention to detail, both in the ship and in the crenellations of the towers, shows careful observation of the original scene. In a slightly later view of a city on the coins of Tarsus, we can see a much less realistic 94 treatment, more symbolic of the power of the city.

Two temple-shrines, also of the 4th century B.C., represent the first purely religious buildings to be illustrated on coins. At Hierapolis Bambyce in Syria, the god is shown 95 in a vaulted shrine, the columns of which have marked Ionic capitals, a Greek detail, which presumably gives a vague outline of the actual building. In spite of the Greek influence, the oriental tradition maintains a flat roof on the shrine. At Tarsus, greater 96 detail is paid to the shrine of the god Anu, in which the local satrap Datames is shown worshipping the cult image. The shrine is flat roofed as at Hierapolis Bambyce and the edge of the roof itself is decorated with palmette antefixes such as have been found on many ancient sites and can be seen on seals and other artefacts of more than a thousand years before. At Tarsus, but at a later date, we have a shrine of the god 97 Sandan. The deity stands on the back of a horned beast, in the typical pose of an eastern god, familiar today from Hittite sculptures. On either side of him are conic baetyls, sacred stones, and the group stands on a base decorated with garlands. A pyramidal structure, or canopy, supports a lantern surmounted by an eagle. Without doubt this is the cult image of the great god of Tarsus, as he would have been seen in his sanctuary.

Several altars are depicted on coins, larger, but not much more substantial than the small altar or puteal visible on the fountain type of Himera. While in the Roman period there are depicted altars which must have been of a monumental nature, in the Hellenistic world they are usually too insignificant to be classed as "architecture." At 98 Parium, for example, the altar is shown to be little larger than the jug which stands beside it; yet the type probably symbolizes the great altar of Hermocreon, one of the largest and most famous altars of antiquity.

Fig. 90 UNCERTAIN, Caria or Dodecanese: Palmette of an architectural form (c. 490 B.C.) BM.

Fig. 91 HIMERA, Sicily: Silenus at a fountain within a sanctuary, in which the local nymph pours a libation (c. 450 B.C.) BM.

Fig. 92 TERINA, Italy: Winged Victory (Terina) seated at a fountain; a bird swims in the pool (c. 420 B.C.) BM.

Fig. 93 SIDON, Phoenicia: Galley drawn up on a slipway before the walls of the city; below, two lions (c. 390 B.C.) BM.

Fig. 94 TARSUS, Cilicia: Lion attacking a bull;
below, the walls of the city (c. 340–335 B.C.)
BM.

Fig. 95 HIERAPOLIS–BAMBYCE, Syria: Shrine of
Hadad, with flattened roof (c. 335 B.C.) Oxford.

Fig. 96 TARSUS, Cilicia: Shrine of Anu, the
flat roof decorated with antefixes (c. 375 B.C.)
BM.

Fig. 97 TARSUS, Cilicia: Shrine of Sandan (Demetrius II
of Syria 129–125 B.C.) BM.

Fig. 98 PARIUM, Asia: Flaming altar in front of which vase (c. 300 B.C.) BM.

Fig. 99 NORTH INDIA: Stupa of Buddha with colonnade of Hellenistic form (Sivadasa, probably late 1st cent. B.C.) BM.

Fig. 100 ROME: The Rostra decorated with ships' trophies, sometimes identified as a harbour installation (45 B.C.) BM.

Fig. 101 ROME: View of the walls and Acropolis at Eryx, Sicily (57 B.C.) BM.

56

From the far east of the Greek world we can illustrate a temple the existence of Fig. which on coins has never been recognized. This is a stupa, or shrine of Buddha. One coin, very stylized, shows that the sacred mountain of Buddha, associated with his birth, a simple man-made pile of rocks, was itself his earliest shrine. Another type, probably minted in the 1st century B.C., represents the shrine as a domed 99 structure above a rectangular Hellenistic colonnade. The dome may have been of wood, since no real domes in stone are known until late in the Roman empire. But there is also a possibility that the coin represents a type of stupa, of which actual examples are known, a building cut deep into the interior of a hillside with rock cut columns under a rock cut stone dome. Later sculptured reliefs show the continuation of the type, but the coins themselves are the earliest representations.

Architectural types are sporadic in the Hellenistic world before 30 B.C., and it is the Romans, themselves great engineers and architects, who began to use such types regularly on their coinage. It is not true to say that they invented the use of architectural coin types but they certainly exploited it; and probably as a direct result of the appearance of buildings on the silver denarii of Rome, other cities saw the attraction of celebrating their own famous buildings in the same way. To illustrate Rome's contribution during the late Republican period, two denarii have been chosen for their particular interest. The coin of the moneyer Palicanus shows a curved set of 100 arches with the prows of three ships set within them and with a magistrate's seat of office above. The coin could represent either the rostra (public platform) at Rome which Sulla had rebuilt in a curved form and which was decorated with ships' trophies, or less probably, some harbour installation showing the ships within their covered slipways. The second coin shows the city walls of the Sicilian town of Eryx with the 101 acropolis topped by the temple of Venus, famous in antiquity. This is reminiscent of our earlier coin of Sidon. The difference in time and technique, however, is emphasized 93 not only by the attention to detail in the walling and gateway, but also by the definite perspective produced by the mountain and the temple on it. The city is identified by its name engraved on the scene.

We are now on the threshold of the Roman Empire founded by Augustus who metaphorically "left a city of marble which he had found built of brick." The commemoration of great building projects in Rome on coinage and the commemoration of similar activity in cities throughout the empire leave us with an impressive picture of one of the greatest periods in the history of architecture.

Fig. 102 ROME: *The Macellum (Nero A.D. 64–66) BM.*

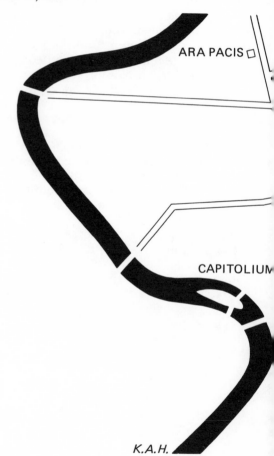

Fig. 105 ROME: *The Ara Pacis (Nero A.D. 64–66) BM.*

Fig. 103 ROME: *The temple of Vesta (Nero A.D. 64–68) BM.*

Fig. 104 ROME: *The Circus Maximus (Trajan A.D. 104–111) BM.*

Fig. 106 ROME: The temple of Janus (Nero A.D. 64–66) BM.

Fig. 107 ROME: The arch of Nero (Nero A.D. 64–66) BM.

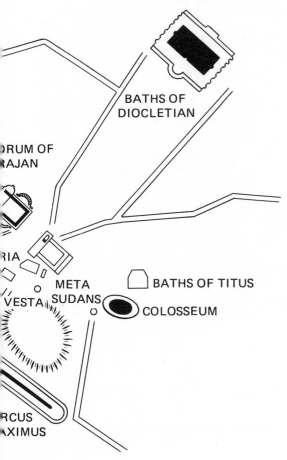

Fig. 108 ROME: The Forum of Trajan (Trajan A.D. 112–117) BM.

Fig. 109 PERGAMUM: The 'temple' of Mars Ultor, an imaginary view (19–18 B.C.) BM.

*Fig. 110 ROME: The Colosseum with the Meta Sudans to left and the Baths of Titus to the right (Titus A.D. 80–81) BM. See colour plate p.67*

*Fig. 111 ROME: The Colosseum. Detail of the relief sculpture from the Haterii Sarcophagus in the Lateran Museum, Rome. (Late 1st. cent. A.D.) Fototeca Unione no. 4753.*

60

# ROME

## THE COLOSSEUM

This Flavian amphitheatre requires no introduction for it is one of the most Fig. fascinating of the secular buildings of the ancient world. The grotesque grandeur of the 110 performances presented there was matched by the building itself. The well-known coin commemorating its dedication by Titus in A.D. 80 gives an excellent view of the architecture, and especially of the tiers filled with spectators watching the sport. In the centre of the audience a single arched opening marks the imperial box from where the decisions of life or death were given. The detailed design of the niches on the exterior of the building and the main entrance surmounted by a chariot group have parallels on a relief in the Lateran Museum. The relief shows that statues of divinities decorated the 111 lower rank of niches, and imperial eagles the second tier. The eagles are, perhaps, symbols of the deified members of the imperial house. The coins show statues in both tiers of niches, and additional decoration above which is omitted on the relief. The actual remains indicate, not niches, but a band of decorations divided into squares. The coins show the rank of squares thus providing a closer guide to the actual architecture than the relief. The wall of the building must have been surmounted by a structure, possibly the trappings for an awning that protected the spectators. On the relief this appears almost as crenellations with cloth stretched between them. On the coins we can see only posts around the top of the wall, a small detail but important enough in the mind of the ancient artist to be included.

The Colosseum coins depict in addition two other monuments which may be linked to the rebuilding programme of Titus. On the left is the Meta Sudans, a conical fountain famous in antiquity. This should be compared with another fountain on Roman coins from which water spurts through the two mouths of the head of Janus 112 set at its apex. The coins emphasize that the Meta Sudans was part of Titus' plan for Rome although it was not completed until after his death. Copies of such a fountain 113 can be seen on coins of Corinth and Nicopolis. Today the brick core has been 76 completely removed to make way for Rome's growing traffic.

Balancing the Meta Sudans on the opposite side of the Colosseum, the coin engraver has depicted tiers of columns which must represent the monumental portico of the Baths of Titus, leading up to the top of the Oppian Hill. Although the plan and architectural details of this building have been preserved by the famous Renaissance architect, Palladio, only the stubbed foundations of the portico can be seen today. It is 114 strange that this equation of the columns on the coin with the Baths of Titus has never been suggested. Yet Titus dedicated the Baths in A.D. 80, the date of the Colosseum itself. Both these buildings and the Meta Sudans must have been part of the same building programme.

Fig. 112 ROME: Fountain, possibly the Meta Sudans itself. The water spouts from a head of Janus (Titus A.D. 80-81) BM.

Fig. 113 CORINTH, Peloponnese: A fountain of the Meta Sudans type, with sculptured decoration of the base (Domitian A.D. 81–96) Berlin.

Fig. 114 The foundations of the Baths of Titus seen to the right of the Colosseum (A.D. 80). Fototeca Unione, no. 3207.

*Fig. 115 ROME: The Capitolium (Vespasian A.D. 76) C.M. Kraay collection.*

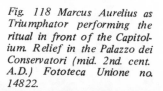

*Fig. 118 Marcus Aurelius as Triumphator performing the ritual in front of the Capitolium. Relief in the Palazzo dei Conservatori (mid. 2nd. cent. A.D.) Fototeca Unione no. 14822.*

*Fig. 116 ROME: The Capitolium with details of the statues on the roof and of the inner cellae (Vespasian A.D. 71) C.M. Kraay collection.*

*Fig. 117 ROME: The Capitolium with three prominent doors (78 B.C.) BM.*

64

# ROME

## THE CAPITOLIUM

The temple of the Capitol, shrine of the Rome triad, Jupiter, Juno, and Minerva, <sub>Fig.</sub> disappeared from the surface of the earth late in antiquity, leaving hardly a trace for posterity. The archaeologists have recently found enough evidence of the original Etruscan building (late 6th to mid-5th century B.C.) to draw the ground plan and elevation and in many respects the coins bear a remarkable resemblance to this early temple. Differences, however, among the various examples of the coin type have led some investigators to conclude that because the temple was rebuilt several times, its style was changed and the coins were issued to commemorate these building programmes. We can show that the coins do portray the original temple and that despite any rebuilding there were little or no important architectural changes to its general form. We know that stone was substituted for wooden portions. But we also know that the Romans had received due warning that the gods did not want the ancient forms changed.

The ground plan and elevation show a building remarkably similar to the description of an Etruscan temple by Vitruvius, the Roman historian of architecture. Squarish in form, the edifice had three separate sanctuaries, the centre one for Jupiter Optimus Maximus Capitolinus, the side halls for Juno and Minerva. The deep porch of eighteen columns, the high podium, the closed back wall, gave prominence in typical Etruscan fashion to the front of the building.

It is the facade of the temple which is shown on all the coins in the Capitoline series. 115—117 By the normal artistic convention, the die engravers have in some cases brought the cult images out of the interior to the facade. This not only identifies the building itself, but also recalls the practice of showing the deity in the facade in an epiphany, a practice that goes far back in early Near Eastern history. That the Capitoline deities were housed in separate shrines is indicated on some examples by showing on the facade the arched baldachinos which covered each of the cult images in the interior. On other examples, the artist has depicted on the facade the three doors which led to the interior.

The die maker of the earliest coin in the series, of the moneyer Volteius, reduced the number of columns in order to show the three doors which in actual fact must have been hidden behind a veritable forest of columns. The same three doors appear on the well-known relief of the 2nd century A.D. where the emperor, Marcus Aurelius, is seen 118 as typical Etruscan triumphator, performing the sacrifice before the Capitolium. To the die-maker of the Volteius coin, the important characteristics of the building to be recorded were the three doors and the decorations of the sloping roofs. The archaeologists in their turn considered the roof decorations interesting because they 119 found Etruscan fictile ornaments that resembled them and were dated to the same period as the early Capitolium. The artist was not working from memory. The building which he illustrated was there for him to see and copy. The coin of 78 B.C. represents the actual decorative details of the original temple building.

Fig. It has never been noticed that the Volteius representation was closely copied by a
120 provincial city, the difference being that the coin of Carallis in Sardinia bears the
legend VENERIS. This coin is an exact copy of the Roman type, but the legend
indicates that Venus held prime position in the worship of the temple. Even so, the
three doors may represent separate sanctuaries; and the Sardinian coin shows how great
an impression the ancient Etruscan shrine made in the first century B.C. on an island,
distant from the Capitol. This same kind of influence is shown by the use of the
142 Capitolium types in Corinth and in Asia.

Because of an ancient report that the pediment of the Capitolium was at one point
in time made higher, it was suggested that a strange coin with a pediment-like design
121 was issued to celebrate the new tympanum. The monster illustrated is a lesser god
named Summanus who, the legend had it, was struck by Jupiter. The same deity
appears in the pediment of the Anatolian issue. Cicero tells us that, in 278 B.C., a statue
of this god decorated the pediment of the Capitolium and was struck by lightning.
There is no firm evidence of any rebuilding during the first century B.C., and so the
reason offered for striking the coin is not valid.

It is often assumed that architectural types on coins of Rome were issued to
commemorate the building, or dedication, or rebuilding of an edifice. This was by no
means necessarily so, and such thinking can lead to absurd theories. The Capitoline
temple appeared first on coins long after it was constructed, not because it was
rebuilt in 78 B.C. but because the Roman world had just begun to use architecture
as coin types. The Capitolium was chosen because it symbolized the most
important cult of the city. Once adopted, it was repeated as a type with the usual
die-makers' variations. In the case of coins bearing a special legend such as the
122 reference to the restoration of the Capitolium in A.D. 82, commemorated on the coin
of the province of Asia, the Anatolian issue mentioned above, the motive for the issue
is self-explanatory: The building was destroyed by fire in A.D. 80 and was rebuilt by
the emperors Titus and Domitian. It should be noted that restoration does not
necessarily imply a change of style or design. All the other types in the Roman
Capitoline series have no legend. Their variations were all inspired directly or indirectly
by a common design, the original temple building itself.

From the coins we can assume that there was a quadriga at the apex, bigae or single
horses as corner acroteria and figures along the raking cornices. There were six columns
on the facade and three main doors to the three cellae. The difference in the number of
columns and in the style of the capitals is immaterial since the coins did not always
emphasize these particular details. The modern elevation, based on actual finds, literary
119 evidence, and the style of Etruscan ornaments, has adopted the quadriga, the decorated
cornices and the acroteria shown on the coins. The statues along the roof are definitely
in the Etruscan tradition.

The main difference between the coins and the Etruscan temple is in the pedimental
sculptures. Also the temple of the coins appears to be a typically Greek or Hellenistic
building, not as on the Volteius coin, or on the late provincial type of Asia Minor, both
of which present a squarish, stunted Etruscan building. There is no evidence that an

66

Fig. 110

*Fig. 110 ROME: The Colosseum. BM.*

Fig. 130

Fig. 133

Fig. 130 ATHENS: The Acropolis. BM.
Fig. 133 ATHENS: The theatre of Dionysus and the buildings of the Acropolis. BM.

Fig. 119 Elevation of the facade of the Capitoline temple (6th–5th cent. B.C.) Courtesy E. Gjerstad.

Fig. 120 CARALLIS, Sardinia: Temple of Venus/Tanit (Late 1st. cent. B.C.) BM.

Fig. 121 ROME: Denarius sometimes said to depict the pediment of the Capitolium (69 B.C.) BM.

*Fig. 122 ASIA: Silver cistophorus celebrating the restoration of the Capitolium at Rome (Domitian A.D. 82) BM.*

*Fig. 123 ROME: The Capitolium with figures apparently reclining in the pediment (Vespasian A.D. 77–78). BM.*

Fig.  Etruscan temple was decorated with figures either in the round or in high relief before the 4th century B.C. Thus if there were any decorations in the tympanum of the Capitolium when it was first constructed, they were almost certainly in low relief, as indicated on some of the ancient models of temples which have survived. The decorations would not be the figures in the round shown by the Roman series. A further remarkable fact should be noted. The figures in the coin pediments duplicate the cult images below. When the cult images between the columns are standing, they are shown standing in the pediment; when Jupiter is portrayed seated and the others standing, the die-maker repeats the composition in the pediment above. An exceptional case is where the two goddesses are shown in the pediment recumbent, but on the facade they are standing. Cult images do not change their positions; it is the die makers 123 who change them when they intend to reproduce something other than an absolutely realistic picture of the temple. Yet we should note the very distinct similarities in the pedimental sculptures between the coin of Vespasian (115) before the destruction, and the relief sculpture of the mid 2nd century A.D. (118). Although much on the coins is truly representative of the actual building, the figures of the pediment, their postures, and the decidedly Greek look of the facade may well be misleading. The Roman citizen who used the coins was not shocked that the familiar Capitolium was pictured as a slender Greek temple. He was used to the mixture of Greek and Roman styles fashionable in all art at that time. One fact must be emphasized that although the coins show a number of variations, the style of the temple itself, symbol of Roman power, remained solidly unchanged.

70

# ROME

## THE CURIA

The Curia is one of the best preserved buildings in Rome, one of the few still Fig. complete edifices along a street of beautiful ruins in the Forum. It owes its 124 preservation to the very religious movement that tried to destroy it. It was turned into a church. The building was planned by Julius Caesar as a meeting place for the Senate, but despite its secular nature, we know from literary sources that it resembled a temple.

The coins which are said to show the Curia, and the Curia as it stands today are, however, patently different. The coin type resembles a temple, although not a typical Roman temple; the present day Curia does not. The unusually well-documented

*Fig. 124 View of the Curia Julia, as restored (End 3rd cent. A.D.) Fototeca Unione 13.*

71

Fig. 125 ROME: The Curia (Augustus
29–27 B.C.) BM.

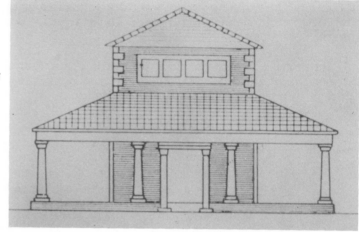

Fig. 126 The temple of St. Ouen-de-Thouberville, France; reconstruction (1st. cent. A.D.) Courtesy A. and J. Picard.

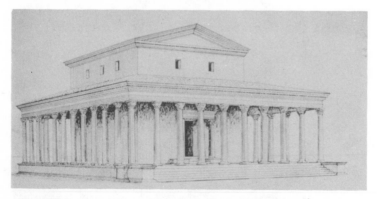

Fig. 127 Reconstruction of temple II at Elst, Netherlands (late 1st
cent. A.D.) Courtesy Staatusiigeverii, Netherlands.

72

*Fig. 128 CAESAREA, Mauretania: The Temple of Augustus (Juba II A.D. 6)*
*BM.*

history of the building not only allows us to explain this anomaly, but permits us to Fig. introduce a series of coins issued in North Africa, the pertinence and importance of which have passed unnoticed.

Caesar undertook to build a new Senate house in the fateful year, 44 B.C. His great 125 nephew and heir, Augustus, completed and dedicated the building in 29 B.C. and in Caesar's honour, named it the Curia Julia. The "Curia" coin was issued at Rome not long after this event. Augustus also dedicated an altar of Victory as an especial reminder of his crushing defeat of Antony and Cleopatra in 31 B.C. and had it installed in the building. The die maker of this coin has placed on top of the building a statue of Victory which in all likelihood represents the Victory dedicated by Augustus, and which actually stood within the Curia. Such shorthand conventions have been discussed in the introduction. They helped the engraver to compress a life-size monument into a very limited space. What is remarkable is that the public could immediately recognize the monument through these engravers' conventions, which today so complicate the interpretation of such coins.

Fig.
What of the further differences between the coin and the building as it stands? It is not possible to know what kind of edifice Caesar was planning; it is possible to hazard a guess. The facade as it is today is so much like that of Gallic temples that it is no wonder that some have thought the coin actually represented some such building and 126—7 not the Curia in Rome. Temples at St. Ouen, at Autun, and several other similar Gallic buildings are dated to the end of the 1st century B.C. or to the 1st century A.D. Caesar spent almost ten years in Gaul, and it is reasonable to assume that he planned a Curia that would resemble a Gallic building as a permanent reminder of his own great triumphs. He planned the windows in the upper part of the facade, the door, and the pediment which exists on both the coins and the building as it stands today. It is worth noting that in the eyes of the pious Republican Roman, the use of a pediment was restricted to sacred buildings.

The coin does not show the most characteristic feature of the Gallic temple, the gallery with pitched roof. Instead, it shows that the Curia was surrounded by an arcade made of low columns, spanned by an horizontal architrave. But the strange openings on the actual Curia building appear to be exactly like those which were found on the core of a temple at Autun, obviously used to receive the beams of a Gallic gallery. Instead of a high pitched gallery, the Curia, as finished after Caesar's death, had a peripteral arcade. The archaeologists have recently announced that they have found evidence of such columns, thus proving the validity of the coins.

128
A fascinating extension of our interpretation brings in a series of coins issued in A.D. 6 by the vassal King Juba II of Mauretania in North Africa. The building on these coins exactly matches the building on the Augustan coin of Rome, except that the inscription honouring Caesar is replaced with one honouring Augustus and a star and crescent, symbol of Juba's Phoenician domain, replaces the statue of Victory on the roof. On some issues of Juba's coins, the surrounding arcades are removed so that the die maker could exaggerate the size and decoration of the door. We know exactly what the door of the Roman Curia looked like because it has survived to the present day, and literary references note that it was something exceptional. The North African die makers emphasized this detail. Juba's father committed suicide after his defeat by Caesar at the Battle of Thapsus in 45 B.C., and as a young boy, Juba II himself was forced to take part in the triumphal march of Caesar through the very Forum where later the Curia Julia was built. The rest of his life is even more dramatic: Augustus befriended him and allowed him to take part in the campaign against Antony and Cleopatra. Juba II subsequently married the daughter of these ill-starred lovers. It is unlikely that Juba's coins represent the Curia at Rome which was so closely associated with the victories of Julius Caesar. Furthermore, provincial cities, with few exceptions, featured their own buildings on their coins. It is certainly possible that Juba II built a temple in honour of Augustus when he moved his capital to Caesareia, and that it was constructed on the model of the Rome Curia.

The well-preserved Curia building stands today among the noble ruins of the Roman Forum much in the same form in which Diocletian restored it. The coins show us how the Curia looked in the golden age of Augustus, a permanent and living record of the building itself.

# ATHENS

In contrast to Rome, the coins of Athens record few of its magnificent buildings so Fig. famous in antiquity. Yet two coins, in spite of their somewhat indifferent workmanship and small size cannot fail to stimulate our interest, representing as they do some of the best known monuments of the ancient world, the buildings of the 129 Acropolis and the theatre of Dionysus. The coins were struck as late as the third century A.D., seven hundred years after the Persian destruction of Athens had forced the citizens to plan again for the adornment of their city, and to crown their citadel with a new temple to their goddess Athena, the Parthenon. Even when these coins were designed, these buildings were ancient, revered in the same way as a Gothic cathedral today.

*Fig. 129 ATHENS: Aerial view of the Acropolis from the North, showing the prominence of the Erechtheum and the caves below Propylaea. Courtesy Greco-Posters Ltd., Athens.*

*Fig. 130 ATHENS: The Acropolis shown from the North, with the Erechtheum, statue of Athena, and Propylaea. The steps of the sacred way lead past cave sanctuaries (mid. 3rd. cent. A.D.) BM. See colour plate p.68.*

*Fig. 132 ATHENS: Statue of Athena which conforms most closely to the Athena Promachos shown on the Acropolis coin (mid. 3rd. cent. A.D.) BM.*

*Fig. 131 ATHENS: A variant view of the Acropolis with prominent gateway below the lip of the hill (mid. 3rd. cent. A.D.) BM.*

The depiction of the whole Acropolis is fascinating, in spite of some stylization, Fig.
since we know the buildings so well today from the ruins. The long stairway, following 130
the line of the famous Panathenaic way from the Agora, climbs up to the Propylaea,
the monumental 5th century B.C. entrance to the sanctuary. There are many versions
of this coin, some of them the right way round on the die, others back to front, and
the most striking variation occurring in the representation of the main gateway. This is
often shown with only two columns and set so far below the lip of the hill that it must 131
be the gateway of the Roman period — the Beulé gate — intentionally omitting for a
reason that may have been clear to the Athenian citizen the more impressive early
Greek propylaea which is situated higher up the hill. On fig. 130 the columns clearly
depict the Greek portico and they flank a squat rectangular object which represents the
great wooden doors that could shut off access to the sanctuary.

On passing through the propylaea, the visitor in ancient times would have been at
once impressed by the gigantic bronze statue of Athena Promachos, sculptured by
Pheidias, which stood directly in front of the entrance. This monumental figure, of
which nothing remains today, dominates the die cutter's representation of the
Acropolis and the same statue appears on another contemporary coin which shows 132
better the general pose of this masterpiece. The remaining building on the hill, a temple
with its altar placed at the East end, presents a problem of identification. One would
expect to find there the most famous temple of the Acropolis, the great temple of
Athena, the Parthenon. The sides however are shown as solid masonry instead of the
usual peripteral colonnade so well known to every visitor today, and although the coins
show columns at the East end, there is no evidence of the Parthenon's West columns.
At other cities, die makers found no difficulty in showing side columns and there is no
reason why they should have lacked the art of doing so at Athens. On the coins
depicting the theatre of Dionysus, the columns of the Parthenon are seen clearly,
crowning the hill. We must therefore consider seriously whether the artist intended to
depict a building other than the Parthenon. Indeed, the structure resembles the
Erechtheum, the smaller temple to the North of the Parthenon, famous for its Caryatid
porch which does have columns on its East facade, as well as a solid masonry wall on
the North. The building occupies so prominent a position in the design and the walling
has been so carefully drawn that we must assume that the die maker intended to show,
not the Parthenon, but the Erechtheum. The reason is that this building housed not
only the ancient cult of the hero Erechtheus, but also the shrine of Athena Polias. It
was the "temple of the archaic image," no less important than the Parthenon itself in
the cult of the goddess Athena. Some of the coins may have been struck to
commemorate the important renovation of the Erechtheum which certainly took place
in Roman times; but the significance of the building would have been clear to the
Athenians of the 3rd century A.D.

The coins plainly show the North wall of the Acropolis much as it is today. In
addition, the artist deliberately distinguished between the masonry of the wall and the
rough rocks of the hill below. Here we find two interesting niches at the side of the
stairway which must represent cults of the deities worshipped in caves on the side of
the Acropolis. One of these was surely the cave of Apollo, situated "just below the
gateway" where the god was supposed to have violated Creusa, the daughter of

77

Fig. Erechtheus. The other famous cave on the hillside was the Grotto of Pan, situated as on our coin near the cave of Apollo. Thus these remarkable coins, in spite of their small size and comparatively poor workmanship, give us a fair impression of the Acropolis in Roman times.

133    Equally interesting is the view of the theatre of Dionysus, a unique design in Greek coinage, showing the auditorium and stairways rising between the seats just as it may be seen today. An upper section of seats is clearly visible. Above these is the cave

134 which now forms the chapel of Our Lady of the Cavern where once stood the choregic monument of Thrasyllos who had dedicated the cave to Dionysus. The buildings of the Acropolis above seem to be a forest of columns as they must have appeared in Roman times. By raising the central portion above the rest, the artist has cleverly created three "buildings." The Parthenon itself appears in the centre with its colonnade and roofing directly above the theatre. On the right is depicted the small temple of Roma and Augustus, the foundations of which are still to be seen to the East of the Parthenon. Balancing this on the left are the columns of either a sanctuary on the South side of the Acropolis or of the Propylaea itself.

   The contribution of the Athenian coins is a considerable one. For those who doubt the reliability of coins — among these are not a few archaeologists — the Athenian series provide simple, interesting, and yet unexpected view of the Acropolis. They show in a most convincing way that Roman Athens was no less proud of her architectural glory than are the modern Greeks today.

Fig. 134 View of the theatre of Dionysus, Athens, with the cavern in the rock of the Acropolis above.

Fig. 133 ATHENS: The theatre of Dionysus with the buildings of the Acropolis above (mid. 3rd. cent. A.D.). BM. See colour plate p. 68

# CORINTH

From its foundation by Julius Caesar in 44 B.C., the Roman colony of Corinth <sub></sub>Fig. possessed an active mint which produced a large and diverse coinage. Architectural types recur frequently and, together with the recent American excavations of the area, provide a good impression of the main buildings of this great city. Pausanias' description of his visit in the middle of the 2nd century A.D. unfortunately leaves much to be desired, but he does name a number of monuments which can be compared profitably with the coins.

Dominating the area is the hill of Acrocorinth on which are still to be seen remains of the famous temple of Aphrodite. This naturally caught the imagination of the 135 designers of the coins and we find not only the temple itself and the cult statues depicted, but also the whole hill with details of its main features: The temple of Aphrodite at the summit, a tree and a rock-cut grotto at lower left which mark the famous fountain of Peirene whose cool waters still provide a fountain for the villagers. On the right there is a gateway probably denoting a sanctuary which has not yet been identified.

*Fig. 135 CORINTH: View of the Acrocorinth surmounted by the temple of Aphrodite and with fountain ? buildings at the foot (M. Aurelius A.D. 161–180) BM.*

Fig. 136 CORINTH: The nymph Peirene giving water to Pegasus; behind, the Acrocorinth (Septimius Severus A.D. 193–211) BM.

Fig. 137 The Acrocorinth with masonry of the fountain of Peirene in the foreground.

Fig.      The fountain of Peirene is also depicted separately on the coins. One shows the
136 nymph of the fountain, personified, pouring water from a jug for the Pegasus, for it
was this legendary winged horse who while drinking at a fountain was tamed by
Bellerophon. Beside the nymph and Pegasus is a tree and in the distance the
137 Acrocorinth surmounted by the temple of Aphrodite. Another coin shows the same
138 nymph with the figure of Scylla in front of her. The connection between the nymph
and Scylla is explained by a third coin which, previously unrecognized, shows a
139–139A straightforward architectural view of the whole Peirene fountain: At the top is the
arcaded facade of the grotto, behind which are catchment basins; flanking this are two
statues which may be Tritons; below, in front, is the rectangular basin with steps
140 leading down to it at the far end. This is exactly as we see the fountain today except
that the statue of Scylla, now lost, is shown on the coin in the rectangular basin of the
forecourt. The excavators found a rough-hewn statue base which stood in front of the
fountain facade and past which the water cascaded on either side into the forecourt.
They assumed that it was a statue of the nymph Peirene, but we can now show that it
was probably a statue of Scylla which occupied this prominent position in the
fountain. The coin itself may have been struck to commemorate the large-scale
embellishment undertaken during period VI, to use the archaeologists' terminology,
which considerably enlarged the fountain's facilities. This, on the basis of the coins,
would have taken place during the reign of Septimius Severus.

80

*Fig. 138 CORINTH: The statues of the nymph Peirene and the monster Scylla (Septimius Severus A.D. 193–211) BM.*

*Fig. 139 CORINTH: The fountain of Peirene showing arcade, court and steps leading down (Septimius Severus A.D. 193–211) Berlin.*

*Fig. 139A CORINTH: The fountain of Peirene (Septimius Severus A.D. 193–211) Courtesy of the Director of the Corinth Excavations.*

*Fig. 140 The fountain of Peirene as it is today. The columns were Byzantine additions to the arcade; but steps and court are as on the coins.*

Fig.    Pausanias underlines the great number of fountains to be found in the city of Corinth and two coins, not previously recognized as fountains are important in this connection. The first shows a statue of Poseidon with a dolphin at his feet which fits

141 Pausanias' description of an impressive bronze fountain and which the archaeologists believe once stood at the West end of the Agora, water gushing out of the dolphin's mouth. At the end of the 2nd century A.D. the fountain was removed to make way for two temple buildings. The second coin, not at once recognizable as a fountain, is an

113 exact copy of Rome's famous fountain, the Meta Sudans, which we have previously discussed under the Colosseum. There is no literary evidence or remains of such a fountain at Corinth. The Corinthians may have built one after the Roman model, perhaps near their own amphitheatre or near the stadium of the Isthmus, but a similar

142 coin copying the Capitolium at Rome suggests that they are Roman not Corinthian monuments represented.

Of the temples represented on the coins, that of Hermes can be identified with the remains of an important shrine at the Northwest corner of the Agora. A temple on

143 coins dated circa A.D. 25 dedicated by an inscription on the architrave to the Gens Julia is probably the temple of "Octavia" mentioned by Pausanias "above the market

144 place." A temple of Artemis Huntress, with prominent half fluted columns, cannot now be identified although the tree indicates a rural setting. On another coin, a tree in a masonry enclosure suggests a cult of non-Greek form. The well-known temple of

145 Poseidon at the Isthmus, the central shrine of the Panhellenic Isthmian games, can be identified on the coins by the statue of the sea-monster Tritons which decorated its roof and which caught the attention of Pausanias. The coins not only show the Tritons but also a tree to indicate the line of fir trees which stood on one side of the road leading up to the sanctuary. On either side of the Isthmus were the harbours for Corinth, at Lechaeum and Cenchreae. These harbours are found on the coins both as

146 personifications and also as actual architectural structures. Cenchreae is identified by the statue of Isis Pharia whose cult shrine actually stood at the end of one jetty, with a

*Fig. 141 CORINTH: The Poseidon fountain (Commodus A.D. 177–192) BM.*

*Fig. 142 CORINTH: The Capitolium at Rome (Domitian A.D. 81–96) BM.*

*Fig. 144 CORINTH: The temple of Artemis Huntress (Plautilla A.D. 202–205) BM.*

*Fig. 143 CORINTH: The temple of Gens Julia (Livia c. A.D. 25) BM.*

*Fig. 145 CORINTH: The temple of Poseidon at the Isthmus (Geta A.D. 198–211) Vienna*

*Fig. 146 CORINTH: The harbour at Cenchreae (Antoninus Pius A.D. 138–161) BM.*

83

Fig. 147 CORINTH: Galley passing the lighthouse at Lechaeum (Commodus A.D. 177–192) Berlin.

Fig. 148 CORINTH: The Agora showing the stoas to North and South (Caracalla A.D. 198–211) ANS

Fig. 149 CORINTH: The column marking the tomb of Lais (Geta A.D. 198–211) ANS.

temple of Asclepius balancing it at the other side of the coin. The lighthouse building Fig. which appears on other coins seems to have no place at Cenchreae and may belong to 147 the Lechaeum harbour. It has always been assumed that the Lechaeum harbour is represented on another coin which shows a temple flanked by two colonnades. But the 148 rectangular arrangement with the strange position of the temple is most unusual, and instead of galleys which normally indicate the water of a harbour, there are two statues both of which seem to be fish-tailed deities holding dolphins, possibly the Tritons which we noticed on the Peirene fountain. It is much more reasonable to suppose that the coins show the main agora of the city with shops down either side. Even the roof tiles are depicted. The temple engraved at the West end, trees growing within its boundaries, is quite clearly the archaeologists' temple E. In spite of a coin of Caligula found in the foundations, the position of the temple fits closely that of Pausanias' temple of Octavia, mentioned above. It stood beyond the actual limits of the Agora and was reached by a flight of stairs. The altar which is shown to the far left of the temple should probably be envisaged as standing between the stairs and the facade.

Other coins of Corinth illustrate many monuments both of the city and of the surrounding country. The tomb of Lais, one of the famous courtesans of antiquity, was 149 a major tourist attraction at the time of Pausanias' visit. He describes the tomb as it appears on the coins; a statue of a lioness with a ram between her forepaws set on a fluted column. The altar of Melicertes stood in a pine grove by the shore at Cromyon. It appears on coins as a large circular structure on a high podium covered by an 150 ornately tiled canopy with dolphin acroteria. A door leads through the podium, 151 presumably to allow access to the statue group of the boy Melicertes lying on a dolphin. Legend had it that the dolphin brought the body of the boy to shore at this spot.

"The gateway from the Agora on the road to Lechaeum is surmounted by two gilded chariots. In one stands Phaethon, son of Helios, and in the other Helios himself". This notable gateway, described by Pausanias, is shown on coins as an 152 ornamental triumphal arch with the chariot groups clearly visible. Finally, one of the most striking monuments of the coins is a column supporting a heroic figure on a large masonry base decorated with equestrian statues. This structure has been identified as a 153 lighthouse, but comparison with the unmistakable lighthouse of the harbour coin-type mentioned above shows that this is most unlikely. It is a quite different form of structure. It has been suggested that it is the so-called circular monument which dominated the East side of the Agora at the end of the centre row of shops, one of the most important monuments in the market place. But the archaeologists have rejected the identification. If it is not that structure, however, it must have been a similar monument somewhere else in the city.

The coins given in this short survey present a truly amazing picture of the grandeur of Roman Corinth in its heyday. We have suggested on the basis of the coins the identification of several important buildings. More will be possible when further remains are unearthed by the archaeologists to become the basis of comparison with the coins.

Fig. 150 CORINTH: The shrine of Melicertes at Cromyon (M. Aurelius A.D. 161–180) Paris.

Fig. 151 CORINTH: The shrine of Melicertes with a doorway in the podium (Septimus Severus A.D. 193–211) BM.

Fig. 152 CORINTH: The gate to the Lechaeum road (Hadrian A.D. 117–138) Oxford.

Fig. 153 CORINTH: Monument or Heroon (Septimius Severus A.D. 193–211) BM.

# DELPHI

## THE TEMPLE OF APOLLO

The representations of the temple of Apollo seem at first glance to be stylized, but Fig. there are several important points of interest which have been overlooked. The temple, the third building on that site of which remains have been found, dates from the middle of the 4th century B.C. It replaced a famous late 6th century shrine which had been completely destroyed circa 370 B.C. by earthquake. The third temple took many years to complete and was not officially opened until 305 B.C. In the Hellenistic period, a world of great monarchies and power politics, Delphi never resumed the position of authority which she had held earlier. It was, nevertheless, a unifying centre for the states of Greece and was held in reverence until the Roman conquerors began to despoil the sanctuary of its treasures. For a hundred years it was a prey to this pillage which ended when the emperor Domitian set about making extensive repairs to 154 the temple circa A.D. 84. Finally time brought the crumbling buildings to ruin and the whole site was in the 19th century covered by a village which had to be removed before the archaeologists could once more reveal the great sanctuary.

*Fig. 154 Delphi before the excavations: from H.W. Williams, Select Views in Greece, London, 1829.*

87

Fig. 155 DELPHI: The temple of Apollo in three-quarter view, with the statue of Apollo Pythios (Faustina I c. A.D. 145) BM.

Fig. 156 DELPHI: The temple of Apollo showing the famous pedimental sculptures and "Mystic E" between the central columns (Septimius Severus A.D. 193–211) Paris.

Fig. 157 DELPHI: The altar (Hadrian A.D. 117- 138) BM.

The actual temple had six columns on the facade and fifteen on the flanks. The Fig. 155 three-quarter view on the coin displays the usual numismatic abbreviation perfectly intelligible to the citizens who knew the temple well. The temple is that of Apollo Pythios whose image stands in the facade and this identifies for us with exceptional clarity the pose of that particular cult statue. This type of Apollo recurs all over the Greek world.

The frontal view of the temple, identified by the mystic E between the columns, 156 gives clear indication of the sculptures which we know from literary sources to have decorated the tympanum. These have recently been re-excavated in Delphi museum. The columns are shown as Doric and on the three-quarter view the roof displays the unusual detail of three horizontal rows of decoration, on the ridge pole, on the tiles, and at the cornice (sima). These have never been shown in a modern reconstruction. It is possible that they belonged to Domitian's renovation, and not to the original temple; but they certainly existed at the time the coins were issued. Such spiky objects, particularly if brightly painted, would have been striking, even dazzling to the onlooker. The frontal view shows standing figures as acroteria.

Another coin of Delphi which has rarely been discussed is that of Hadrian showing 157 an "altar." It is difficult to escape the conclusion that this must represent the great altar of the sanctuary, the altar dedicated by the Chians. In favour of the identification is the fact that the structure is placed on a most unusual podium, exactly as the actual 158 altar of the Chians appears when seen from the Sacred Way. The coin also definitely shows that the altar had a pediment, an unusual architectural feature for an altar 91 but by no means unknown. No modern reconstruction, however, has acknowledged this exceptional detail. It is entirely possible that the pediment was a false one, decorating the eastern facade of the altar, and thus dominating the Sacred Way. Insufficient stones of the upper courses survive so that we cannot know whether this pediment was a Roman addition to the original Greek structure.

*Fig. 158 The altar of the Chians and the temple of Apollo, Delphi, as restored by the excavators*

Fig. 159 AMASEIA: View of the city on the mountainside with temple and altar of Zeus Stratios above (Alexander Severus A.D. 229) Price Collection. See colour plate p. 101.

Fig. 159A AMASEIA: The city defences under construction (Alexander Severus A.D. 229) BM.

Fig. 160 View of the city of Amaseia from across the gorge. From G. Perrot and E. Guillaume, Exploration archéologique de la Galatie....executée en 1861, Paris, 1862–1872.

# AMASEIA

"Our city lies in a deep and impressive gorge through which the river Iris runs; and it has been built with so marvellous a combination of skill and nature that it serves both as a habitation and as a fortress. The high cliff falls sheer to the river; at the foot, on the banks of the river, there is a wall which supports the town itself, and on either side the fortifications rise to the very tops of the mountain. For there are two actual summits, connected by a spur to each other which are both splendidly fortified. Within the wall which surrounds the town are to be found the palace and the tombs of the Pontic kings. The summit may be reached only by a path on a narrow ledge and whether you come from the river or the outskirts of the town, the ascent is still some five or six stades; and there is a further steep climb of one stade to the summits which can be defended easily against any attack."

Strabo, Geography III, 39.

The city of Amaseia is described today as one of the most impressive sights in Turkey; and the description of the Roman geographer Strabo of his own home town makes a most poignant commentary on the fine coin of the city issued in A.D. 229/30. The walls are not depicted there as continuous stretches of masonry as at Bizya and in other city views, but as independent towers. A previously unpublished coin shows these under construction and a look at the terrain will show that fortifications at strategic points on the sheer face of the mountain were all that were necessary or practicable. The city itself lay at the foot of the mountain with two bridges only across the river. Dominating it was the ledge some way up the mountain side, on which stood the palace of the Pontic kings, and which still has Hellenistic walling supporting the Turkish fortress. On the coin, this position is taken by a large temple with six columns on the facade. There is no clear identification of this building, but it probably represents the temple of the Imperial cult for which the city was endowed with the coveted title Neocoros in the middle of the second century A.D. Certainly no better position in the city could have been found as a mark of respect to the Roman emperors. *(Fig. 159)* *(24)* *(159A)* *(160)*

To the left of this temple the coin shows a strange niche in the rock, fully explained by Strabo's remarkable description, and visible on the mountain side from across the gorge. It is one of the famous rock cut tombs of the kings of Pontus, some of which

91

*Fig. 161 One of the rock-cut tombs of the kings of Pontus, Amaseia. From G. Perrot and E. Guillaume, Exploration archéologique de la Galatie...Paris 1862–1872.*

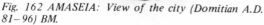

*Fig. 162 AMASEIA: View of the city (Domitian A.D. 81–96) BM.*

Fig. 161 were placed within the walls and some outside. If it represents a particular tomb, that of Mithradates I, the founder of the dynasty, is the most probable.

At the top of the design is another temple, placed in three-quarter view, with an altar in front of it to the right. The side wall of the temple can be made out behind the topmost tower. This sanctuary was most certainly dedicated to the chief deity of Pontus, Zeus Stratios. Close inspection, however, reveals that it is not actually standing on the mountain. If you remove it entirely from the design, the mountain top appears with the twin peaks exactly as described by Strabo and as it appears today. The temple and altar were not on the mountain. Another example of the coin proves this: No temple and altar are shown; only the two mountain summits are seen.

Fig. 162

The presence of the sanctuary on some of the coins is easily explained. It was placed there by the same numismatic convention we have so often seen used, showing above what actually stood behind. The sanctuary of Zeus Stratios was not at Amaseia itself, but to the East, behind the mountain, on the high plateau at Buyuk Evlia. In order to show the temple of the high plateau, the die-makers have added it to the design. Mithradates the Great is reported to have sacrificed at the altar of Zeus Stratios and the flames of the altar were said to be visible from the Black Sea. The altar on the coin has flames clearly visible.

92

*Fig. 164 AMASEIA: Temple of Zeus Stratios (?) (Trajan A.D. 116) Berlin.*

*Fig. 163 AMASEIA: The altar of Zeus Stratios with chariot of Helios above, and sacred tree (Caracalla A.D. 209) BM.*

This great monumental altar of Zeus Stratios also appears as a coin type of the city, Fig. 163 always accompanied by a tree or a flower which would seem to have some connection with the cult. As at Ephesus, Sardis, and in many ancient local cults, it may well be that an altar existed before the temple was built. The temple itself is probably the fine building shown on a coin of Trajan of A.D. 116/7. Such details as are clear fit with the 164 temple as it appears in the city view. We should note the prominent parotids as on the Trajan temple at Pergamum. It is clear, therefore, that the great sanctuary of the plateau has been brought into the design of the city view to complete the picture of 3 the religious life of the city. The three great monuments of its territory — the sanctuary of Zeus Stratios, the Neocorate temple, and the tomb of the Pontic Kings — are brought together within the protection of the walls of one of the most famous citadels of the ancient world.

Fig. 165 NEOCAESAREA: Gate to the sanctuary with closed doors (Caracalla A.D. 209–10) Berlin

Fig. 166 NEOCAESAREA: Gate to the sanctuary with open doors (Septimius Severus A.D. 209–10) Berlin.

Fig. 167 NEOCAESAREA: Gate to the sanctuary with two radiate busts and decorated doors (Septimius Severus A.D. 205–6) Paris.

# NEOCAESAREA

## THE SANCTUARY OF MA

The pre-Roman name of Neocaesarea is not yet known with certainty. In the 3rd Fig. century A.D., it is clear from the coins that the town assumed considerable importance as a centre for the cities of Pontus. The focal point of worship of the Pontic League was the monument which is found on numerous coins of the Severan family. Each engraver gives us different details and so it is therefore necessary to consider each variety in the search for the true reconstruction. No other building on 165– coins has attracted so many different details. 172

With few exceptions the coins show a tetrastyle facade usually with carefully delineated Corinthian capitals. One variety depicts a building of five columns which is 173 unknown in actual architectural remains. This may indicate the exact number but could also be attributed to an artist's carelessness. All show one and the same building. The altar in the centre of the columns is the key to the function of the monument; for when the die maker used it, he intended to represent, not a temple, but a gate, as on the several examples listed in the introduction. All the architectural details and figures shown in the facade actually stood behind it. The variety and multiplicity of cult objects and images presuppose a large sacred area. The monument of the coins, then, is a gate; not the door of a temple, but the gate of a sanctuary.

*Fig. 168 NEOCAESAREA: Altar and radiate bust within the gate to the sanctuary of Ma (Geta A.D. 209–10) BM.*

95

Fig. 169 NEOCAESAREA: Niche within the gate to the sanctuary (Septimius Severus A.D. 209–10) Berlin. See colour plate p. 49.

Fig. 170 NEOCAESAREA: Three busts between the columns of the gateway (Geta A.D. 209–10) Vienna

Fig. 172 NEOCAESAREA: Gate with bust and door knocker (Septimius Severus A.D. 209–10) BM.

Fig. 171 NEOCAESAREA: Statues and busts within the gate to the sanctuary (Geta A.D. 209–10) Vienna

Fig. 173 NEOCAESAREA: 'Pentastyle' gate to the sanctuary (Septimius Severus A.D. 209–10) BM.

96

*Fig. 174 NEOCAESAREA: Statue of Ma/Zeus on a pedestal within the gateway (Caracalla A.D. 209–10) BM.*

*Fig. 175 NEOCAESAREA: Temple of Zeus (Gordian III A.D. 238–244) Paris.*

We are dealing with a sanctuary of an inland city of Pontus where Iranian influence [Fig.] persisted throughout the Roman period. The standing statue in the centre of the coins [174] is identifiable as Zeus, who, as the great sky god, was a celestial divinity. He appears [175] again seated, on a later coin, with a rosette sun-symbol in the pediment. The radiate bust may well represent the great local sky god, Ma ('she' was both male and female), who dominated the beliefs of indigenous Oriental Pontus and the duplication reflects perhaps Zeus' dual role in the Dioscuri. Her standing figure appears on other Pontic issues, of Comana, associated with the eagle of Zeus in the pediment. Ma was the [176] object of the celestial cult of the Pontic kings whose coins are decorated with stars and [177] crescents. It would appear therefore that the coins show the gate of a sanctuary dedicated to the worship of the supreme sky god, Ma, the Magna Mater of Pontus, associated with the celestial, Graeco-Roman Zeus.

On the question of cult, the coins have even more to offer. One example shows what must be an imperial bust within a niche; another, three busts. The simplest explanation [169–70] is that these are the busts of the emperor Septimius Severus and of his two sons Caracalla and Geta. If so, we have the imperial cult inextricably linked with the local [178] cult of Ma/Zeus. This appears to be confirmed by the fact that later the city can boast [179] two neocorates under Severus Alexander, the first of which must have been given by Septimius Severus.

Thus from the coins which at first seemed so enigmatic, we may deduce that the main sanctuary of Neocaesarea was dedicated to Ma in whom the Greeks recognized Zeus, and under the Roman empire this was shared by the imperial cult. The artistic treatment of the facade on the coins has enabled us to lift the veil from this strange persistence of Oriental traditions into the Roman period.

Fig. 176 COMANA, Pontus: Temple of Ma
(Trajan A.D. 98–117) ANS.

Fig. 177 PONTUS: Silver tetradrachm depicting
the celestial deity, Ma (Pharnaces I 185–159
B.C.) BM.

Fig. 178 NEOCAESAREA: Two neocorate
temples (Alexander Severus A.D. 234–5) BM.

Fig. 179 NEOCAESAREA: Two neocorate
"temples" with altars within (Alexander
Severus A.D. 226–7) BM.

# NICAEA

The city of Nicaea, mentioned in Pliny's letters quoted in the preface, has left a rich Fig.
series of coins on which architectural types play a notable part. At least four different
temples are shown, as well as gates and a view of the walls, and they tell us a good deal
about the city itself. Architecturally, ancient Nicaea was most noted for the
gymnasium which formed the central focal point of the city, and for the colonnades
which were erected along the main thoroughfares in early imperial times.

Two coin issues under Claudius may well refer to this programme of adorning the 180—3
city: One shows a double storied arcade sometimes with no roof decoration and
sometimes with a roofline of two half pediments sloping inwards and a rounded
moulding as a barrelvault. The second coin type shows a similar structure but with a
normal pediment and sometimes an arcuated lintel on the second story. While it is
possible that these are but two variants of the same type, with the engraver of the first
merely doodling at roof level, it seems more probable that there is an intended
difference. It may be suggested that the half pediments are to be seen as continued to
left and right of the building, the whole forming a continuous line of pediments and
arches at the roofline of an arcade — the famous colonnades in fact along the main
streets. The second type, more clearly a single structure, has walling clearly delineated
on some examples at either side. It is a gate much like the gate of the Athena Polias 184
sanctuary at Pergamum, and the steps would suggest that it is the gate, not of the city,
but of another main building. At the cross roads of the main streets stood the
gymnasium, and it is here that this gate would be most suitable, at the end of the
colonnaded streets shown by the other coins. The relieving arch on the upper storey is 185
clearly seen on the existing remains of one of Nicaea's city gates.

Most of the temples on the coins can be identified either by the cult figure or by an
inscription mentioning the deity; but the buildings are usually undistinguished. That 186—7
most commonly present is the temple of "Agathe Tyche" which together with the
imperial cult clearly formed the central point of the city's worship. The capitals are of
the Ionic order, and it is therefore possible that the fine three-quarters view of an Ionic
temple represents this one. A fine coin, uncertainly attributed to Nicaea, depicting a 188
monumental altar of Zeus which must have been as imposing as the Ara Pacis of Rome,
should be noted. It could be that Nicaea was the mint city of this Bithynian issue since
the altar of Zeus Litaios, found on other coins of Nicaea, shows the importance of the
cult there.

A most unusual building, apparently religious in nature, occurs on a unique coin in 189
Paris. It looks more like a gate than a temple, having two decorated pilasters at the
side, with capitals of the Corinthian order and a heavy superstructure pierced by three
windows. Its identification, not as clear to us as to the ancients, is given by three
statues which stand in the openings in the facade. The central figure is an imperial
statue of the so-called Prima Porta type, hand outstretched. This must be the emperor
Septimius Severus, traces of whose name are inscribed around the coin. To the left,
there is a similar figure in similar pose but hand not outstretched. The other figure on

Fig. 180 NICAEA: Arcade with garland on the upper story (Claudius A.D. 41–54) Berlin.

Fig. 181 NICAEA: Colonnade with line of alternate pediments and arches at the roofline (Claudius A.D. 41–54) BM.

Fig. 182 NICAEA: Gate reached by a flight of steps (Messalina A.D. 41–48) BM. See colour plate p. 14.

Fig. 183 NICAEA: Gate with walling on either side (Messalina A.D. 41–48) Paris.

Fig. 24

Fig. 159

Fig. 24 BIZYA: View of the city. Berlin.
Fig. 159 AMASEIA: View of the city. Price coll.

Fig. 329                                              Fig. 201

Fig. 49                                               Fig. 330

Fig. 329 TYRE: Baldachino or shrine with caryatid figures (Gallienus A.D. 253–268). Berlin.
Fig. 201 CYZICUS : The sanctuary of Demeter. Paris.
Fig. 49 PRUSA AD OLYMPUM: Scene of sacrifice before the round building of a shrine. Paris.
Fig. 330 ZELA : Portico within which altar (Caracalla A.D. 206/7) ANS.

*Fig. 184 Gate to the sanctuary of Athena Polias from Pergamum (2nd. cent. B.C.) Pergamum Museum, Berlin, DDR. Courtesy Elisabeth Rohde.*

*Fig. 185 The Istanbul Gate, Iznik. Courtesy Rudolf Naumann.*

Fig. 186 NICAEA: Temple of Agathe Tyche (Commodus A.D. 177–192) ANS.

Fig. 187 NICAEA: Three-quarter view of an hexastyle temple (Maximinus A.D. 235–238) BM.

Fig. 188 BITHYNIA: Monumental altar of Zeus (Trajan A.D. 98–117) BM.

Fig. the right, also wearing a short tunic, has the attributes, thyrsus and cantharus, of the
189 patron of the city, Dionysus. This is in fact Severus' son Caracalla in his role as Neos Dionysus. The figure on the left is Severus' other son, Geta. All the figures stand on low bases and the general appearance of the building is of a quasi-oriental altar court, although the inscription around the coin shows that it is in some way connected with the imperial cult. The exact identification must await further evidence.

190 The most dramatic of the architectural coins, however, are those which commemorate the construction of the walls of the city in the mid-third century A.D. In 256 the invading Gothic tribes from the north completely overran the city, destroying much of it. On their retreat, it was rebuilt with new fine walls completely
191 encircling it, which are still well preserved today. The date of the rebuilding is given by
192 an inscription on the gate of Yenisehir and this coincides with the issue of a series of coins which show the great walls, two main gates heavily fortified, with short stretches of a wall easily defended from the many towers. If few of the buildings illustrated by the coins of Nicaea have been preserved today, it is doubtless because of the devastation caused by the Gothic capture of the city; but as the result of this same event we are permitted to see one of the best examples of Roman city walls to survive.

Fig. 189 NICAEA: Entry to a sanctuary, with statues of Septimius Severus and his two sons Geta and Caracalla (Septimius Severus A.D. 193–211) Paris.

Fig. 190 NICAEA: The city walls (Gallienus A.D. 253–268) Berlin.

Fig. 191 The ancient walls of Iznik, built after the destruction of the city by the Goths. Courtesy Rudolf Naumann.

ΑΥΤΟΚΡΑΤΟΡΙΚΑΙΣΑΡΙΜΑΥΡΚΛΑΥΔΙΩ ΕΥΣΕΒΕΙΕΥΤΥΧΕΙΣΕΒΔΗΜΑΡΧΙΚΗΣΕΞΟΥΣΤΑΣΤΟΔ ΕΥΤΕΡΟΝΑΝΘΥΠΑΤΩΠΑΤΡΙΠΑΤΙΔΟΣ
ΚΑΙΤΗΙΕΡΑΣΥΝΚΛΗΤΩΚΑΙΤΩΔΗΜΩΤΩ ΡΩΜΑΙΩΝΗΛΑΜΙΟΤΑΤΗΚΑΙΜΕΓΙΣΤΗΚΑΤΑΡΙΣΤΗΝΕΙΚΑΙΕΩΝΠΟΛΙΣΤΟΤΕΙΧΟΣΕΠΙΤΟΥΛΑΜΠΡ
ΥΠΑΤΙΚΟΥΟΥΕΛΛΕΙΟΥΜΑΚΡΕΙΝΟΥΓΡΕΣΒΕΥΤΟΥΚΑΙΑΝΤΙΣΤΡΑΤΗΓΟΥΤΟΥΣΕΒΚΑΙΣΑΛΛΙΟΥΑΝΤΩΝΙΝΟΥΤΟΥΛΑΜΠΡΛΟΓΙΣΤΟΥ

Fig. 192 Inscription on the Yenisehir Gate, Iznik, commemorating the completion of the rebuilding of the walls by Claudius Gothicus A.D. 268–270. Courtesy Rudolf Naumann.

*Fig. 193 The remains of the terrace of the temple of Athena, Troy. Courtesy C.H. Anscombe.*

*Fig. 194 Sealstone (Sard), depicting Achilles dragging the body of Hector around a Roman Troy (Imperial period) BM.*

*Fig. 195 ILIUM, Asia: The only surviving coin presenting the temple of Athena (M. Aurelius A.D. 161–180) Berlin.*

106

# TROY

## THE TEMPLE OF ATHENA

> "And when they came to the temple of
> Athena in the upper city....she sent up her
> prayers to the daughter of Great Zeus: 'Oh,
> Goddess Athena, divine guardian of cities,
> break the spear of Diomedes and hurl him
> head-long from on high before the Scaean
> gates."
>
> Homer, Iliad VI, 297 f.

Long after the great days of Homer's Troy, in the 3rd century B.C., the citizens built Fig.
a new temple to Athena, proud of their sacred heritage and of their ancient cult image.
The top of the hill on which the city stood was levelled to make room for a large
sanctuary and the temple was erected within it. Parts of the surrounding colonnade and
its gate have long been known and in recent years the foundations of the temple itself 193
have been uncovered. An imaginative view of the city is preserved on a small seal-stone.
The victorious Achilles drags the body of Hector around the walls of an incongruously 194
Roman Troy, as in the Renaissance Christ was pictured in an Italian setting. In spite of
the fact that most of the buildings on this seal cannot be identified, the temple of
Athena is seen standing at the left hand limits of the city, slightly marred by a crack in
the seal-stone.

A coin issued by the city under Marcus Aurelius, today surviving in a single 195
specimen, gives us a further more detailed view of the temple. The building has a
facade of six columns just as the archaeologists have conjectured from the remains;
sculpture which once adorned the pediment is represented by a shield. The famous cult
image, the Palladion, is brought out to the front, and it is shown on the exceptionally
high base that is characteristic of many other representations of it on coins. This detail
emphasizes that the statue was not like the monumental statue of Athena at Athens,
overpowering by its very size; but that it was a small image which could be easily
carried off, as indeed it was in Homer's epic by that guileful pair, Odysseus and 196
Diomedes, to assure the fall of Troy.

The reliability of the temple coin is confirmed by the representation of the temple
of Athena on a famous marble relief of the Roman period, the Tabula Iliaca. Coin and 197
relief together establish what the archaeologists subsequently found in the
Graeco-Roman levels: A temple in the dominant position of the city, a colonnaded
portico surrounding the sanctuary, and an altar in front of the temple. Although the

Fig.196 ARGOS, Peloponnese: Diomedes carrying off the statue of Athena Ilias (4th cent. B.C.) BM.

Fig. 197 The Tabula Iliaca, showing the walls of Troy and the temple of Athena in the upper city (1st. cent. A.D. ?) Museo Capitolino, Rome. photo. Alinari 27113.

Tabula Iliaca was the work of a western Roman artist, there is no reason to doubt its accuracy. Troy was a tourist spot during all of its historic existence. Indeed during the Roman period, the city's coin types continuously hark back to the stories of the Homeric age in contrast to the standardized types of the nearby military colony at Alexandria Troas. It can truly be said that Troy was never forgotten. For centuries collectors searched through Europe for coins minted in the ancient city. It should be remembered that between 1453 and 1822, Turkey closed the way to travellers. It was not until Schliemann's world-shaking discovery at Hissarlik in 1870 that the actual city of Troy was given again to mankind.

# CYZICUS

"Coin types are notoriously bad evidence for architecture". This scepticism coming Fig.
from Hasluck, the early 20th century historian of Cyzicus, reveals an unfortunate
misunderstanding of the material. The numismatic evidence not only records the
existence of ancient monuments of the city now lost, but also clarifies the ambiguities
in literary and archaeological sources. Five buildings are represented on the coins of
this city: three of them are temples, to Hadrian, Caracalla, and Hermes. Another two,
it will be seen, are monuments connected with the Mysteries, the most important cult
at Cyzicus.

One of the buildings has been incorrectly identified as a sacrificial altar of the
temple of Hadrian because on some examples it appears at the side of the temple. It 198—9
appears sometimes on the right and sometimes on the left of the temple. Such
numismatic juxtaposition does not signify that the so-called altar necessarily stood in
reality next to the temple. Furthermore, a sacrificial altar would normally require the
presence of a burning fire which is never found on the many representations.

The coins show us a round building with plain masonry walls, a two-leaved door 200—1
unusually high up on the facade, no steps leading up to it. The structure has no roof;
but three female figures holding up torches decorate the rim. On one example, two

Fig. 198 CYZICUS: The temple of Hadrian and
the sanctuary of Demeter (Caracalla A.D.
198–211) Paris.

Fig. 199 CYZICUS: The sanctuary of Demeter
and the temple of Hadrian (early 3rd. cent. A.D.)
ANS.

Fig. 200 CYZICUS: The sanctuary of Demeter surmounted by statues and flanked by snake entwined torches (early 3rd. cent. A.D.) Paris.

Fig. 201 CYZICUS: A similar view of the sanctuary of Demeter (Hadrian A.D. 117–138) Paris. See colour plate p.102.

Fig. 202 CYZICUS: The Demeter sanctuary surmounted by a chariot group and figures (Gallienus A.D. 253–268) ANS.

110

Fig. 203 Fragment of an inscribed stele from Samothrace (late 2nd. cent. B.C.) Courtesy J.R. McCredie.

Fig. 204 Manuscript of Cyriac of Ancona depicting an inscribed stele with the name Asklepiades (14th cent. A.D.). Courtesy the Bodleian Library, Oxford, Ms. Lat. Misc. d. 85, fol. 140r.

horses, possibly a chariot, seem to be running to the side between the figures. ꜰɪɢ. Snake-entwined torches, an unmistakable symbol of the mystery cult, always flank the 202 building. It is difficult to distinguish Demeter from Kore on coins. Here, however, one can say with certainty that both mother and daughter are represented at the top of the building, accompanied by another of the many female deities involved in the cult. The central group of horses could certainly be an illustration of the rape of Persephone (Kore).

For the identification of this so-called altar coin, we can draw on an unusual amount of non-numismatic evidence. It will turn out however that this evidence will not only throw light on the coins but will, by a kind of reflection, be itself clarified and strengthened by the coin. From Samothrace we have extant fragments of several reliefs which were copied by the famous traveller Cyriac of Ancona on his trip to the East in the 15th century, whose drawings are preserved in several manuscripts.

Fig. 205 Reconstruction of the Arsinoeion at Samothrace, (289–281 B.C.) From A. Conze, A. Hauser, G. Niemann, Archaologische Untersuchungen auf Samothrace, Wien, 1875.

Fig. 206 Elevation of the Sphinx tomb/shrine from Xanthos, facade B of Building H combined with pediment in the British Museum (470–460 B.C.) Courtesy H. Metzger and D.E.L. Haynes.

One of the Samothracian reliefs actually preserved was a stele dedicated by a citizen Fig. of Cyzicus, one Asklepiades, son of Attalos, late in the 2nd century B.C. Asklepiades 203 was sent to Samothrace for some purpose — the inscriptions are not clear on this point — connected with his profession as architect. The building engraved on his stele decorated other Samothracian stones, which were also the gifts of citizens from Cyzicus, and all these visitors from Asia Minor were initiates both at Cyzicus and at Samothrace.

It is surprising that the building pictured on the Samothracian reliefs and in the 204 manuscripts of Cyriac is so close to the so-called altar on the coins of Cyzicus, that it could easily be called the model for the coin-type. The manuscripts have some charmingly naive variations introduced by the copyists: male instead of female figures, staffs instead of small torches. These details are consistent on the coins. By a recognizable convention, the figures shown above on the roof could actually have decorated the interior of the building. The monumental torches shown to the side of the building on the coins were in reality, by a similar artistic convention, in front of the building as is clearly shown by the manuscript and relief.

The building on the Samothracian reliefs — in each case the badge, as it were, of citizens of Cyzicus — is exactly the same as that found on the coins of Cyzicus. More important, the fact that the building is found on coins minted in Cyzicus also means that the building was situated in Cyzicus. Mrs. Lehmann has recently recognised in this a "Samothrakeion" and has described it as a copy of the famous Arsinoeion of Samothrace, derived from the great cult of the island.

In its style of architecture, the Cyzicus building bears some resemblance to the 205 Arsinoeion, dedicated by Queen Arsinoe at Samothrace in the early 3rd century B.C. In adopting the form of a round building, Cyzicus deliberately imitated the Samothrace Rotunda. But there the similarity ends. Missing is the most unusual part of the Arsinoeion, the upper drum of solid masonry, decorated with engaged columns and a rank of windows. Missing also is the domed roof with a prominent lantern at its top, restored by the archaeologists on the roof of the Arsinoeion. In addition, the door positioned as if it was a window means that the Cyzicus monument did not serve the same purpose as the Arsinoeion: The Samothracian building with its steps was obviously accessible to the outside world, while the Cyzicus building does not appear to have been.

What was the function of the Cyzicus monument? The door-window itself, curiously enough, supplies the answer. Just such a detail has been found on actual buildings and is represented on coins and other objects. Called a "sacred portal," it was from prehistoric times onward the symbol of structures that were tomb/altar/shrines at one and the same time. One reconstructed most recently is the Sphinx monument at 206 Xanthos where a series of false door-windows, framed with typically Near Eastern receding frames or embrasures, decorates the facades and pediments. The Cyzicus monument, if it has a roof at all, undoubtedly had a flat roof which may be compared with the eastern altar/shrines, such as the so-called Fire Temple on the coins of Persia, 50—1

113

*Fig. 207 Detail of the relief from the gravestone of Attalos (mid. 2nd. cent. B.C.) Louvre. Courtesy photo. Musées nationaux, Paris.*

*Fig. 208 CYZICUS: The round aedicula of Demeter (c. A.D. 200) Paris.*

and it may therefore itself have been a tomb/altar/shrine, a most appropriate edifice for Fig. a mystery cult that celebrated the death of Persephone.

By a rare coincidence, there is preserved a grave relief of another citizen of Cyzicus, named Attalos, son of Asklepiodoros, who was not only an architect, a devotee of the Samothracian and Cyzicene Mysteries, but also the father of our first architect, Asklepiades. The miniature building of the relief in the hands of a female figure is 207 without doubt a copy of the Arsinoeion. It is not the tomb/altar/shrine of Cyzicus. The upper drum with engaged columns, the hallmark of the Samothracian Rotunda, is clearly depicted. More important, the very top of the miniature building, obviously broken off, was a lantern which duplicated the lantern of the actual Samothracian Rotunda, a truly exceptional detail. All other known examples of such lanterns are found only on coins and ancient models. Why the father-architect was favoured with the Samothracian monument, and the son with the Cyzicene building, approximately 150 years after the Arsinoeion was constructed, even the good Cyriac obviously could not know.

The lantern above a domed roof, however, is found on another coin-type of Cyzicus. 208 It appears on an open round building with peripteral columns. Tie-beams between the columns form a balustrade around the whole building. In the centre, the cult image of Demeter or Kore stands on a prominent base. Although the building resembles the Arsinoeion in some respects, it lacks the enclosing walls, stairway, peripteral steps, and the very characteristic upper drum and windows. But the domed roof with lantern of the Rotunda is a close architectural parallel.

It follows, therefore, that in the cult of Demeter at Cyzicus, there were two sacred buildings, both used in some way or other for the Samothracian Mysteries and both with architectural forms inherited from Samothrace. One may have been a tomb/altar/shrine. The other may have had the same function as the Arsinoeion. Unfortunately, as in all mysteries, what took place in Arsinoe's sacred building has not yet been revealed.

It is possible that Cyriac saw these two cult buildings at Cyzicus. The creatures of the Mystery cult, Demeter, Kore, horses, and others of the Samothracian records, appear in Cyriac's report of the temple of Hadrian at Cyzicus, the manuscripts even preserving the same kind of errors, mixing up the sexes (the three graces are shown as males!), changing torches to staffs, etc. The manuscripts do not make it clear whether the statues of the deities involved in the Mysteries decorated the sanctuary of Demeter and Kore or the temple of Hadrian, or both. Very little of the temple has been found; its unmistakable octastyle facade, however, is confirmed by the coin representations. Crypts, for the practice of Mysteries, were discovered under the temple and Cyriac's drawings suggest that the temple was also used in the celebration of the ritual.

The connection between the Imperial and Mystery cults was close: emperors and empresses were initiated and thereby achieved mystic union with other deities. Faustina at her death was worshipped as a new Kore Soteira, the principal deity of the

Fig. 209 Drawing of the temple of Hadrian at Cyzicus in the Destailleur copy of Cyriac (14th cent. A.D.) Courtesy B. Ashmole.

Fig. 210 CYZICUS: Temple with herm as the cult image (Faustina I c. A.D. 145) Paris.

<sup>Fig.</sup> city and of the Mystery cult. Hadrian may also have had a place in this Pantheon as a neos Hermes. In Cyriac's drawing of Hadrian's temple, the circle of the pediment is filled not with the bust of the emperor, as has always been assumed, but with a head set on a herm. This fact is confirmed by the Byzantine author Malalas who reports — the Greek has always been translated without a close look at the drawing — that <sup>209</sup> Hadrian placed a marble herm with his own bust at the "top of the temple." A herm <sup>210</sup> with the head of the god Hermes appears as the cult image of another Cyzicus coin-type. Although herms of rulers are known, the herm of an emperor in this context is so extraordinary that it must have had some meaning. Was Hadrian also honoured in the temple of Hermes, the god of the Mysteries, the god who played the part of guiding the dead to the kingdom of Hades? Caracalla also had a temple at Cyzicus which appears on the coins; but whether he too played a part in the Mysteries is not known.

Nearly all the coins of Cyzicus show that the imperial cult was inextricably linked to the worship of the great gods of Samothrace, the sacred island that gave Cyzicus its cult, its religious conventions, and, to some extent, its architecture.

116

# PARIUM

## THE TOMB/ALTAR/SHRINE

Some of the most adventurous, although not the most artistic of Anatolian dieFig.
engravers, produced the series of 3rd century A.D. coins of Parium. By using the
convention of "above instead of behind," they were able to show on a single coin both
an arch and portions of a monumental altar court behind it.

Several different examples represent the triumphal arch, made of masonry blocks, 211
with four columns on the facade, and three entrances between the columns. An
elephant chariot group is shown above the arch, an unusual motif for arches. One other,
known from coins, is the arch of Domitian at Rome, and Malalas described yet another 212
at Antioch in Syria. Several other details are shown as well on the arch-coins. One is a
naked male figure with spear of staff who seems to stand above the elephants on one
example, or between their heads and tails on another. Two statues appear either above 213
the arch or at the sides on apparently separate columns.

The whole design becomes clearer when the arch is removed, as it were, to show
what is behind. This occurs on another series of 3rd century A.D. coins to reveal an 214
altar which is quite unlike any other found on coins. Here the two statues on columns
appear attached to the masonry wall of a court in which an altar stands. The male
figure also pictured on the arch-coins is now shown decorating the altar. The
monument itself is set high above the pavement of the court and is reached by a flight
of steps.

Fig. 211 PARIUM: Gateway, surmounted by
elephants and figures (Gallienus A.D. 153–168)
Berlin.

Fig. 212 ROME: Arch (Domitian
A.D. 85) Paris.

*Fig. 213 PARIUM: Gateway showing elephant heads and statues (Gallienus A.D. 253–268) Berlin.*

Fig.
215
216
Some examples show a chariot group above the altar instead of the male figure. Within the chariot stands a radiate figure who could be Apollo Helios or the Roman emperor. As mentioned previously, by far the best known building at Parium was the altar which Hermocreon built from stones taken from an oracular temple of Apollo Aktaios and Artemis that stood outside the city. This was famous in antiquity for its size and beauty. The Apollo Aktaios of the city's Hellenistic tetradrachms shows that this cult was probably the leading cult of the city. It is tempting to connect the "Apollo" of the chariot group on our coin with Apollo Aktaios and so suggest that this monument is the altar of Hermocreon. Regrettably there is insufficient evidence.

The identity of the nude male figure, however, is revealed by several examples of the coin which show him flanked by snakes. He is Parius, one of the Ophiogeneis, who were changed from snakes to human beings, the legendary founder of the city which bore his name. He appears here in the very moment of metamorphosis from snake to human. As a hero, his cult was chthonic, his tomb was an altar. Athenagoras reports a tomb at Parium. The passage is admittedly garbled because at one point he seems to refer to Alexander, inventor of snake-shaped Glycon, and at another to Paris of Troy where Athenagoras quotes Homer, in both cases apparently referring to the same person. But he may even have meant Alexander the Great whose father, according to legend, was Zeus in snake form! The names Paris and Parius are almost the same in Greek, as well as in other languages. Both had equal antiquarian relevance for Athenagoras. But the coins would suggest that the tomb was almost certainly that of Parius.

The altar dedicated to the cult of Parius may also have been dedicated to Apollo who lost his temple outside the city. That the famous altar of Apollo Aktaios stood within an altar court is suggested by Strabo's remark that its sides were a stade in length. Strabo was undoubtedly referring not to an altar but an altar court. The altar on the Hellenistic coins which was discussed previously is assumed usually to be Strabo's monument; but it is only a small puteal for sacrifices, the vase and fire indicating the small size. As an altar court with a tomb/altar/shrine, the Roman coins of Parium depict a typical prehellenic structure, the artistic origin of which is in the oriental, non-Greek world.

98

118

Fig. 217

*Fig. 217 PERGAMUM: The altar of Zeus. BM.*

Fig. 221

Fig. 32

Fig. 221 EPHESUS: *The temple of Artemis. BM.*
Fig. 32 EUMENEIA: *The temple of Artemis Ephesia. BM.*

*Fig. 214 PARIUM: Altar surmounted by a statue of the hero Parius set within an open court (Gallienus A.D. 253–268) Paris.*

*Fig. 215 PARIUM: The altar of Parius surmounted by a chariot group (Gallienus A.D. 253–268) BM.*

*Fig. 216 PARIUM: Silver tetradrachm depicting Apollo Aktaios at an altar (c. 150 B.C.) Paris.*

121

# PERGAMUM

## THE ALTAR OF ZEUS

"And to the angel of the Church in Pergamum write: These things saith he which hath the sharp sword with two edges. I know thy works, and where thou dwellest even where Satan's seat is....where Satan dwelleth...."

Revelations II, 12, 13

The great "altar" of Pergamum shown on the coin of Septimius Severus was Fig thought to be the seat of Satan mentioned in Revelations. There is no way of proving 21 or disproving this, yet it is noteworthy that the concept of an altar as a throne is known from very early times. A century after St. Paul, the Latin writer, Lucius Ampelius, called the Pergamum altar, one of the wonders of the world, and it is certainly one of our most interesting numismatic wonders because so much of the famous monument has been discovered. It must be said at once that the term "altar" used for the building is misleading: The structure is a monumental colonnaded altar court on a terrace with a very elaborate entrance portico.

An early 20th century numismatist insisted that the coin did not help in the reconstruction of the altar court, but that the monument, once restored, helped to explain the coin! The opposite, as it turned out, was actually the case. The first reconstruction of the marbles in the Pergamum Museum of Berlin, made without an understanding of the coin conventions, was universally recognized to be incorrect. Even as the altar court appears now in the recent reconstruction, to some extent based 21 on the coins, there is more than a suspicion that the die maker's image and conventions were not sufficiently analyzed.

At one time the altar court was set up with two stairways in the facade of the entrance. Now the entrance has one monumental flight that leads up to the colonnade of the court terrace. The coins display the sacrificial altar in the centre of the facade, but this altar actually stood behind within the court. The steps shown below the small altar, spreading out as they descend, were taken to represent the monumental entrance stairway.

A question will immediately arise in the mind of the reader. If the altar itself should be considered as an object brought out from the interior, why wasn't this true of the stairway immediately below it? The answer is that the steps should perhaps be considered exactly in that way and the small altar may be reconstructed with the steps as a stepped altar, a form well-known in ancient art and one which appears on a good 15 number of coin-examples. Thus the steps themselves would serve the double function 257

122

of showing the exterior and interior of the building. The tiny sacrificial altar of the Fig.
actual reconstruction in the Museum does not begin to measure up in size to the altar
as indicated on the coins and, of course, it lacks the stepped podium just suggested.
The die maker seems to have been especially impressed with the size of the altar and its
podium. The baldachino was undoubtedly of bronze and was probably erected in the
Imperial period when a Roman altar replaced an earlier Hellenistic round edifice. On
the tomb of the Haterii there is found a good example of just such a baldachino which 219
provides an answer to those who doubt the practicality of such an arrangement.

In addition to the sacrificial altar and baldachino, the artist has also emphasized on
the coin the colonnades and bulls. The columns seemed far more important to him
than the famous sculptured frieze which holds an honoured place in every book on
Hellenistic art. The bulls shown in front of the monumental portico screen the famous
sculptured frieze of the portico from our vision. We may suppose that they have been
given this prominence because to the visitor they were indeed typical of the altar itself.
Possibly we have here a remnant of a familiar Near-Eastern tradition, lines of facing
animals framing the sacred way to the sanctuary. Just as at Didyma we have lines of
facing figures, so at Pergamum we may have had a line of facing bulls.

Another objection to the Berlin reconstruction concerns the statues placed on top of
the colonnade at roof level. In this instance the archaeologists followed too trustingly
the picture on the coin, without recognizing the numismatic convention of "above
instead of behind." In other words, the statues now on the colonnade should have been
placed behind in the courtyard. Fragments of figures found in the excavations identify
the Pergamene figures as Poseidon, Cybele, and priestesses of Athena. The coins of 165–72
Neocaesarea show a similar altar-court entrance and indicate that there were various
statues in the court behind the gate.

No other coin type is exactly like the Pergamene issue, but another building never
associated with it before is amazingly similar: The temple of the Severi in Leptis Magna 220
in North Africa. There is every reason to believe that the same artist who built it
worked on the repair of the Pergamum altar in about 200 A.D. The architect, the
master builder of the North African Severan city, is reported to have come from the
Near East; the marble for his temple at Leptis was actually imported from near
Pergamum. In regard to two architectural elements, the monumental stairway with
spreading steps, and the double podium which supports the columns, the temple is
similar to the "altar." The temple has the usual uninterrupted facade of columns which
in proportion to the platform are much taller than those of the reconstructed altar.
This, we might suggest, should perhaps be altered in the latter building.

The whole design of the Pergamum "altar" is typically Near Eastern, with
prototypes in Hittite, Mesopotamian, and Iranian art, where men worshipped in
sanctuaries open to the skies. The interpretation of the coins is perfectly intelligible in
the context of the conventions outlined elsewhere in this book, and they lead to a
more plausible reconstruction of the altar than did the archaeological remains alone.

Fig. 217 PERGAMUM: *The altar of Zeus. The portico has been opened to insert the stepped altar and baldachino (Septimius Severus A.D. 193–211) See colour plate p. 119.*

Fig. 218 *The reconstructed altar of Zeus from Pergamum (180–160 B.C.) Pergamum Museum, Berlin, DDR. Courtesy Elisabeth Rohde.*

124

*Fig. 219 Altar and baldachino from the Haterii sarcophagus (late 1st. cent. A.D.) Lateran Museum, Rome. photo Anderson 1875 B.*

*Fig. 220 Restoration of the temple of the Severi at Leptis Magna (c. A.D. 216). Courtesy J.B. Ward-Perkins.*

Fig. 221 EPHESUS: Newly discovered coin showing the temple of Artemis, with details of sculptures in the pediment, at the base of the columns, and within the cella (Maximus A.D. 235–238) BM. See colour plate p. 120.

Fig. 222 Elevation of the facade of the temple of Artemis at Ephesus made by S. Shaw in 1945. The steps in fact continued across the facade, and there were no parotids. Courtesy Metropolitan Museum of Art.

126

# EPHESUS

## THE TEMPLE OF ARTEMIS

> "For a certain man named Demetrius, a
> silversmith which made silver shrines for
> Diana....said...."This Paul has persuaded and
> turned away much people."..... and they were
> full of wrath and cried out saying, "Great is
> Diana of the Ephesians."
>
> Acts 19, 24—28

A recently discovered coin preserves one of the most exciting views of the great Fig.
temple of Artemis of Ephesus which was once reckoned amongst the seven wonders of 221
the world. The Artemisium was built in the 4th century B.C. on the model of an earlier
temple erected in the time of Croesus, which had been burned to the ground by the
infamous Herostratus. Virtually unchanged thereafter, the coin of the 3rd century A.D.
shows us how the temple looked at the time of St. Paul's visit to the city. Today the
temple of Ephesus is preserved only as a line of foundations and a few beautiful
architectural fragments.

The reconstruction is based on a number of different coin types, as well as on the 222
finds in the excavation of the site. The features that impressed Pliny the Elder were the
sculptured drums and pedestals, fragments of which are now in the British Museum. 223
One of the drums is nearly complete. Early reconstructions of the temple placed the
round sculptured drums upon the square pedestals as decorations of the columns of the
facade. The only coin which might suggest an arrangement is a silver cistophorus, 224
ornately decorated, which shows prominent horizontal bands at the base of the
columns. We believe that the artist wished to indicate in this way that there was
decoration in this position — not that this was a decorated drum on a square plinth.
The facade columns were decorated only with the round drums; the rectangular
pedestals stood elsewhere. The Ionic order of the capitals shown on the coins is also
confirmed by the finds in the excavations.

Further details appear in the pediment of the coins. Three windows figure
prominently and in addition there are four statues, two recumbent in the angles and
two probably female standing on either side of the central window. Each has one arm
raised towards the window and one lowered. These may have been the famous
Amazons which decorated the 5th century B.C. altar and which may have been moved
to the pediment of the 4th century temple in the rebuilding. The large circular detail in
the apex of the tympanum appears to be a head of Medusa decorating the end of the
great beam that supported the roof.

127

*Fig. 223 Column base from the temple of Artemis, as originally reconstructed on a rectangular plinth. Courtesy D.E.L. Haynes.*

*Fig. 224 EPHESUS: The temple of Artemis, a decorative representation on a silver cistophorus (Hadrian A.D. 117–138) Corpus Christi College Cambridge*

*Fig. 225 MAGNESIA AD MAEANDRUM, Asia: Temple of Artemis Leukophryene (Trajan A.D. 98–117) Righetti collection.*

128

Fig. 227 Clay model of a shrine from the Argive Heraeum (c. 700 B.C.) Courtesy National Museum, Athens.

Fig. 226 LAODICEA, Asia: Caracalla sacrificing in front of a hexastyle temple with windows in the pediment (Caracalla a. A.D. 215) Berlin.

Fig. 228 Model of a shrine of Ashtoreth from Beisan, Palestine. (12th cent. B.C.) Courtesy the University Museum, Philadelphia.

Fig. 229 EPHESUS: Temple of Artemis with a priestess (?) in the central window of the pediment (Antoninus Pius A.D. 138–161) Berlin.

129

*Fig. 230 West facade of the church of Mshabbak, Syria (4th cent. A.D.) Courtesy
Princeton University Press.*

Fig.
225—6

227
228
320

229

Most important are the three windows. Recently, a door or window jamb which once formed one of the pedimental windows was discovered, built into the Byzantine church near the site of the temple. There are many parallels now known both on the coins and on actual buildings of the Near East, but the earliest known example is that of the Artemisium. Evidence of such pedimental openings, however, is available from earlier times: In the Greek world we have the Argive Heraeum model; from Egypt a tomb relief found at Saqqara; and from Palestine, a 2nd millenium model of a shrine. In each case, the window appears to have served a specific ritualistic function, an epiphany at which the deity or the deceased appeared. At Ephesus an epiphany is specifically mentioned in an inscription (Dittenberger SIG 867.35) and there are several parallel Graeco-Roman shrines with pedimental windows at which there was probably a similar epiphany. Pliny (Natural Histories XIV 1, 9) tells us that at Ephesus there was a staircase to the roof level which, for all practical purposes, should have led to those openings in the pediment. A coin, a single specimen in the Berlin collection, appears to show a figure standing in the central opening, in the very act of an epiphany.

*Fig. 231 Frieze on the north side of the choir depicting the epiphany of Christ (?) at St. Paul-les-Dax, France (12th cent. A.D.). Courtesy Akademie Verlag, Berlin, DDR.*

In front of the temple was a court in which a great altar stood, recently recovered Fig. and restored by the archaeologists. We can now visualize the people assembled before the temple waiting for the epiphany of the goddess or a symbol of her divinity in the windows. Such a ritual is known from remote Mesopotamian and Egyptian origins.

Christian architecture continued the tradition of Ephesus as Ephesus had continued the traditions of the Orient. Early Christian churches provide many close parallels. A 230 tomb relief at St. Paul-les-Dax leaves no doubt about the functions of the pedimental 231 window: Christ actually rises through the window. The windows of the cathedral of St. Pantaleon at Cologne are a vivid example of the medieval age. The tripartite design is 232 still to be seen in the sanctuary windows of modern churches.

Traditions follow traditions: Long ago crowds of worshippers assembled in the courtyard of Uruk and of Babylon and of Ephesus. Today crowds wait in patient faith 233 in the court in front of St. Peter's to receive the blessing of the Pope standing at the central window high above them.

*Fig. 232 Facade of St. Pantaleon Church, Cologne (A.D. 980) Courtesy the Pharramt, St. Pantaleon.*

*Fig. 233 Crowd outside St. Peter's, Rome, receiving the blessing of Pope Paul, Courtesy Religious News Service, Wide World Photos.*

132

# SAMOS

## THE NAISKOS OF THE TEMPLE OF HERA

One of the longest series of coins to depict a single building — from Domitian to <sup>Fig.</sup> Gallienus — represents the famous temple of Hera at Samos and her cult image. The [234—5] sanctuary was as ancient as it was renowned, for the site was considered sacred as early as 2500 B.C. The latest results of the excavations show that the gigantic Ionic octastyle temple of the 6th century B.C. stood at the West end of a vast temenos. An altar was in front, to the East of the temple, but their facades were not exactly in line. The sacred lygos tree, famous in antiquity, stood behind the altar within a separate courtyard. Between the archaic temple and the altar there was built a small Roman Doric shrine with six columns on its facade.

With the excavations now quite advanced, the coins play an important role in settling problems of the architectural scheme. They show the altar and tree either on [236] the left or right of a temple. This indicates, as we know from the excavations, that the altar and tree were in fact positioned in front (a good comparison is found on the coins [237] of Tyre which show altar and tree in front). An illustration of the convention used on the Samian coins is found on those of Tripolis where the gate of the sanctuary is [238] depicted to the side of the Temple of Zeus Hagios.

*Fig. 234 SAMOS: The aedicula housing the cult image of Hera (Etruscilla A.D. 249–251) BM.*

*Fig. 235 SAMOS: The Ionic temple of Hera (Domitian A.D. 81–96) BM.*

133

Fig. 236 SAMOS: The aedicula of Hera with altar and Lygos tree to the right (Gordian III A.D. 238–244) Paris.

Fig. 237 TYRE, Phoenicia: The temple of Astarte with altar and date palm in front (Elagabalus A.D. 218–222) BM.

Fig. 238 TRIPOLIS, Phoenicia: The temple of Zeus Hagios with the gate to the sanctuary on the left (Caracalla A.D. 215–6) BM. See colour plate p.32

Fig. 239 MILETUS, Asia: Naiskos of the temple of Apollo at Didyma (Gordian I, II, and Balbinus A.D. 238) Paris.

134

Some claim that the temple of the coins of Samos represents the large Greek Ionic <sup>Fig.</sup> temple, others, the small Roman Doric building. It has also been claimed that the roof of the Greek building was never completed and that the temple was abandoned in the Roman period and turned into a picture gallery. Because the Roman architect Vitruvius called the temple of Hera a Doric shrine, it was inferred that during the Roman period the goddess was housed, not in the Greek building, but in the Doric. There is, however, no archaeological evidence that the Ionic building was ever abandoned. On the contrary, there is proof that a monumental entrance stairway was constructed to the complex during the Roman period. Also we know that many temples beside housing the deity were, like modern cathedrals, the focal point of tourists, treasure houses of the arts.

The image of Hera shown on this long series of coins was the actual cult statue of the earlier Greek period. It is the typical figure created in the Hellenistic period, based on the prehellenic type like so many Anatolian cult images. The 'temple,' unusually stereotyped for such a long series, is invariably shown with Ionic capitals, never with Doric; and with the exception of the earliest series it appears with an arcuated lintel. Furthermore, when fluted, the columns almost always appear with spiral fluting, a distinctly Roman form. The building cannot represent the 6th century B.C. Ionic temple, nor on the other hand, the Roman Doric temple. The details are so consistent that the type with arched lintel must refer to an interior, free-standing naiskos or aedicula in which the cult image was housed in Roman times. The coin of Domitian 235 alone shows the facade of the Ionic temple. There is a very strong possibility that the arched lintel, so rarely found in actual architecture, was present on this structure. At Miletus, similarly, the coins show not the great facade of the famous Didymaion, but 239 the naiskos that housed the cult image within the open courtyard. In the same way the artists at Samos could have been hinting that the great archaic shrine was actually open to the skies, as some archaeologists have suggested, and as was certainly the case at Didyma.

It does not seem possible that a city would have celebrated a temple on its coins with such regularity if the temple had not been the principal shrine of the principal deity. Nor do we believe that the architectural details would be so consistent if they were not recognizable as indicating an actual structure. Altar, Lygos tree, and Ionic facade are all accounted for by the coins. These must therefore illustrate for us the naiskos, the Holy of Holies, in which the cult image of the goddess stood, the essential element in the worship of the sanctuary.

Fig. 240 SARDIS: *Cult image of Artemis/Kore with pomegranate and corn ears (Commodus c. A.D. 175) BM.*

Fig. 241 SARDIS: *The temple of Artemis/Kore, symbol of the city on a medallion struck for the League of Ionian cities (Aurelius c. A.D. 140) Paris*

Fig. 242 SARDIS: *The three neocorate temples of the imperial cult, and the temple of Artemis/Kore (Elagabalus A.D. 218–222) BM.*

Fig. 243 EPHESUS, Asia: *The four neocorate temples – to Artemis, Hadrian, Caracalla, and Elagabalus (Elagabalus A.D. 218–222) BM.*

136

# SARDIS

Through the work of archaeologists in recent decades, we now know that many of <sup>Fig.</sup> the great cities of Western Asia Minor had a history as ancient as Troy's. Such a city is Sardis, the site of one of the largest excavations of modern times. Although a considerable number of monuments has been found, only one temple has so far been excavated. It was dedicated to Artemis and was the centre of the main cult of the city. The coins show us her cult image in a strange pre-Greek form, decorated with ears of corn and pomegranate, which, as the archaeologists have surmised from other evidence, link her in turn with the neighbouring cemetery. For these are the attributes of Kore, 240 the goddess of the Mysteries.

The temple of Artemis/Kore was erected in the Hellenistic period. It was once thought that it was originally constructed with two separate cellae and that it was also dedicated to Zeus Lydios, but the archaeological evidence suggests that the cella was not divided until a later period. A colossal head of Faustina the Elder was found near the centre of the temple together with a portion of the base *in situ*. Faustina, whose daughter at Cyzicus became identified with Kore Soteira, was thus at Sardis given a place in the temple of Artemis/Kore. Kore herself, as we know from the coins, continued to be the main deity of the shrine late into the Roman period, and her cult image stood on a base found in the western cella. Recent excavations at the West end of the temple revealed a stepped altar. Its foundations are dated to the 6th century B.C., and the whole site had an even earlier history as a sacred area. The coins of Sardis show Artemis/Kore in her temple, and it is her temple that is used on the coins of the 241 League of Ionian Cities, as a symbol of Sardis, with the cult image of the goddess dominating the facade.

The temple of Artemis/Kore is also represented on coins which show it with other temple buildings. One issue represents four buildings, two of them identified by cult images of Artemis and an emperor. The inscription around the coin demonstrates that Sardis was honoured three times with the neocorate title, probably under Hadrian, Antoninus Pius, and Elagabalus. Unlike the great Artemis of Ephesus, the people of Sardis did not gain the prized neocorate for the temple of Kore. A comparison of the coins of Sardis with the numismatic conventions of other cities shows without any doubt that the four-temple-type does not represent four aspects of the shrine of 242—3 Artemis/Kore as was supposed by the early archaeologists and by writers of recent handbooks. The coins show that there are at least three temples dedicated to the Imperial cult, still to be discovered by the archaeologists.

Another temple occurs on the coins of Sardis quite different in appearance. This is the shrine of Aphrodite of Paphos, clearly modelled on the well-known sanctuary in Cyprus and its prehellenic prototypes. The coin almost certainly represents a sanctuary located at Sardis, for it is rare that a city shows on its coins any but its local

*Fig. 244 SARDIS: The great altar of Zeus Lydios, with the cult statue and a tree to the right. Fine figure sculpture is shown as the relief decoration on the altar (Elagabalus A.D. 218–222) Paris. See colour plate p. 49*

*Fig. 245 SARDIS: The great altar of Zeus Lydios with statues of Heracles and Zeus Lydios (Philip I A.D. 244–249) Courtesy Museum of Fine Arts, Boston.*

138

*Fig. 247 A and B SARDIS: Zeus Lydios and Heracles on the two sides of the same coin (c. A.D. 225–250). BM.*

*Fig. 246 SARDIS: Statue of Heracles and the bull (Caracalla A.D. 211–217) BM.*

monuments. In the same way, the shrine of Aphrodite Paphia on the coins of Fig. Pergamum illustrated her sanctuary in Pergamum, not Cyprus. But the architectural 268 pattern of a traditional Oriental tower and courtyard was dictated by the ancient cult 266 of Cyprus and the great temple there.

By far the most spectacular coin of Sardis is that which shows a monumental altar, 244 the size of which is emphasized by the statue of Zeus Lydios on a pedestal beside it. The accompanying tree refers to a pastoral setting much as is found on many other coin types. The decoration of the altar consists of three statues in high relief seen against a masonry wall. The coin is precious evidence for other altars such as the Hellenistic altar at Priene where only one such statue has survived, and the 5th century B.C. altar at Ephesus, which was decorated with the famous Amazons sculptured by Pheidias, Polycleitus, Cresilas and Phradmon.

The altar of Zeus Lydios is identified by the god standing on a pedestal next to it, a prehellenic deity worshipped widely in the cities of central Asia Minor. Among the numerous archaeological references to this god at Sardis is a head recently found and thought to have been the head of a cult image. It is also suggested that this cult image was of Zeus Poleus or Zeus Olympios. However, no cult image or cult building of Zeus Lydios has as yet been discovered at Sardis. Given the great antiquity of the cult of the deity, the altar may have stood alone, open to the skies in a sacred grove, symbolized by the tree, at a distance from the city. The altar itself would then have been the focal point of the worship of the god.

A variant of the coin places a statue of Heracles dragging a bull by the horns to the 245 left of the altar, thus balancing that of Zeus Lydios on the right side. The same Heracles and bull, undoubtedly a statue group, appear more clearly on another coin. 246

*Fig. 248 SARDIS: Queen Omphale of Lydia dressed in Heracles' lion skin (c. A.D. 175) BM.*

*Fig. 249 SARDIS: The bull of Heracles before two altars on which snakes (mid. 3rd. cent. A.D.) BM.*

*Fig. 250 Heracles and the lion on the back of a model depicting a shrine of Cybele (mid. 6th. cent. B.C.) Courtesy G.M.A. Hanfmann.*

Fig. And still another issue represents Zeus Lydios, so named by legend with his image on
247 the obverse and Heracles on the reverse. So many coins represent the famous hero that
he must have played as important a part in the life of the city as Zeus Lydios.
Mythology in fact explains this. Heracles was sent as a slave to the Lydian Queen Omphale
to expiate the murder of Iphitus, brother of Iole, one of his loves. A coin of Sardis
248 illustrates his affair with the legendary Omphale in dramatic manner: the hero appears
on one side, the Queen on the other, naked except for Heracles' lion skin draped
around her shoulders. From this compromising scene, we can understand how the
legend grew that Croesus and the whole dynasty of Lydian Kings were descended from
Heracles and Queen Omphale. Thus both Heracles and Lydian Zeus belong to the local
Lydian cycle of Sardis' history.

Numismatic evidence also links Heracles with another prehellenic cult of Sardis. The
249 same bull which formed part of the Heracles-statue group, appears on another type, in
the same attitude, vainly stretching its forefeet in resistance. But this time the bull is
shown with two snakes on low pedestals. The snakes were without doubt part of the

*Fig. 251 Facade of the same model as Fig. 250, showing the image of Cybele flanked by snakes (mid. 6th. cent. B.C.) Courtesy G.M.A. Hanfmann.*

same group as the statue on the altar-coin. Since Heracles appears so early in the Fig. myth-history of Sardis, his snakes can be associated with two equally unusual snakes that decorate a 6th century B.C. model recently found at Sardis. The snakes frame the 250—1 figure of Cybele portrayed in half-round on the long side of the rectangular model. Heracles and the lion appear on the back of the shrine. The other sides are decorated with figures of moving females and lions in panels. This decorative pattern can be paralleled in Hittite art and Cybele, as Magna Mater, also goes back into pre-history. On the eastern bank of the river Pactolus, the archaeologists have discovered an altar together with a Lydian graffito naming Cybele. Lions decorated its corners, as lions decorate the model. It seems reasonable to conclude that the model was a representation of the altar which stood alone and open to the skies almost exactly in the manner of the Zeus Lydios altar of the coins. The Lydian monument was undoubtedly an altar/shrine.

The altar-coin which linked Zeus Lydios, the great male god of earliest Lydia, with Heracles, the founder of the Lydian royal dynasty, is now linked with an equally early deity worshipped at Sardis, Cybele, Magna Mater. In addition, the altar represented on the Roman coin, purely Greek in style but similar in function to the pre-Greek altar of Cybele on the hillside (the Hittite Magna Mater always emerged from a mountain!) illustrates the continuity of an ancient form and ritual for over a thousand years. Myth and legend grow into history as archaeology makes discoveries. We may yet find remains that will throw further light on the prehellenic cults and monuments of Cybele, Heracles, and Zeus Lydios. Meanwhile, the main cult within the city was that of Artemis/Kore — a goddess whose attributes show that her origins were shrouded in the prehellenic past. As at Ephesus and Perga and other cities, she assumed a Greek 334 name and a Greek temple; and it was her building that the people of Sardis recognized as a symbol of their city.

Fig. 252 SELGE: *Sanctuary of Zeus and Heracles on a high masonry terrace (Alexander Severus A.D. 222–235) Berlin. See colour plate p. 154.*

Fig. 253 SELGE: *Sanctuary of Zeus and Heracles (Alexander Severus A.D. 222–235) Paris.*

Fig. 254 *Painting with scene of ritual between sacred trees, from Mari on the Euphrates (18th cent. B.C.) Louvre. Courtesy A. Parrot.*

# SELGE

## THE PREHELLENIC SANCTUARY

The most extraordinary monument found on the coins of Anatolia is the one at Fig. Selge. Many attempts to identify the structure have been unsuccessful. The tree-like objects on high pedestals are set on a high terrace. In front of each stands an altar and 252 to the left and right are columns supporting eagle and Nike. A high substructure supports the terraced platform reached by a monumental stairway to the right. Some 253 examples show two ranks of steps.

The thunderbolt and club symbolize Zeus and Heracles, but the cult objects and the architectural form of the monument point to prehellenic deities. The cult trees have generally but incorrectly been called styrax trees; the styrax flower was said to have produced incense or perfume. The cult trees, however, are without doubt sacred trees, not pastoral ornaments. Hittite sources mention an "eya tree" on which a bag of gifts was hung. The duplication of the trees and of the columns takes us even further back arranged as they are in so-called Mesopotamian symmetry. Two such sacred trees are 254 found on the painting from Mari of the 18th century B.C., framing a ritual scene in a sacred area. Two trees, not as well-known, frame the tripartite shrine with characteristic semicircular court on an early geometric vase from Cyprus. 255

*Fig. 255 Geometric vase depicting tripartite shrine and sacred trees (8th cent B.C.) Courtesy Director of Antiquities and the Cyprus Museum.*

143

Fig. 256 SAGALASSUS, Pisidia: Double shrine in which two altars with their baldachinos (Valerian A.D. 253–258) BM.

Fig. 258 **Drawing of an Akkadian seal, depicting a deity seated upon an altar of flat stones (c. 2000 B.C.) Courtesy B. Goldman.**

Fig. 259 SELGE: Shrine in which round cult object entwined by snakes; below, thunderbolt of Zeus (Aurelian A.D. 270–275) BM.

Fig. 257 BOSTRA, Arabia: Altar of Dusares on a terrace (Trajan Decius A.D. 249–251) Paris.

Fig. 260 SELGE: Star entwined by snakes (Faustina A.D. 160–175) BM.

Fig. 262 SELGE: **The sanctuary of Zeus and Heracles with a barrier in front** (Commodus A.D. 177–191) BM.

Fig. 261 SELGE: The sanctuary of Zeus and Heracles with the "mystic E" inscribed on the platform (Etruscilla A.D. 249–251) BM.

144

Twin columns or pillars also have a long history in the Near East. The most famous [Fig.] are the twins, Jachin and Boaz, which were free-standing in front of the Phoenician temple of Solomon at Jerusalem. Very like the columns described in the Bible are the [277] decorated pillars on the Sidon bronze coin.

The architectural and religious traditions of Selge can be seen elsewhere in Pisidia. At Sagalassus, two altars are shown within a gate or aedicula, decorated with elaborate [256] columns. The stars over the altars symbolize a Near Eastern celestial cult related to the Greek Dioscuri. It is clear from the many examples of altars within portals on coins that this type at Sagalassus indicates a cult shrine situated within an open courtyard.

Closest to the monument of Selge is that of Bostra. The coins show a high terrace [257] reached by steps on which the altar of Dusares rises above, but by convention actually standing behind, three small altars or baetyls. He must have been a humourist, the numismatist who years ago described the flat stones as a pile of cakes. That they are the artist's device for showing an altar is evident from an Akkadian seal where a deity is [258] shown seated on an altar portrayed by means of the same type of stones.

The substructure at Selge is surprisingly like that at Baalbek. It is noteworthy that at Baalbek, twin columns stood on either side of a monumental altar/shrine in the open court above the crypt. Both at Baalbek and Selge, the god was an early deity who became Zeus/Jupiter. At Baalbek, the rites of both a mystery cult and an oracular cult [286] were practised in the substructure. The same can be deduced for Selge.

A simple aedicula on a Selge coin has a strange cult object, a shield decorated with [259] snakes. A similar shield is found on earlier Hellenistic coins, as are the attributes and heads of Zeus and Heracles. A flower-like object, surrounded by snakes, a star — it is [260] not the styrax bloom — also appears on the coins. The shield was clearly of special significance at Selge, since a great many shields decorate building blocks still to be seen at the site. Snakes, in their turn, may indicate a chthonic mystery cult as we have seen in the Sacred Sanctuary at Cyzicus. That the cult of Selge involved an oracle is further suggested by the mystic epsilon, the strange sacred letter of the oracle at Delphi, [261] engraved on the platform.

The sanctity of the enigmatic monument is emphasized by a low barrier occasionally [262] shown in front. The most famous barrier of this type is the one which stood in front of the temple of Solomon ostensibly to keep out the gentiles. One found at Zela closes [263] the gateway itself. At Sebastopolis a barrier stands at the entry to a court flanked by [8—9] columned porticos. Similar structures are found on a Roman coin in front of the temple [264] of Antoninus Pius and Faustina, and from the area of Pisidia itself, on the temple of [265] Men on the coins of Antioch, and on the subject of our next section, the temple of Aphrodite at Paphos.

Much more will be learned about this strange monumental altar complex when Selge is further explored. Future archaeologists must be fully aware that Selge continued her prehellenic religious beliefs and prehellenic architectural forms into the Roman imperial period.

145

Fig. 263 ZELA, Pontus: Temple with barrier across the entrance (Caracalla A.D. 206/7) Paris.

Fig. 264 ROME: *Temple of Antoninus Pius and Faustina. An altar stands between the barrier and the facade of the building (Antoninus Pius A.D. 141–161) BM.*

Fig. 265 ANTIOCH, Pisidia: Temple of Men with barrier in front (Gordian III A.D. 238–244) BM.

Fig. 266 CYPRUS: The sanctuary of Aphrodite at Paphos (Septimius Severus A.D. 193–211) BM. See colour plate p.154.

146

# PAPHOS

## THE SANCTUARY OF APHRODITE

> "But Aphrodite, lover of laughter, went to
> Paphos in Cyprus, where were her priests and
> her altars of incense."
> Homer, Odyssey VIII 361—2

Of all the great cults in the ancient Greco-Roman world that which preserved its Fig. prehellenic characteristics most clearly was at Paphos in Cyprus. Today, only the site and a few stones of the portico may be seen; but in Homer's day it was believed to be the authentic birthplace of the goddess Aphrodite, the home to which she returned in shame after being discovered with her lover, Ares, by her husband, the limping blacksmith god, Hephaestus. The coins show us the temple in the 2nd century A.D., a 266 strange oriental-looking building which owes practically nothing to the Greek and 268 Roman cultures. Everything in its style bespeaks the Bronze Age.

The central feature of the tripartite structure is a tower, opened to reveal the cult image within, the sacred stone-baetyl. The three windows in the top storey of the building are reminiscent of the pedimental windows of the temple of Ephesus, which 229 we have suggested were used in the ritual of an epiphany. Here at Paphos, the openings likewise recall the triglyph frieze of later Doric architecture. Are they the origin of this decorative motif? The line of the two outer pilasters is continued above the roof of the tower, surmounted by crenellations symbolic of horns of consecration, the typical prehellenic objects of adoration in the East. The building has three parts: On each side of the tower are side porticos with doves perched on the roofs; these birds were sacred to Aphrodite. Inside each of the two porticos are the "altars of incense" of Homer, thymiateria or incense burners, on tall stands, to show the ritual purpose of the shrine.

The whole complex is on a low platform, and a semicircular courtyard, shown on gems as well as on coins, is enclosed by an open lattice-work fence with gates at the front. The stone slabs of the court are clearly delineated by the die engraver: On them he has placed a long, low slab which was undoubtedly a table for offerings to the goddess, relished perhaps by her doves. To the right of this table, three circular details, always present and always in the same position, were also presumably places of offering or dedication. The whole design is crowned with the star and crescent, the symbol of an Eastern celestial cult, in ancient as well as in modern times.

Nothing of the 6th century shrine has been discovered. The coins and gems, the sole 267 evidence for the temple, not only show its appearance in ancient times, but also help to trace the development of its extraordinary architecture up to Roman times. The tripartite design and prehellenic cult objects appear on Minoan and Mycenaean 269 documents. A model from Lemnos delineates a later shrine, a divided entrance behind the typical semicircular court. This indicates that the shape of the court was not 270

147

Fig. 267 Gold plaque showing the shrine of Aphrodite at Paphos, with details of the courtyard. (Imperial period) Courtesy Ashmolean Museum, Oxford.

Fig. 268 PERGAMUM, Asia: Sanctuary of Aphrodite Paphia (mid. 3rd. cent. A.D.) Berlin.

Fig. 269 Gold ornaments from Mycenae, each with a tripartite shrine (16th century B.C.) Courtesy National Museum, Athens.

148

*Fig. 270 Model of a shrine from Lemnos (7th cent. B.C.) Courtesy National Museum, Athens.*

dictated by the shape of the coins: Such a form actually existed. A similar tripartite ᶠⁱᵍ· structure is pictured on a vase of the Geometric period, forming a link between the 255 Bronze Age and the Hellenic examples.

The tripartite design is also known in early North Syria. Actual remains have not yet been found in mainland Phoenicia; but the evidence of the coins, summarized below under Sidon is clearly important for the history of architecture; and in the lands under North Syrian influence we have temples with three cellae. Again actual tripartite temples have been excavated at Xanthos and in the Phoenician West. It is no coincidence that the sacred Eastern baetyl is found as an object of adoration both in Phoenicia and in Cyprus.

The fame of Paphian Aphrodite was world-wide and on coins we have two further illustrations of her cult at Pergamum and at Sardis, both emphasizing the semicircular 268 court in front of the temple. The former coin issue identifies the temple with the word 31 "Paphia." But neither at Pergamum nor Sardis are the side colonnades of the Cypriot complex shown: instead there are free-standing torches or incense burners, and columns surmounted by doves. Partly because of these differences, it is reasonable to suppose that the shrines depicted on the coins of Pergamum and Sardis are illustrations not of the sanctuary at Paphos, but of local shrines to Paphian Aphrodite, based on the design of the great Cypriot sanctuary. It would follow that the worship of Paphian Aphrodite required a special ritual which dictated the architectural form.

Fig. 271 BYBLOS: Detail from a coin depicting a view of the sanctuary of
Aphrodite (Macrinus A.D. 217–8) BM. See colour plate p.153.

Fig. 272 The temple of the obelisks, Byblos (18th cent. B.C.). Courtesy Nina Jidejian.

150

# BYBLOS

## THE SANCTUARY OF APHRODITE

"And I also saw a great sanctuary in Byblos, that of the Aphrodite of Byblos, and in it they celebrate the ritual of the death of Adonis....First of all they weep for Adonis, as if for a corpse, but on the next day, they declare that he is alive."

Lucian, De dea Syria, 6.

From Byblos, a city where Eastern influence was always strong, comes a monument Fig. that is unlike any other on coins. We do not know where the original building was 271 located since no remains of such a sanctuary have been found. The impression from the coins is of a most unusual architectural arrangement. It is most probable that the literary references to the celebration of the death of Adonis at Byblos should be linked with the sanctuary of this coin.

An equally exceptional sanctuary has actually been found at Byblos, dated to approximately 2000 B.C. and known as the Temple of the Obelisks. A large number of 272 sacred stones or baetyls, arranged strangely in a rectangle, were found on the site. Ordinarily only one such baetyl was used as a cult object. Otherwise the plan was like other Semitic sacred areas. Almost contemporary with this shrine is the sanctuary of 273 Nini-Zaza at Mari on the Euphrates which is remarkably similar to the courtyard pictured on the Byblos coin; for in both there is a single baetyl in the centre of the open area. Thus the Byblos coin type, like that at Paphos, is a direct descendant of the Bronze Age sanctuaries. It is interesting to note that a later development of the same arrangement is the Islamic shrine, the Mosque at Mecca with its Ka'ba.

The details of the coin have provoked much comment and one of the points of controversy is the porch portrayed on the left. It is sometimes claimed that this was an ancillary building, reserved for the temple priests. It has even been thought that it was a separate temple. However, the coins clearly show that the building is joined to the side of the courtyard. It will be further noted that there is an altar pictured in the facade of the porch and, as we have seen, this invariably identifies the building as an entrance way, not a temple or shrine, or for that matter a separate room for temple priests.

151

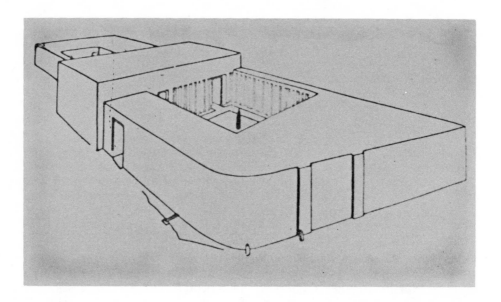

*Fig. 273 Restoration of the temple of Nini Zaza, Mari (18th cent. B.C.) Courtesy A. Parrot.*

Fig.    If this porch is the entrance, what is the colonnaded structure reached by steps that fills the lower side of the court? This colonnaded structure is not attached to the rest of the arcade of the courtyard. Further it is shown surmounted by a "horned" altar and this in turn is once more surmounted by the baetyl. In order to show this complicated monument, the die maker deliberately opened up the enclosing wall of the courtyard and replaced the wall with this structure which in reality stood inside the court. The baetyl on the horned altar is shown above although in reality it stood behind the colonnaded portico reached by a flight of steps. In effect, this colonnade acted as a barrier within the large central court and behind it stood the sacred baetyl either on the horned altar or behind it. The porch, the monumental Graeco-Roman portico, delineated to the side, may be envisaged as filling the fourth side of the court.

214    Thus interpreted, the Byblos monument is very like the tomb/altar/shrine of Parium. As an essentially oriental sanctuary, the altar/shrine complex is remarkably like the great court sanctuaries at Pergamum and Baalbek, and effectually links them as well to the Bronze Age temples of Byblos and Mari.

Fig. 271

Fig. 271 *BYBLOS: The sanctuary of Aphrodite. BM.*

Fig. 252

Fig. 266

*Fig. 252 SELGE: The sanctuary of Zeus and Heracles. Berlin.*
*Fig. 266 CYPRUS: The sanctuary of Aphrodite Paphia. BM.*

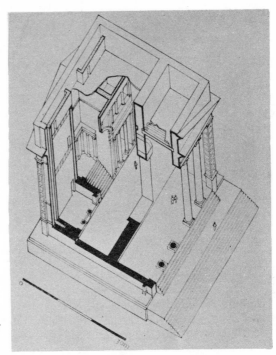

Fig. 274 Reconstruction of the temple, Kasr Fira'un, Petra (2nd cent. A.D.). Courtesy J. B. Ward-Perkins.

Fig. 275 BERYTUS, Phoenicia: The temple of Astarte (Diadumenian A.D. 217–218) BM.

Fig. 276 BERYTUS, Phoenicia: Marsyas within a gate surmounted by horned altars (Elagabalus A.D. 218–222) BM.

155

# SIDON

## THE TEMPLE OF EUROPA—ASTARTE

> And there is even another large sanctuary in
> Phoenicia, one which the Sidonians possess.
> They themselves say it is dedicated to Astarte,
> but I myself think Astarte was Selene; and as
> one of the priests explained to me, it was
> dedicated to Europa, the sister of Cadmus.....
> And Zeus in the form of a bull took Europa to
> Crete.... and the coins which the Sidonians
> use portray Europa on the bull, who is Zeus."
>
> Lucian, De dea Syria, 4.

Fig.
277 One of the coins of Sidon, known through only a few examples, gives us a rare and
extraordinary view of an oriental sanctuary. A simple form of perspective is adopted.
The temple building is shown directly above the columns that marked the entry to the
sanctuary. Looking at the coins from an architectural point of view, there are four
main elements. In the front stand the two great columns finely decorated with floral
scrolls. Between the two columns, but actually behind, is an open courtyard in which
the statue of Marsyas and the torchbearers on their pedestals are shown. The temple
behind is open to reveal the main cult statue of Europa on the Bull and smaller figures
in the side aisles. Colonnades stand rather incongruously on the roof of the side
chapels.

The columns at the entrance of the sanctuary are in the same tradition as the twin
columns "Jachin and Boaz" set up by Solomon's architect in front of the Temple of
Jerusalem, the capitals of which were also decorated with a floral pattern. Similar
columns are known from many Near Eastern documents and are the hallmark of a
sacred area. The Phoenician architect of Solomon's Temple, Hiram, came from Tyre
and the legendary temple of Melqart-Hercules of that city also had such columns. The
temple of Europa at Sidon, like so many other Syrian temples, has a tripartite
275–6 sanctuary. The two small figures appear to be cult images which stood in the side
chapels. The columns on the facade have been opened to show these small cult images
and the curious arrangement of columns on the second storey may be compared with
274 a temple at Petra where the two columned chapels are parts of an elaborate adyton.

The legend which brought Europa to Crete, there to become the mother of King
Minos, clearly reflects the penetration of Near Eastern influences into the Greek
mainland and islands in the Bronze Age. The Greek Europa can through mythology be
identified with the early Semitic Asherat whose name was later Hellenized to Astarte
or Atargatis. This Mother-goddess was a member of an early Phoenician triad. The
coins show Astarte in numerous Graeco-Roman temples, often accompanied by figures

156

*Fig. 277 SIDON: The sanctuary of Astarte/ Europa. Two decorated columns mark the entrance to the court, and the cult image is shown within the temple (Elagabalus A.D. 218–222) BM. See colour plate p.13.*

of celestial nature, such as the celestial twins whom the Greeks called the Dioscuri, best known under their Roman names Castor and Pollux. Here, at Sidon, the two cult figures in the side chapels were such celestial divine beings, connected with the Graeco-Roman cult image of Europa on the Bull. The torchbearers emphasize the celestial nature of the cult as does the Silenus Marsyas, the devotee of the great male sky god, Dionysus. This comic little figure with his wine skin is North Syrian in origin but is best known as the Silenus from Phrygia who challenged Apollo to a contest in playing the pipes. Just as Silenus accompanied Dionysus in the Greek world, so Marsyas was found with Astarte in the Near East. In contemporary Roman thought, he had been adopted as the symbol of the freed slave, and thus of the freedom, the *jus Italicum*, enjoyed by certain Greek cities. His presence on this coin may have such overtones for Sidon, itself a Roman colony.

The coins which represent the temple of Sidon, and many others dedicated to Astarte, reflect a surface veneer of Graeco-Roman culture over the ancient forms of Phoenician ritual, religion, and sacred architecture. The great court in front of the temple is particularly characteristic of this Semitic sanctuary. This is dramatically illustrated in the story of Christ's cleansing of the Temple of Jerusalem. The money changers are "in the temple, those that sold oxen and sheep and doves.....He drove them all out of the temple, and the sheep and the oxen... and overthrew the tables...." Money changers' tables, oxen and sheep certainly had no place inside a relatively small temple building. Even the worshippers may not have been allowed into the building itself. Thus it was not from the building that the money changers were driven out, but from the sacred courtyard, the place where the worshippers gathered.

157

*Fig. 278 HELIOPOLIS: Detail depicting the temple of Jupiter (Septimius Severus A.D. 193–211) Berlin.*

# BAALBEK—HELIOPOLIS

An unlikely legend attributes the founding of Baalbek to King Solomon and its Fig. destruction to Tamburlane the Great. It was, however, a Graeco-Roman city founded apparently no earlier than the Hellenistic period. Many years have been spent excavating to uncover and restore the monumental sanctuary and the other buildings 279 that attract travellers today from all parts of the world.

The sanctuary was dedicated to a Semitic-Roman divine family, Hadad-Jupiter, Atargatis-Venus, and Simios-Mercury. The temple of Jupiter, dating from the end of the 1st century B.C., appears on several coins identified by the accompanying 278 inscription I(ovi) O(ptimo) M(aximo) H(eliopolitano) and by its decastyle facade. The high podium with the flight of steps on the main facade is typical of a Roman building while the typically oriental window fills the centre of the pediment. This window was reconstructed in the tympanum of the large temple on the basis of the coins and because a similar pedimental opening was actually found on the smaller temple just outside the great sanctuary of Jupiter.

*Fig. 279 View of the sanctuary of Jupiter Heliopolitanus, Baalbek. The reconstructed columns at the rear of the complex mark the temple of Jupiter. Courtesy George Taylor.*

*Fig. 281 HELIOPOLIS: The temples of Venus and Jupiter (Valerian A.D. 253–268) Paris.*

*Fig. 280 HELIOPOLIS: The temple of Jupiter with rays projecting from the raking cornices and prominent pedimental window (Septimius Severus A.D. 193–211) Paris.*

Fig. 280   On the rare frontal view of the temple on coins appear strange decorations along the raking cornices, the importance of which has not been recognized. It is usually claimed that they are rudely depicted statues such as are found on the coins showing the Capitolium at Rome. They were in fact added and deliberately slanted to symbolize the rays of the sun, and to identify the building as the shrine of a deity who in one of his aspects was the god Helios, from which the Greek name of the city derives.

The temple of Atargatis-Venus, today called the shrine of Bacchus, was built in the middle of the 2nd century A.D., parallel to the larger temple of Jupiter. It was dedicated to the same Triad, but here a private mystery cult, associated with the worship of Bacchus was also practised. It appears somewhat stylized in detail combined

281 with the main temple; but the die maker, although a poor artist, was an adventurous one. Instead of making the two temples exactly the same, which was often done with types of two or more temples, he tried to show what he saw, that one building was larger and set back from the other. The so-called temple of Bacchus had stairways to the roof or attic, and part of the roof was flat. It was once suggested that the window in the pediment was used to reach the eaves in order to clean away bird-droppings; for some of the temples at Baalbek without pedimental windows were protected by metal screens. It was also supposed that the sole purpose of the window was to let in light. The far more plausible function of the window is that it was purely ritualistic. The stairway, the partially flat terrace, and the window permitted a sacred object such as

221 the cult image, or a copy of it, to be shown, as at Ephesus, to the devotees in the courtyard below. Such an epiphany is known at other sanctuaries in the Near East and in Egypt. At Edfu and Dendera, for example, the gods were carried up to the roof and there in the presence of the people, sacrifices and offerings were made to them.

*Fig.* 282 HELIOPOLIS: *The sanctuary of Mercury on the hill. The temple shows marked similarities with the temple of Jupiter (Philip I A.D. 244–249) BM. See colour plate p. 171.*

*Fig. 283 The ancient stairway recently found on the hill of Shekj Addallah and depicted by the engraver of coin fig. 282. Courtesy George Taylor*

Atargatis-Venus was the main deity of the Bacchus temple. The goddess is also Fig. shown on a coin which may represent the so-called round temple just outside the great sanctuary where she was also worshipped. The most junior member of the Triad, Mercury, also had a second shrine at a distance from the main sanctuary. A coin 282 depicting the temple is identified by a caduceus, Mercury's famous snake-entwined 283 staff, and by a great stairway leading up the wooded hillside to a walled sanctuary at the top. Ruins of a temple were found in just such a position on top of the hill Shekj 'Addallah, and part of the stairway itself leading up to the sanctuary has also been discovered. The coin shows two characteristic details of Semitic architecture: By engraving a border around the temple, the die maker has emphasized the typical oriental court in which the temple stood; by indicating the great flight of steps, he has made allusion to the "High Places" referred to in the Old Testament, and to the hilltop worship so common in the East. It would not be surprising if this sanctuary were not older, if less sophisticated, than the great sanctuary of Jupiter in the plain below.

161

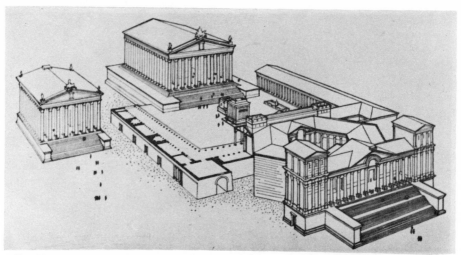

*Fig. 286 Axonometric view of the sanctuary of Jupiter, Baalbek. Courtesy J.B. Ward-Perkins.*

*Fig. 284 HELIOPOLIS: Monumental stairway and portico to the sanctuary of Jupiter (Philip I A.D. 244–249) BM. See colour plate p.171.*

*Fig. 285 CAPITOLIAS, Syria: Gateway to the sanctuary of Zeus (M. Aurelius A.D. 166–7). BM. See colour plate p.13.*

Fig. 287 The remains of the portico and court of the sanctuary of Jupiter, Baalbek. Courtesy George Taylor.

Fig. 289 Detail of a scabbard found at Mainz, showing a "Syrian" arch (A.D. 17) BM. Courtesy D.E.L. Haynes.

Fig. 288 ABILA, Syria: Gate to an altar court (Verus A.D. 161–168) R. Laurence collection.

163

*Fig. 290 HELIOPOLIS: Temple of Jupiter, showing 10 columns on the facade and 17 on the sides (Philip I A.D. 244–249) Paris. See colour plate p.171.*

Fig. 284  One of the most valuable of all coins depicting architecture is that showing the great gate and its flanking towers of the entrance portico to the enormous sanctuary of Jupiter. The remains of this portico were considerable and together with the coins provide good evidence for the reconstruction. However, it is worth noting that in the 286 latest reconstruction the heavy lantern so prominent on the coins has been reduced to a mere coping stone of the pediment. The Baalbek coins must be compared with those 285 of Capitolias and Abila to show that such towered monumental entrances were not uncommon in Syria and were as dramatic as the facade of a mediaeval cathedral. The coins of Heliopolis and Capitolias show that the central tower was clearly more 86—8 prominent than the archaeologists would like to admit. One might even compare the three towers of the military gates in other parts of the empire. Both the towers and the 287 arched gateway are inheritances from early Mesopotamia. The 'arcuated lintel' shown so clearly on the portico of the Baalbek coin, and found in the remains, is found as early as 1000 B.C., although it is best known from its reappearance in the 1st century 289 A.D. The name given to this motif is 'Syrian arch,' but surprisingly one of the earliest examples of the 1st century A.D. is on a scabbard found in Mainz, but perhaps of eastern origin. The earliest example on a coin is probably the strange building at 367 Caesareia, Samaria, under Trajan. This arched lintel so commonly found on coins is often not intended to represent architectural exactitude, but rather to indicate the arched or canopied aedicula over the cult image. Here, however, at Heliopolis, Capitolias, and Abila, it is clearly the mark of the gate to the sanctuary, and was almost certainly part of the actual architecture.

164

Fig. 292 NEAPOLIS, Syria:
Image of Zeus Hypsistos (M.
Aurelius A.D. 161–180) ANS.

Fig. 291 Image of Jupiter
Heliopolitanus (2nd cent. A.D.)
Louvre. Courtesy musées
nationaux, Paris.

Fig. 293 HIERAPOLIS–BAMBYCE,
Syria: Hadad and Astarte with shrine in
which standard (Alexander Severus A.D.
222–235) Vienna.

The ear of wheat in the gateway symbolizes the nature of the deity honoured in the Fig.
sanctuary. It is not the thunderbolt of the Graeco-Roman Zeus-Jupiter, but a reference
to Hadad-Jupiter as god of creation and fertility. The same ear of wheat also appears at 290
the side of the main temple of Jupiter of the coins mentioned above. A number of
reliefs and statues show the cult image of Jupiter Heliopolitanus as a typical fertility 291
deity; and in both shape and decoration, with registers of panels, it is like those of
Egyptian mummy-cases. The immediate parallel for the style of the Baalbek figure was
the cult image of Artemis Ephesia. It is important to note that the "window of 221
appearance" is found on both temples. Flanked by bulls, the deities on coins of 292
Syria, as at Chalcis and Neapolis, are close to the figure of Jupiter of Baalbek. At
Hierapolis Bambyce we have Hadad seated outside his shrine also flanked by bulls. At 293
Chalcis and Neapolis the images of the gods are anthropomorphic, but they both hold

Fig. 294 CHALCIS, Syria: Statue of Helios —
Helios Hieros usually called Helioseiros (Trajan
98–117) Courtesy R. Myers.

Fig. 295 HELIOPOLIS: The ferculum (portable
shrine) on which radiate bust of Jupiter
(Gallienus A.D. 253–268) BM.

Fig. ears of wheat, and at Chalcis, the name of the deity is identified by the inscription on
294 the coin — "Helioseiros" — a name clearly derived from, if not equivalent to, the sun
god himself. Similar figures are found on the coins of Rabbathmoda, Dium, and
Ascalon, supporting evidence for the wide-spread worship of such a celestial deity. At
Baalbek, Jupiter was, as Hadad, god of storms and fertility, but also, as Helioseiros
of Chalcis, the great sky god of Eastern Religion.

Two altars stood in the large court between the great entrance portico and the
temple of Jupiter during the Roman period. The larger one, the tower-altar, stood
closer to the entrance, its Semitic nature emphasized by the traditional twin columns
that flanked it. The altar was so gigantic that it obliterated the facade of the temple
from the view of someone entering through the portico. An ancient literary source
295 refers to a "ferculum" at Baalbek, a portable shrine which carried a sacred object or
image around the sanctuary. The pedimental window of the temple of Jupiter is no
coincidence. As at Ephesus, Magnesia, and Nysa, the portable shrine can be linked with
the epiphany of the deity at this high central window. Similarly the tower/altar derived
from the ziggurat must have played a part in such an oriental ritual.

Such was the sanctuary of Baalbek, dedicated to an early Eastern cult with
Graeco-Roman veneer, for which the coins supply invaluable evidence hardly
appreciated heretofore.

166

*Fig. 296 EMISA: Temple of Elagabal (Caracalla A.D. 215) BM.*

Fig. 297 EMISA. *Temple of Elagabal opened to reveal the cult stone above a prominent altar (Caracalla A.D. 216) Munich.*

Fig. 298 EMISA: *Temple of Elagabal (Caracalla A.D. 216) Paris.*

Fig. 299 EMISA: *Temple of Elagabal in three-quarter view, emphasizing the high podium (Caracalla A.D. 216) Paris.*

168

# EMISA

## THE TEMPLE OF ELAGABAL

> "The temple of Emisa, rising high, glistens in
> the first rays of the sun, the city spreads over
> wide fields, her towers reaching for the sky.
> Citizens with well-ordered, active lives
> worship the flaming Sun. Higher than the
> Lebanon peaks, green with opulent cedar, the
> temple of Emisa jealously competes, boasting
> of its tall triangular top."
>
> Avienus, Descriptio Orbis Terrae, 1083ff.

The late Latin poet, Avienus, left us a grandiose description of the ancient city of Emisa, but in an archaeological sense, quite inadequate. In all the centuries between Avienus and today, no archaeologist has explored the city (modern Homs). The coins, however, show the main sanctuary in its original form during the Roman period. They are, therefore, the only available evidence for the existence and appearance of this famous temple. Fig. 296—9

The great sanctuary dedicated to the sun god, called by the Romans Heliogabalus, appears on several series of coins. A conflation of all of them gives us a clear picture of the over-all design of the building as well as significant architectural decorative details. The lower drums on the facade were decorated. The example that exists both on coins and in actual fragments is on the temple of Artemis of Ephesus discussed above. At Emisa, we possess only the miniature reliefs of the coins which thus contrast with the majestic size stressed by Avienus. 221

The coins also show that the temple had a windowed-pediment similar to those at Ephesus, Baalbek, and elsewhere. The cult image in the centre of the facade is not the usual anthropomorphic cult figure, but the age-old Semitic sacred stone or baetyl which symbolized the divinity or the abode of the divinity. The eagle which decorates the baetyl symbolizes the supremacy of the sun god Elagabal, and also serves as a contemporary reference to the power of the Roman emperor. 280 296

Varius Avitus, a Syrian priest of the god Elagabal, a cousin and allegedly the bastard son of the Roman Emperor, Caracalla, became emperor of Rome through the intrigues of his grandmother and great aunt. Such was his devotion to the worship of Elagabal that he determined to make it the chief cult of the empire and had the god's stone transported from Emisa to the Capitol at Rome. His assumption of a divine name, and the orgiastic Eastern rites that came with it, shocked even the Romans. The activities 300

Fig. 300 ROME: Procession with the sacred stone of Elagabal (Elagabalus A.D. 218–9) BM.

Fig. 301 EMISA: The altar of the temple of Elagabal (Julia Domna A.D. 193–211) BM.

Fig. of this emperor are commemorated on the coins minted at this time: they depict, for example, the sanctuary at Emisa, the cult image, and the cortege bearing the baetyl to Rome.

Later in the third century, another claimant to the Roman throne, Sulpicius Uranius Antoninus, also issued coins depicting the temple of Elagabal. By this time, the baetyl had been restored to its original place in the temple at Emisa. Another coin type shows the great altar of Emisa, one of few such monumental structures found on coins, decorated as it is with ranks of statues in round-headed niches. The altar is shown 300 flaming and the presence of the window in the temple suggests that the altar was an auxiliary shrine in the court below the windowed facade much as at the sanctuary of Baalbek and of Ephesus discussed above. This may be the same altar which is shown underneath or in front of the baetyl within the temple facade, and, if so, it is possible that the court and temple could have been conflated into the same design. The interior of all Oriental temples, from the time of the ziggurats, was inaccessible to the general public. Only the priests were allowed into the Holy of Holies. At Emisa, therefore, we may surmise that the sacred object was brought out from its secret place into the open courtyard so that its worshippers could "behold and see."

170

Fig. 290

Fig. 282

Fig. 284

*Fig. 290 BAALBEK: The temple of Jupiter. Paris.*
*Fig. 282 BAALBEK: The sanctuary of Mercury. Berlin.*
*Fig. 284 BAALBEK : The portico to the sanctuary of Jupiter. BM.*

Fig. 56

Fig. 302

Fig. 56 PELLA, Syria: View of city with temple of the Acropolis. Paris.
Fig. 302 NEAPOLIS, Samaria: Mount Gerizim with the temple of Zeus Hypsistos. Paris.

# NEAPOLIS, SAMARIA

The remarkable medallions of Neapolis furnish details which the archaeologists can Fig. 302—3 use to supplement the meagre remains of the monuments on the site. A conflation of all the varieties minted during the second and third centuries A.D. gives the following details: A peripteral temple on the top of Mt. Gerizim, standing on a large platform; an upright male cult image with arms raised between the central columns of the left 292 facade of the temple; a horned altar to the right of the temple; an elaborate stairway descending from the temple to a colonnade at the foot of the mountain; several one-storeyed buildings on both sides of the stairway; a path with arches at both ends winding up the valley between the spurs of Mt. Gerizim; the right-hand peak crowned with an altar.

From ancient authors we learn that Hadrian commanded that a temple be built on top of Mt. Gerizim for the worship of Zeus Hypsistos, and that for its adornment the doors of the temple of Jerusalem be brought from the sacred city. Five hundred years earlier, in the time of Alexander the Great, the Samaritans under Sanaballet built a temple on the same mountain.

Recent excavations have uncovered the temple that Hadrian built. The coins show the correct orientation, north-south, but they have much of value to add since nothing but fragments of the superstructure remain today. They show that the building was a typical peripteral Graeco-Roman shrine, its main facade facing South.

*Fig. 302 NEAPOLIS: Mount Gerizim surmounted by the temple of Zeus Hypsistos. Altars stand to the right of the temple and on another spur of the mountain; and a terraced stairway leads from a colonnade, past sanctuary buildings, to the temple (Antoninus Pius A.D. 138—161) Paris. See colour plate p.172.*

173

*Fig. 303 NEAPOLIS : Mount Gerizim. A variation of fig. 302 (Antoninus Pius A.D. 138–161) Paris.*

*Fig. 304 ZELA, Pontus: Flaming altar on top of mountain (Caracalla A.D. 205/6) Vienna*

174

*Fig. 305 The arcaded terrace below the temple of Trajan at Pergamum. Drawing from the model in the Pergamum Museum, Berlin, DDR. Courtesy Elisabeth Rohde.*

The coins do *not* show the statue of the god standing in *front* of the temple, as has been incorrectly proposed, nor was the temple necessarily tetrastyle. It was once thought that a structure found under the Hadrian temple was the pre-Roman Samaritan building, but it is now recognized that the rubble and other fragments form part of an altar or a podium dated many years earlier. There is no doubt, however, that this heap of rubble became part of an extended platform to support the larger Roman temple. The coins show the platform as an arched structure which resembles the podium prominently delineated on the coin of Pella in the Decapolis. Actual remains 56 of such a supporting platform have been found as the terrace of the temple of Zeus 305 Philios and Trajan at Pergamum. The archaeologists who are still working on the site may be fortunate enough to find traces of these arches.

Remains were also found on the elaborate stairway variously described in the ancient sources as of three hundred or fifteen hundred steps. It consists of a series of small terraces up the side of the hill, connected by a short flight of stairs. Even this detail has been faithfully shown on some of the coins. The buildings on either side of the stairway stood on wider-terraced areas. Made up of two storeys, they were undoubtedly of a sacred nature belonging to the mountain-sanctuary itself, similar to those at Delphi. No remains of the colonnade have yet been found, but judging from the coins, it may have enclosed the whole sacred mountain complex.

The antiquity of the sacred nature of Mt. Gerizim is emphasized by the passage in the Old Testament (Deuteronomy 27.2). Joshua is charged to make the Israelites stand, some on Mt. Gerizim to bless the people, and some on Mt. Ebal to curse them. Similarly the altar on the right hand spur of Mt. Gerizim may be compared with an identical structure on a coin of Zela in North Turkey. The tradition that led to such 304 sacred places on the top of mountains, the same tradition that influenced the style and construction of the ziggurat, is here shown to be very much part of Roman Neapolis.

*Fig. 306 JUDAEA: Symbolic view of the temple of Jehovah, Jerusalem with barrier in front (Bar Kosiba A.D. 134–5) BM.*

*Fig. 307 Relief from the arch of Titus, Rome (A.D. 81) Fototeca Unione no. 14823.*

176

## THE TEMPLE OF THE JEWS

The temple of Solomon stood, as did its successor restored by Herod the Great, in ᶠⁱᵍ·

The temple of Solomon stood, as did its successor restored by Herod the Great, in Fig. the section of Jerusalem now dominated by the Dome of the Rock (the mosque Abd el Malik, the so-called mosque of Omar) and the mosque el Agsa. The Old Testament and other ancient literary sources give generous descriptions of the temples but the written word is so ambiguous that there is no agreement on the appearance of these two famous buildings. When, however, the Jewish rebel, Bar Kosiba, sought a symbol for his coins to epitomize the idea of Hebrew freedom in his conflict with Hadrian, he 306 chose to represent the great temple as it stood before its destruction by the Romans in A.D.70.

The coins display a facade of four heavy columns and a flat roof sometimes surmounted by a wavy line. In the centre of the facade is the Ark of the Covenant, the sacred chest that held the Tables of the Law. Below the building, instead of steps, there is a fence which extends the full width of the facade.

The numismatic conventions are easily explained. The four-columned facade represents the main entrance of the temple. The Ark of the Covenant occupies the position between the central columns usually taken by the cult image on a Graeco-Roman coin. Since there was no "graven image" allowed to the Hebrews, they adopted one of the sacred objects used in the ritual. Here it was the Ark of the Covenant. The Ark in fact is shown as a portable shrine with dots marking the frontal 307 view of the carry-bars. We know that in the triumphal procession of Titus at Rome, the Ark was carried high on the shoulders of slaves. On the walls of Santa Maria Maggiore, the Ark is seen being transported by soldiers.

The flat roof of the temple is typically Phoenician, consistent with the sort of building that the original Phoenician architect, Hiram, would have designed. The wavy line interprets itself as a row of Oriental crenellations such as appear on the shrine of Anu on the 4th century B.C. coins of Tarsus. A close parallel may be seen in the 96 representation of the temple of Artemis at Ephesus depicted with decorative rather 224 than architectural emphasis on a silver cistophorus. A fence is shown in the space below the building; in reality it stood in front. This is without doubt the barrier of stone which we know to have been set in front of the temple, engraved in Greek and Latin with a warning that Gentiles were not to pass into the sanctuary on pain of death. We have noted such a barrier on other coins in our study above of the sanctuary 263—6 of Selge.

The building on the Bar Kosiba coins is strikingly similar to the representation of the temple that has survived in the wall paintings of the synagogue of Dura Europos. However, here, on the tetrastyle facade, instead of an Ark, there is a representation of 308 the Torah shrine with prominent doors. A similar picture of the Torah shrine appears

*Fig. 308 Detail of a painted panel above the arch of the Torah shrine in the Synagogue at Dura Europos (3rd cent. A.D.) Courtesy Princeton University Press.*

*Fig. 309 Glass from the catacombs at Rome, depicting a Torah shrine between columns. Courtesy B. Goldman.*

Fig. 310 *JUDAEA: The seven branched candlestick on a coin of Mattatiyah Antigonus (40–37 B.C.) BM.*

*Fig. 311 AELIA CAPITOLINA (Jerusalem): Temple of Astarte (Diadumenian A.D. 217–218) Paris.*

*Fig. 312 AELIA CAPITOLINA (Jerusalem): Temple of the Capitoline Triad (Hadrian A.D. 117–138) Paris.*

on a well-known glass from a Roman catacomb. For the die-maker, the symbol of the temple was the Ark of the Covenant; for the Dura and Catacomb painters, the Torah shrine. Both objects were used in the ritual of the temple. The die-maker could have chosen another symbol of Hebrew piety, the seven-branched candlestick, which was used as a coin type by Mattatiyah Antigonus. Both candlestick and Ark decorate the arch of Titus at Rome. To this victorious emperor, they were symbols not only of Jewish religious belief, but also of the temple itself which he had destroyed. Fig. 309 310

The building on the Bar Kosiba coins is admittedly an abbreviated view of the great temple of Jerusalem although it does have a characteristically Phoenician facade and other Oriental architectural details. It is academic to insist either that the structure was the temple of Solomon, built in the 10th century, or the temple restored by Herod in the 1st century B.C. The later temple maintained the traditional scheme of the earlier, although it may have been enlarged to suit Herod's dreams of grandeur. But neither was extant at the time the coins were issued, Herod's temple having been destroyed sixty years before. Thus the coins commemorate a temple that not many men could have seen at the time of the revolt against Hadrian.

The coins really commemorate a sacred house of Jewish dreams of religious freedom like the temple of Ezekiel. But Jewish hope was lost soon after the coins were issued. Bar Kosiba was defeated. The Roman city of Aelia Capitolina was built on the ruins of Jerusalem. Today archaeological excavation of the sacred precinct is inhibited by the very sanctity of the site. Hopefully some day conditions may change and the great temple be brought to light again. 311–2

Fig. 313 ALEXANDRIA: The Pharos, the doorway
reached by a long flight of steps (Antoninus Pius A.D.
142) BM.

Fig. 314 Lamp made in the shape of the Pharos of
Alexandria (Imperial period) Courtesy Istituto della
Enciclopedia Italiana.

# ALEXANDRIA

## THE PHAROS

The Pharos was the Tour Eiffel of ancient Alexandria. In spite of an abundance of <sup>Fig.</sup> ancient and mediaeval descriptions and representations in many different media, the appearance of this famous monument is still a matter of debate. Although the coins[313] have always been used as important evidence for the statues, the stairway, and the division into storeys, there has been a remarkable neglect of the shield-like objects which appear without exception on every example of the coin type issued under successive emperors. These have been taken to be shorthand versions of rectangular windows.

The meaning of the shield-like details on the walls of the lighthouse becomes clear when they are compared to the round holes of Egyptian ceramic lamps which were [314] shaped to represent the Pharos. The lamps show that without any doubt the walls of the Pharos were pierced by circular openings and identical details decorated a glass vase found in Afghanistan. [315]

Alexandria was always a fortified city. Under the Pharoahs, the Rhakotis on the Acropolis, later a sacred area, was used as a fortified post against sea raiders. In post-Roman times, the Pharos was rebuilt as a fortress. In the Hellenistic and Roman periods, the Pharos served both as a guide to incoming friendly ships as well as a watch tower against unfriendly ships. We know, for example, of a mirror which was used on the Pharos until the 8th century A.D. to give signals to the mainland of approaching vessels. Fortifying the Pharos was in the Egyptian tradition. The Greek architect, Sostratos, designed the Pharos for Ptolemy II (286—246 B.C.) at a time of considerable political disturbances. A mosaic shows the Pharos with defensive crenellations in two [316] tiers, identical to those of a city wall Even the pylons of sanctuaries were protected against enemies, so that it should come as no surprise to find that the Pharos was a [64] fortified structure. For its function we can compare the look-outs and armed guards on [66] 'lighthouses' at Berytus and Aegeae. [485]

In describing the Pharos, a late Arab writer spoke of peep-holes in its walls. These then are the round openings shown on the coins, archer-holes through which arrows and other things could be hurled to cripple the crews of enemy ships entering the harbour. It is time that the high-rise dwelling proposed by Thiersch, and the modern [317] rectangular windows, be rejected. The Pharos was a fortified building with archer holes up and down its rectangular walls.

Fig. 315 Glass vase from Begrame
engraved with a view of the Pharos (mid.
3rd. cent. A.D.) Kabul Museum.
Courtesy Imprimerie Nationale.

Fig. 317 The old reconstruction of the Pharos from H.
Thiersch, Der Pharos, Leipzig/Berlin, 1909. Courtesy
B.G. Teubner, Stuttgart.

Fig. 316 Detail from a mosaic depicting the Pharos as a
crenellated fortress, Qasr-el-Lebia, Cyrene (6th. cent.
A.D.) Courtesy H.G. Bray.

182

# ALEXANDRIA

## THE SANCTUARY OF SERAPIS

> "In the city of Alexandria....the Serapeum is distinguished above all the other temples — because words are inadequate, this must be an understatement — the sanctuary is decorated with so many arcaded courts and life-like statues and so many other objects of art that, with the exception of the Capitolium in which Rome takes so much pride as a symbol of her venerable years and immortality, the whole world could point to no more splendid monument."
>
> Ammienus Marcellinus, Res Gestae V, xxiii, 16, 12.

So many Alexandrian coins are extant that it is as if the sands of Egypt deliberately Fig. preserved them for posterity. Their abundance, however, and this applies to the architectural types as well, has not added to their reputation. The many representations of temples are very stylized, and have limited use as evidence since so little of ancient Alexandria has been excavated, lying as it does beneath the modern city. But one important area has been exposed and with it the famous sanctuary of Serapis, begun in the Hellenistic period. The coins, therefore, which represent the Serapeum, are invaluable. 318

The worship of Serapis, Isis, and Harpocrates, the main cult of Graeco-Roman Alexandria, satisfied all the polyglot citizenry. The Ptolemies, the Greek successors of Alexander the Great, had changed Osiris of the Egyptians into Serapis; Isis had been given "ten thousand names" to account for her various attributes, and Horus was transliterated into Harpocrates. The Roman temple itself was not the Serapeum, but part of it. The Serapeum was a large open sacred area with corridors, subterranean crypts, and a labyrinth of shrines.

The principal function of a Serapeum — we have evidence also from other similar sanctuaries in the Near East — was the practice of the mystery cult. An army of divinities, Greek and Egyptian, crowded into the temenos, all of them related in one way or another to Serapis, Isis, or Harpocrates. We know, for example, that in the Hellenistic period, there were three niches in the portico of the East wall of the sanctuary for the images of the three deities. In the Roman period a large base in the open court could have supported a statue group.

Most significant is a 1st century A.D. inscription found in the Serapeum: "....to Zeus, Helios the Great, Serapis, and the gods of the same temple." Julian the Apostate amplifies this and calls Serapis "one" with Zeus, Hades, and Helios, a version of "three

Fig. 318 ALEXANDRIA: The Serapeum (Verus A.D. 161–168)
ANS

Fig. 320 Stele with false door of appearance from the tomb of Nefer-Seschem-Ptah,
Saqqara (2494–2345 B.C.) Berlin. Bildarchiv Foto Marburg no. 86916.

*Fig. 319 ALEXANDRIA: Serapis in procession saluting his alter ego (Verus A.D. 166) Paris.*

divine natures in one God." He was Zeus to the Greek population and Helios to ᶠⁱᵍ· accomodate the creed of the Egyptians, in a mixture of traditions that can be seen in the extraordinary coin which represents the Serapeum.

This coin has rarely been equated with the great sanctuary. Yet it presents a conflation of both the facade of the sanctuary and the facade of the temple building itself. The head of the main deity, Zeus-Serapis, appears in the pediment. As Helios—Serapis, the god's head is engraved radiate in the transom window, thus positively identifying the building on the coin. We know from other sources that such a window was built in the facade of the temple building and that through it the sun entered to "kiss" the statue of the deity. A transom window is not known on any other coin, but is directly derived from the window of appearance of Egyptian funerary reliefs. At Ephesus, three windows decorated the pediment of the Roman Serapeum, an architectural detail borrowed from the temple of Artemis of Ephesus, but owing its ritualistic origin to the Alexandrian Serapeum.

Looking carefully at the coin, we can see drapery under the facade-window, the tell-tale mark of a portable shrine. With this detail the diemaker has indicated that during a festival the godhead was carried out of the temple in a portable shrine. Another coin of Alexandria shows the deity Serapis as Zeus in a processional car facing his alter ego, Helios, high above in the Heavens, a reference to the ritual 319 associated with the Serapeum.

Three doors decorate the facade of the coin, signifying the presence of three chapels on the interior. The design at Kom Omba is similar: here two doors led to the cella which was divided into two chapels. The two guardian figures on the coin appear to be male and female, the deities, Isis and Harpocrates perhaps. The facade is remarkably like the screen wall of a Fifth Dynasty tomb. Note the traditional "window of 320 appearance" and the three false doors of Egyptian tomb architecture. Serapis himself was a chthonic deity associated with death.

Fig. 321 ALEXANDRIA: Personification of the Nile beside a domed Nilometer with steps (Antoninus Pius A.D. 133) ANS.

Fig. 322 ALEXANDRIA: The Nile reclining with a hippopotamus; above, a "genius" recording the level of the water on a stele (Trajan A.D. 114) ANS.

Fig. 323 Detail from a silver trulla with the representation of a Nilometer (6th. cent. A.D.) Courtesy Hermitage Museum.

186

# ALEXANDRIA

## THE NILOMETER

Throughout Egypt's history, the maximum rise of the waters of the Nile was <sup></sup>Fig. measured, mainly to establish a tax rate based on the average flood height of the river. To some extent, the actual taking of the measurement was always a priestly ceremonial, and at various stations along the Nile there were curious structures used to measure the flood, usually near a temple, and later called by the Greeks "Nilometers."

Although numismatists many years ago identified the Nilometer on the coins, it is 321–2 now possible to equate it with an actual Roman building found in the excavations outside the gate of the Serapeum. The archaeologists have established that there was a long flight of stairs descending into a deep pit resembling a well, which must have been channelled to the Nile itself. The coins show that in addition to the steps and pit, the Nilometer included a domed superstructure. The steps leading to it can be made out below the domed building. But other examples of the coin type show only a tall pillar or stele. In both series, a little "genius" of the Nile is shown recording the level of the water. In both cases the Nilometer is reduced in size to accomodate it to the small space allowed at the side of the larger figure of the river god.

The difference in the coin types can be explained by reference to another document, a silver plate which is usually but incorrectly interpreted as a representation of the 323

*Fig. 324 Mosaic from the 'Villa of the Nile', Leptis Magna (2nd–3rd cent. A.D.)*

187

*Fig. 325 Tapestry with the representation of a Nilometer (5th cent. A.D.) Louvre. Courtesy photo musées nationaux, Paris.*

Fig. Pharos. It is however quite clearly the Nilometer. The artist has deliberately raised the columned stele so that the viewer could see the "genius" marking it with Greek numerals. The stele actually stood within the building and within the pit, covered by the dome. It was a component part of the Nilometer and was displayed alone on some coins as an abbreviated view of the interior so that the "genius" could be shown. Such 324 a stele associated with the god Nile is found on a mosaic of Leptis Magna. Another 325 representation on an early Byzantine tapestry bears a striking resemblance to the domed structure of the coins, as does a lamp recently published and thought to be — in error — the pyramid-shaped tomb of Alexander the Great. To those who discovered the pit and stairway at Alexandria, it may come as a surprise that the Nilometer had a superstructure. The coins show it; the tapestry and trulla suggest it. The archaeologists have yet to find it.

# VARIOUS BUILDINGS ARRANGED BY TYPE

*(For figs 326–330 see colour plates)*

### DISTYLE TEMPLES

Fig. 331 *ARIASSUS, Pisidia: Temple of Pergaean Artemis. (J. Mamea A.D. 222–235) Trell collection.*

Fig. 332 *MYLASA, Asia: Temple of Zeus Osogoas (Elagabalus A.D. 218–111) Paris.*

Fig. 333 *MYRA, Lycia: Temple of Artemis (Gordian III A.D. 328–244) Paris.*

Fig. 334 *PERGA, Pamphylia: Temple of Artemis (Verus A.D. 161–168) BM.*

Fig. 335 *ABDERA, Spain: Temple with prominent door, fish replacing two columns, and neo-Punic inscription in the pediment (Late 1st. cent. B.C.) BM.*

189

Fig. 336 GERMA, Galatia: Military standards and city Tyche in imperial temple (Commodus A.D. 177–191) Paris.

Fig. 337 PERGAMUM, Asia: Shrine of Telesphorus on podium (Antoninus Pius A.D. 138–161) Paris.

Fig. 338 PERGA, Pamphylia: Imperial eagle in shrine flanked by standards (Gallienus A.D. 253–268) Paris.

Fig. 339 ANAZARBUS, Cilicia: City Tyche in shrine (Severus Alexander A.D. 222–235) Paris.

Fig. 340 ARADUS, Phoenicia: City Tyche in shrine with marked shell in arch decoration (Elagabalus A.D. 218–9) ANS.

Fig. 341 TANAGRA, Greece: Shrine of Dionysus with caryatids supporting a flat roof (Antoninus Pius A.D. 138–161) BM.

Fig. 342 HADRIANOPOLIS, Asia: Temple with prominent bases in which oil basin (Hadrian A.D. 117–138) Berlin.

Fig. 343 HERACLEA AD LATMUM, Asia: Temple of Tyche with marked antae (Caracalla A.D. 198–211) BM.

190

Fig. 344 PERGA, Pamphylia: *Temple of Artemis with barrier before the image (Tacitus A.D. 275–276) Paris.*

Fig. 345 CREMNA, Pisidia: *Temple of Luna (Gordian III A.D. 238–244) BM.*

Fig. 347 EDESSA, Mesopotamia: Temple within a gate? (Severus Alexander A.D. 222–235). Paris.

Fig. 346 CAESAREA, Cappadocia: *Temple of Artemis of Perga, on a silver cistophorus (Trajan A.D. 112–117) Corpus Christi College, Cambridge.*

Fig. 348 ALEXANDRIA, Egypt: Serapeum? (Antoninus Pius A.D. 149) ANS.

Fig. 349 PERGAMUM, Asia: Temple of Roma and Augustus (Early 1st. cent. A.D.) BM.

Fig. 350 APOLLONIA AD RHYNDACUM, Asia: Temple of Apollo, crater in pediment (Antoninus Pius A.D. 138–161) Berlin.

Fig.351 COMANA, Pontus: Temple of Ma (Septimius Severus A.D. 198) Berlin.

Fig. 352 AMISUS, Pontus: Temple of Demeter (Caracalla A.D. 209–10) BM.

*Fig. 353 MYLASA, Asia: Temple of Zeus Labraundeus (Geta A.D. 198–211) BM.*

*Fig. 354 SILANDUS, Asia: Temple of Dionysus (Verus A.D. 161–168) BM.*

*Fig. 355 EPIDAURUS, Peloponnese: Temple of Asclepius (Antoninus Pius A.D. 138–161) BM.*

Fig. 356 TEOS, Asia: Temple of Augustus (Augustus 31 B.C. – A.D. 14) BM.

Fig. 358 CAESAREA PANIAS, Palestine: Temple in which patera (?) On the podium an unexplained cruciform indentation (Herod Philip I 4 B.C. – A.D. 34) BM.

Fig. 357 COLYBRASSUS, Cilicia: Temple in which oil basin (Saloninus A.D. 258) Paris.

Fig. 359 SIDON, Phoenicia: Temple on a podium, flanked by columns of a colonnade; in front, altar (Early 1st. cent. A.D.) Paris.

Fig. 360 SAGALASSUS, Pisidia: Shrine of Tyche surmounted by mountain and two figures (Etruscilla A.D. 249–251) Paris.

194

Fig. 361 SIDON, Phoenicia: Temple of Astarte/Tyche
(Elagabalus A.D. 218–222) BM.

Fig. 364 COMANA, Pontus: Gate with broken pediment
(Septimius Severus A.D. 198) Berlin.

362

363

Fig. 362–3 ZELA, Pontus: Gate to an altar court
(A.D. 209/10) 362, Oxford: 363, Paris.

195

Fig. 365 BLAUNDUS, Asia: Temple of Apollo
(Philip A.D. 244–249) Paris.

Fig. 366 ATTUDA, Asia: Temple of Cybele (Mid.
3rd cent. A.D.) Paris.

Fig. 367 CAESAREA, Samaria: Altar, with barrier
and temple of city goddess beyond (Trajan A.D.
98–117) BM.

Fig. 368 THYATEIRA, Lydia: Temple of Roma
(Severus Alexander 222–235) BM.

Fig. 369 CYPRUS: Temple of city Tyche with narrow, central stairway (Caracalla A.D. 211–217) In trade.

Fig. 370 METROPOLIS, Ionia, Asia: Temple of Ares, with steps to the cult image (Septimius Severus A.D. 193–211) ANS.

Fig. 371 HIERAPOLIS, Phrygia: Temple of Apollo (Philip I A.D. 244–249) Paris.

Fig. 372 LAMPSACUS, Asia: Temple of Priapus (Philip I A.D. 244–249) BM.

Fig. 373 TYRE, Phoenicia: Altar in front of temple of Astarte (Elagabalus A.D. 218–222) BM.

Fig. 374 DIUM, Arabia: Entrance to altar court (Caracalla A.D. 198–211) Paris

Fig. 375 BYBLOS, Phoenicia: Temple of Astarte (Caracalla A.D. 198–211) BM.

Fig. 376 ORTHOSIA, Phoenicia: Tripartite temple of Astarte (Caracalla A.D. 198–211) Paris.

Fig. 377 TRALLES, Asia: Temple of Zeus (Verus A.D. 161–168) Paris.

197

Fig. 378 CAESAREA, Cappadocia: The neocorate temple of the imperial cult (Caracalla A.D. 206) Paris.

Fig. 379 ANKYRA, Galatia: The imperial temple (Nero A.D. 54–68) Paris.

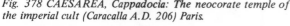

Fig. 380 SARDIS, Asia: The temple of Dionysus? (Faustina I. c. A.D. 145) Paris.

Fig. 381 ASPENDUS, Pamphylia: Temple of Serapis, (Macrinus A.D. 217–8) Trell collection.

*Fig. 382 HYPAEPA, Asia: Temple of Artemis Anaitis (Trajan Decius A.D. 248–251) BM.*

*Fig. 383 MARONEA, Thrace: Temple of Dionysus with broken pediment (Caracalla A.D. 211–217) Berlin.*

*Fig. 384 ZELA, Pontus: Temple or gate with broken pediment (Septimius Severus A.D. 206–7) BM.*

Fig. 385 DIOCAESAREA, Cilicia: Altar to the left of temple (Septimius Severus A.D. 193–211) Paris.

Fig. 386 MYRINA, Asia: Temple of Apollo at Grynium, with prominent Doric entablature with Corinthian capitals to the columns (Septimius Severus A.D. 193–211) BM.

Fig. 388 NYSA, Asia: Temple of Men (M. Aurelius A.D. 161–181) Berlin.

Fig. 389 HIERAPOLIS, Asia: Temple of the emperor? (Caracalla A.D. 198–211) Berlin.

Fig. 387 PHILOMELIUM, Asia: Temple of Asclepius (Severus Alexander A.D. 222–235) Berlin.

200

Fig. 390 NICOMEDEIA, Bithynia: Neocorate temple (Geta 198–209) BM.

Fig. 391 TRALLES, Asia: Temple of Mercury? with elaborate figured acroteria (Augustus 31 B.C.–A.D. 14) Berlin.

Fig. 392 PATRAS, Peloponnese: Corinthian temple with bust in roundel in the pediment, and tall figured acroteria (Julia Domna A.D. 193–211) Berlin.

Fig. 393 *APOLLONIA, Pisidia:*
*Imperial temple (Gallienus A.D.*
*253–268) ANS.*

Fig. *394 SAGALASSUS, Pisidia:*
*Large bust above altar in temple*
*(Volusian A.D. 253–258) Paris.*

Fig. *395 AEGEAE, Cilicia:*
*Temple of Asclepius (Macrinus*
*A.D. 218) Paris.*

Fig. 396 *BITHYNIA: Imperial temple (Hadrian A.D.*
*117–138) BM.*

Fig. 397 *ERESUS, Lesbos: Imperial temple (?) (Anton-*
*inus Pius A.D. 138–161) BM.*

Fig. 398 APOLLONIA, Illyria, Temple of Apollo
(Caracalla A.D. 198–211) Berlin.

Fig. 399 ANKYRA Galatia:
Temple of Men (Trajan A.D.
98–117) BM.

Fig. 400 CORCYRA: Temple of Apollo (Plautilla
A.D. 202–205) Berlin.

203

Fig. 401 ALEXANDRIA TROAS, Asia: Temple of Apollo
Smintheus (Commodus A.D. 177–191) BM.

Fig. 402 NICOPOLIS AD ISTRUM, Moesia: Temple of
Serapis (?) (Elagabalus A.D. 218–222) BM.

Fig. 403 HIERAPOLIS, Asia:
Temple of Dionysus (Elagabalus
A.D. 218–222) Paris.

Fig. 404 ARGOS, Peloponnese:
Prostyle temple (Julia Domna
A.D. 193–211) BM.

Fig. 405 DARDANUS, Asia:
(Commodus A.D. 177–191)
ANS.

Fig. 406 AEGEAE, Cilicia:
(Valerian A.D. 253–258)
Vienna.

Fig. 407 SIDE, Pamphylia:
(Valerian A.D. 253–258) Paris.

Fig 408 PHILADELPHIA-
EPHESUS, Asia (Trajan Decius
A.D. 249–251) Paris.

204

Fig. 409 ROME: Prostyle temple of Neptune
(41 B.C.) BM.

Fig. 410 DOCIMEUM, Asia:
Corinthian temple (Macrinus
A.D. 217–218) Paris.

Fig. 411 AEGINA, Greece: Prostyle temple
(Septimius Severus 193–211) ANS.

Fig. 412 EPHESUS, Asia: Neocorate temple (?) (Nero, A.D.
54–68) BM.

Fig. 413 DAMASCUS, Syria: Temple on podium over a spring; an altar stands in front of the steps (Otacilia A.D. 244–249) Paris.

Fig. 414 NEOCAESAREA, Pontus: Neocorate temple (Gallienus A.D. 253–268) Berlin.

Fig. 415 TYRE, Phoenicia: Temple of Melqart (Macrinus A.D. 217–8) BM.

Fig. 416 PHILIPPOPOLIS, Thrace: Temple held by Apollo and the emperor (Elagabalus A.D. 218–222) Berlin.

Fig. 417 NESIBIS, Mesopotamia: Seated city Tyche within pilastered facade (Philip I A.D. 244–249) BM.

Fig. 418 CARRHAE, Mesopotamia: Tripartite shrine of a celestial deity (Verus A.D. 161–168) Paris.

Fig. 419 RABATHMODA, Mesopotamia: Hadad-Ares standing on his temple (Septimius Severus A.D. 193–211) Paris.

Fig. 420 TRIPOLIS, Phoenicia: Tripartite temple of Astarte, (Elagabalus A.D. 218–222) ANS.

Fig. 421 SABRATHA, Africa: 'Pentastyle' temple with cella extending above the architrave and supporting a pitched roof (Late 1st. cent. B.C.) BM.

Fig. 422 NEAPOLIS, Samaria: Temple of Astarte (Faustina II A.D. 158–9) Paris.

Fig. 423 EUMENEIA, Asia: Round ? naiskos of Artemis (Philip I A.D. 244–249) Paris.

421

422

423

Fig. 424 PATARA, Lycia: Aedicula with
caryatids (Gordian III A.D. 238–244) Paris.

Fig. 426 AMISUS, Pontus: Altar and temple of
Zeus (Hadrian A.D. 131–2) Paris.

Fig. 425 SICYON, Peloponnese:
temple or tall column flanked
by herms (Julia Domna A.D.
193–211) Paris.

Fig. 427 TANAGRA, Greece:
Shrine of Artemis Huntress with
ship below (Antoninus Pius A.D.
138–161) Paris.

Fig. 428 CLAUDIOSELEUCEIA,
Pisidia: Snake on altar, with
flaming altar to right of shrine
(Tranquillina A.D. 238–244)
Paris.

208

*429*

*430*

*431*

Fig. 429 (Maximinus A.D. 235–238) Paris.

Fig. 430 (Maximus A.D. 235–238) Berlin.

Fig. 431 (Maximus A.D. 235–238) Paris.

*Figs. 429–431 Various views of the tripartite shrine at ANAZARBUS, Cilicia.*

209

Fig. 432 ROME: Temple, with large figured acroteria, between colonnades (Trajan A.D. 104–111) BM.

Fig. 434 PAUTALIA, Thrace: Two altars, Asclepius in tree, and tetrastyle temple of Asclepius (Caracalla A.D. 211–217) Paris.

Fig. 435 DALDIS, Asia: Mythological scene in front of the temple of Apollo (Gordian III A.D. 238–244) Paris.

Fig. 433 DAMASCUS, Syria: Shrine in which Marsyas and river in grotto (Otacilia A.D. 244–249) BM.

Fig. 436 APOLLONIA, Illyria: Temple of Zeus (Julia Domna A.D. 193–211) Paris.

Fig. 437 SELINUS, Sicily: Sanctuary of the river god Hypsas (Mid. 5th. cent. B.C.) BM.

Fig. 438 EPHESUS, Asia: Altar and worshippers before the temple of the emperor (Macrinus A.D. 217–218) BM.

Fig. 439 PERGAMUM, Asia: Sacrificial scene before the temple of Caracalla as Dionysus Kathegemon (Caracalla A.D. 211–217) Paris.

Fig. 440 COLOPHON, Asia: Worshippers before the temple of Apollo at Claros (Valerian A.D. 253–258) BM.

211

*Fig. 443 SEBASTOPOLIS – HERACLEOPOLIS, Pontus: Naiskos and altar of Heracles. See figs. 8–9 (Geta A.D. 198–211) Berlin.*

**Fig. 441 APOLLONIA, Thrace: Monumental altar (Faustina II A.D. 160–175) BM.**

Fig. 444 CHALCIS, Syria: Naiskos of Helios (Trajan A.D. 98–117) BM.

**Fig. 442 ADRAA, Arabia: Altar of Dusares (Commodus A.D. 177–191) Berlin.**

Fig 445 SELEUCIA PIERIA, Syria: Naiskos of Zeus Kasios (Trajan A.D. 98–117) BM.

212

Fig. 446 NICOMEDEIA, Bithynia: Galley with two neocorate temples above (Commodus A.D. 177–191) BM.

Fig. 447 TRALLES, Asia: Temples of Zeus and the imperial cult (Caracalla A.D. 198–211) Paris.

Fig. 448 CYZICUS, Asia: The two neocorate temples (Caracalla A.D. 211–217) Paris.

Fig. 449 ANKYRA, Galatia: The gates to two altar courts (Gallienus A.D. 253–268) ANS.

Fig. 450 PERGAMUM, Asia: Column and two imperial temples (Commodus A.D. 175–191) Paris.

Fig. 451 BEROEA ?, Macedonia: Column and two neocorate temples (Severus Alexander A.D. 222–235) Berlin.

Fig. 452 DAMASCUS, Syria: Two imperial temples, and aedicula of the city Tyche (Philip I A.D. 244–249) BM.

Fig. 453 SIDE, Pamphylia: The temple of Apollo and two imperial temples (Trebonianus Gallus A.D. 251–253) Paris.

*Fig. 455 SMYRNA, Asia: The temples of Tiberius, Roma, and Hadrian (Caracalla A.D. 211–217) Paris.*

*Fig. 454 PERGAMUM, Asia: The three neocorate temples (Caracalla A.D. 211–217) Paris.*

*Fig. 457 NICOMEDEIA, Bithynia: Galley with three temples (Valerian A.D. 253–258) ANS.*

*Fig. 456 NICOMEDEIA, Bithynia: Temple of Demeter and two neocorate temples (Severus Alexander A.D. 222–235) BM.*

*Fig. 458 THESSALONICA, Macedonia: Four neocorate temples (Trajan Decius A.D. 249–251) BM.*

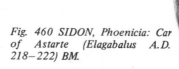

*Fig. 459 EPHESUS, Asia: Horse drawn aedicula (Valerian A.D. 253–258) BM.*

*Fig. 460 SIDON, Phoenicia: Car of Astarte (Elagabalus A.D. 218–222) BM.*

*Fig. 461 ANAZARBUS, Cilicia: Elephants drawing carriage on which replica of temple (Julia Maesa A.D. 222–235) ANS.*

*Fig. 462 PALTUS, Syria: Shrine fitted with carry bars (Septimius Severus A.D. 193–211) Paris.*

*Fig. 463 PTOLEMAIS, Phoenicia: Flat roofed shrine of Hadad with carry bars (Macrinus A.D. 217–218) Berlin.*

464

465

*Figs. 464 and 465 TYRE, Phoenicia: Oriental shrines fitted with carry bars (Gallienus A.D. 253–268). 464, ANS; 465 Berlin.*

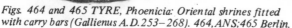

216

Fig. 466 ASCALON, Palestine: Oriental shrine with receding embrasures (Antoninus Pius A.D. 150) Vienna.

Fig. 467 DAMASCUS, Syria: Shrine of Astarte-Tyche, fitted with carry bars; below image, rectangular area decorated with ram (Philip II A.D. 244–249) Berlin.

Fig. 468 TYRE, Phoenicia: Shrine of Astarte-Tyche (Gallienus A.D. 253–268) BM.

Fig. 469 LAODICEA AD MARE, Syria: Bust of Julia Domna in shrine (Septimius Severus A.D. 193–211) ANS.

Fig. 470 SIDE, Pamphylia: Shrine of Tyche with prominent conical roof topped with pomegranate (Salonina A.D. 253–268) Vienna.

217

Fig. 471 TOPIRUS, Thrace: Round monument (Antoninus Pius A.D. 138–161) Paris.

Fig. 472 TOPIRUS, Thrace: Round monument flanked by equestrian statues (Caracalla A.D. 211–217) Berlin

Fig. 473 HERACLEA, Bithynia: Stadium building with temple at one end (c. A.D. 240) Berlin.

Fig. 474 ALEXANDRIA TROAS, Asia: Bouleuterion in session (Trebonianus Gallus A.D. 251–253) BM.

*Fig. 477 ROME: Two storied portico; Basilica Aemilia (61 B.C.) BM.*

*Fig. 475 PAESTUM, Italy: Two storied building with pitched roof and arcade (Late 1st cent. B.C.) ANS.*

*Fig. 478 BURA, Peloponnese: Portico or arcade (Septimius Severus A.D. 193–211) Oxford.*

*Fig. 476 NYSA, Asia: Double storied arcade with large figures at roof level (Gallienus A.D. 253–268) Berlin.*

*Fig. 479 CORINTH, Peloponnese: Enclosure and tree (Verus A.D. 161–168) BM.*

Fig. 481 SIDE, Pamphylia: Harbour and arcades
(Gallienus A.D. 253–268) BM.

Fig. 480 PTOLEMAIS, Phoenicia:
Harbour with colonnades around
(Elagabalus A.D. 218–222) P. Franke coll.

Fig. 483 SOLI-POMPEIOPOLIS,
Cilicia: Harbour and the god
Oceanus (Antoninus Pius A.D.

Fig. 482 MEGARA, Greece: Ornate gate and
the harbour at Pagae (Geta A.D. 198–211)
Berlin.

Fig. 484 MOTHONE, Peloponnese:
Harbour with statue at entrance (Geta
A.D. 198–211) Berlin.

Fig. 487 OLBA, Cilicia: Crenellated tower (Early 2nd cent. A.D.) Paris.

Fig. 485 AEGEAE, Cilicia: Ship sailing past a guarded tower (Trajan Decius A.D. 249–251) Paris.

Fig. 488 ALEXANDRIA, Egypt: Fountain with three spouts in lower part, four columns above, between which three figures; flat roof decorated with eagle and acroteria (Trajan A.D. 109) Paris.

Fig. 486 ABYDUS, Asia: Heroic scene of ships with trumpeter in tower (Septimius Severus A.D.193–211) Paris.

Fig. 490 AUGUSTA TRAIANA, Thrace: Shrine
of Apollo (Caracalla A.D. 198–211) Berlin.

Fig. 489 ALEXANDRIA (Aphroditopolite Nome) Egypt:
Shrine with two sacred cats on pedestals (Trajan A.D.
98–117) BM.

Fig. 491 ALEXANDRIA (Aphroditopolite Nome) Egypt: Shrine of Isis
with sacred birds on pedestals (Trajan
A.D. 112) Paris.

Fig. 492 ALEXANDRIA, Egypt:
Shrine of Harpokrates of Mendes
(Hadrian A.D. 134.) Paris.

Fig. 493 ALEXANDRIA, Egypt:
Shrine with Canopi (Hadrian A.D.
134) Paris.

Fig. 494 ALEXANDRIA,
Egypt: Shrine with griffin
(Hadrian A.D. 137) ANS.

Fig. 495 MEGARA, Greece: Shrine with
herm (Geta A.D. 198–211) Berlin.

222

Fig. 496 NICAEA, Bithynia: Tyche crowned with city gate
(M. Aurelius A.D. 161–180) Paris.

Fig. 497 BIZYA, Thrace: Ornate
city gate (Antoninus Pius A.D.
138–161) Courtesy Dr. H.A.
Cahn.

Fig. 498 PAGAE, Greece: City gate with
figures (Septimius Severus A.D.
193–211) Berlin.

Fig. 499 MARCIANOPOLIS, Thrace: City gate
(Gordian III A.D. 238–244) Paris.

Fig. 500 TOMI, Thrace: City gate
(Maximus A.D. 235–238) ANS.

223

Fig. 501 MARCIANOPOLIS, Thrace: Crenellated gate (Gordian III A.D. 238–244) Paris.

Fig. 502 ISAURA, Crenellated gate with central tower (Septimius Severus, A.D. 193–211) Paris.

Fig. 502 SIDE, Pamphylia: Crenellated gate (Valerian A.D. 253–258) BM.

Fig. 504, HADRIANOPOLIS, Thrace: City gate (Gordian III A.D. 238–244) ANS.

Fig. 505 PRUSIAS AD HYPIUM, Bithynia: City gate (Gallienus A.D. 253–268) P. Bastien coll.

224

Fig. 506 ROME: Ornamental triumphal arch (Trajan A.D. 104–111) BM.

Fig. 507 DIOCAESAREA, Cilicia: Arch with figures (Otacilia A.D. 244–249) Paris.

Fig. 508 MAURETANIA: Portico with narrow stairway; cella wall and roof visible above (Juba I 60–46 B.C.) Paris.

Fig. 509 ALEXANDRIA, Egypt: Pylon to the sanctuary of Isis (Hadrian A.D. 135) Berlin.

*Fig. 511 TARSUS, Cilicia: Ornamental gate (Caracalla A.D. 198–211) ANS.*

*Fig. 510 ALEXANDRIA (Heracleopolite Nome) Egypt: Shrine of Heracles (Trajan A.D. 110) BM.*

*Fig. 512 PAGAE, Greece: Two storey gate with image of Heracles (Septimius Severus A.D. 193–211) ANS.*

*Fig. 513 CAESAREA GERMANICA, Bithynia: City walls and gate (Germanicus c. A.D. 40) ANS.*

*Fig. 514 ZELA, Pontus: The Propylaea on the Acropolis (Caracalla A.D. 198–211) Berlin.*

226

515

516

517

Fig. 515 PTOLEMAIS, Phoe-
nicia: The Acropolis (Elagabalus A.D. 218–222) Paris.

Fig. 516 ANAZARBUS,
Cilicia: The Acropolis with
head of Zeus in the foreground
(Claudius A.D. 45) Berlin.

Fig. 517 GANGRA, Paphlag-
onia: Towers and two secular
buildings (Caracalla A.D. 198–
211) Berlin.

Fig. 518 EPHESUS, Asia; Jupiter Pluvius seated above the city (Antoninus Pius A.D. 138–161) BM.

Fig. 521 EMERITA, Spain: Gate and city walls (Tiberius A.D. 14–38) BM.

Fig. 519 SARDIS, Asia: Lion before the walls of the city (Caracalla A.D. 198–211) Vienna.

Fig. 520 EPHESUS, Asia Galley carrying image of Artemis with the city in the distance (Gordian III 238–244) Paris.

Fig. 522 PELLA ? Macedonia; The city walls (Late 1st. cent. B.C.) BM.

# BIBLIOGRAPHY

This selection of references to earlier work is intended to lead the reader to a more intimate acquaintance with the problems involved. It does not set out to be a comprehensive list of all relevant works, but supplements the chapters of this book both as a guide to further reading and as explanation of certain remarks which we have felt it necessary to make.

## NUMISMATIC

**(For reference to the catalogues of cabinets, see Grierson)**

**L. Anson,** Numismatica Graeca, 1–11, Greek Coin-Types Classified for Immediate Identification, London, 1910–1916 (reprint, 1967).

**Antonio García y Bellido,** Hispania Graeca, Tome II (Instituto Espãnol de Estudios Mediterraneos, Publicacions sobre arte y arquelogia), Barcelona, 1948, 219-231.

**A. Beltran,** "Los Monumentos en las monedas Hispano-Romanas," Archivo Espaõl de Arqueologia, xxvi, 1953, 39–66.

**C. Bosch,** "Die kleinasiatischen Münzen der römischen Kaiserzeit," Jahrbuch des Deutschen Archäologischen Institutes, Archäologischer Anzeiger, Berlin, 423–455.

**British Museum,** Coins of the Roman Republic in the British Museum, 1910 (1970) (H. Grueber).

**British Museum.** Coins of the Roman Empire in the British Museum, 1923 (in progress) (H. Mattingly).

**G. Dattari,** Numi Augg. Alexandrinii. Catalogo della Collezione G. Dattari, Cairo, 1901 (reprint, 1969).

**L.F.J.C. De Saulcy,** Numismatique de la Terre Sainte, Paris, 1874.

**T.L. Donaldson,** Architectura Numismatica, London, 1859 (reprint, 1966).

**Thomas Drew-Bear,** "Representations of Temples on the Greek Imperial Coinage," American Numismatic Society Museum Notes 19, 1974, 27–63.

**Günter Fuchs,** Architekturdarstellungen auf römischen Münzen der Republic und der frühen Kaiserzeit (Deutsches Archäologisches Institut, Antike Münzen und geschnittene Steine, ed. Erich Boehringer, No. 1) Berlin, 1969.

**Philip Grierson,** Bibliographie numismatique, Bruxelles, 1966.

**Konrad Kraft,** Das System der Kaiserzeitlichen Münzprägung in Kleinasien, Materialien und Entwürfe, Berlin, 1972.

**Fernand Chapouthier,** Les Dioscures au service d'une déesse. Étude d'iconographie religieuse, Paris, 1936.

**Tony Hackens,** "Architectura Numismatica, à propos de quelques publications récentes," L'Antiquité Classique, xli, 1972, 244–254.

**F. Imhoof-Blumer and P. Gardner,** A Numismatic Commentary on Pausanias, London, 1887 (Journal of Hellenic Studies, 6, 1885; 7, 1886, 8, 1887) (reprint, 1964).

**Harald Küthmann** et al, (Antike) Bauten Roms auf Münzen und Medaillen, München, 1973.

**L. Lacroix,** Les reproductions de statues sur les monnaies grecques, Liège, 1949.

**Josef Liegle,** "Architekturbilder auf antiken Münzen," Die Antike, Zeitschrift für Kunst und Kultur der Klassischenaltertums, xii, 1936, 202–228.

**Mattingly, Sydenham, Sutherland, Kent, and Carson,** Roman Imperial Coinage, British Museum, 1923 (in progress).

**George C. Miles,** "Mihrab and Anazah: A Study in Early Islamic Iconography," Archaeologica Orientalia in Memoriam Ernst Herzfeld, New York, 1952, 156–171.

**J.C. Milne,** University of Oxford, Ashmolean Museum, Catalogue of the Alexandrian Coins, Oxford, 1933, (New Edition, 1971).

**J.C. Milne,** "Pictorial Coin Types at the Roman Mint in Alexandria," Journal of Egyptian Archaeology, 1943, 1950, 1951, continued by J.W. Curtis, ibid., 1955.

**Erwin Ohlemutz,** Die Kulte und Heiligtümer der Götter in Pergamon, Darmstadt, 1940 (reprint, 1968).

**M. Jessop Price,** "Architecture on ancient coins," The Classical Tradition (The British Museum Yearbook I, 1976) 33–47.

**Kurt Regling.** "Die Münzen als Hilfsmittel der archäolgischen Forschung," Walter Otto, Handbuch der Archäologie, München, 1939, 134–144. (Reprint, 1969).

J. Rouvier, "Numismatique des villes de la Phénicie," Journal internationale d'archéologie numismatique, Athens, 3, 1900, 125–168, 237–312; 4, 1901, 35–66; 5, 1902.

Henri Seyrig, Antiquitées Syriennes, 5 volumes, Paris, 1934–1958.

Bluma L. Trell, Architectura Numismatica, Part II, Temples in Asia Minor, New York University, 1942, diss. unpublished.

Bluma L. Trell, "Architecture on Ancient Coins," Archaeology, 1976, 6–13.

W.H. Waddington, E. Babelon, Th. Reinach, Recueil générale des monnaies grecques d'Asie Mineur, 1904–1924.


## GENERAL


A. Boëthius and J.B. Ward-Perkins, Etruscan and Roman Architecture, Harmondsworth, 1970.

V. Chapot, La colonne torse et le decor en hélice dans l'art antique, Paris, 1907.

L. Crema, L'architettura romana (Enciclopedia classica, sezione, III: Archeologia e storia dell'arte classica, xii, 1), 1959; idem., Manuale di storia dell'architettura antica, Milano, 1962.

W.B. Dinsmoor, Architecture of Ancient Greece, An Account of its Historic Development, London/New York, 1950.

M. Leglay, Saturne Africain, Monuments I, 1961; II, 1966; Histoire (Bibliothèque des études Françaises d'Athènes et de Rome, fasc. 205), 1966.

A.W. Lawrence, Greek Architecture, London, 1957.

W.H. Plommer, Ancient and Classical Architecture (Simpson's History of Architectural Development, vol. 1) London/New York, 1956 (reprint, 1961).

D.S. Robertson, A Handbook of Greek and Roman Architecture, Cambridge, 1945.

P. Romanelli, Topographia e archeologia dell'Africa Romana; Rome, 1970.

G. Taylor, Roman Temples of Lebanon, A Pictorial Guide, Beyrouth, 1967.

Enciclopedia dell'arte antica, classica e orientale.

Theodor Klauser, Reallexikon für Antike und Christentum (in progress).

Paulys, Realencyclopädie der classischen Altertumswissenschaft.


## HARBOURS


Aline A. Boyce, "The Harbour of Pompeiopolis, A Study in Roman Ports and Dated Coins," American Journal of Archaeology, 62, 1958, 66–78.

Lionel Casson, Ships and Seamanship in the Ancient World, Princeton, 1971, bibliography p. 367, note 22.


## PORTABLE SHRINES


Henri Seyrig, Syria, xviii, 1937, 368–378; xlix, 1972, 104–108.


## TOMB/ALTAR/SHRINE


Paul Collart, "La Tour de Qualaat Fakra," Syria, 1, 1973, 137–161.

Paul Collart, and Pierre Coupel, L'Autel monumental de Baalbek, Paris, 1951.

René Dussaud, "Temples et cultes de la Triade Héliopolitaine à Baalbek," Syria, xxiii, 1942/3, 33–37.

Ernest Will, "La Tour funéraire de Palmyre," Syria, xxvi, 1949, 89–116; Idem, "La tour funéraire de la Syrie et les monuments apparentés," Ibid., 258–313.

Klaus Shippman, Die iranischen Feuerheiligtümer (Religionsgeschichtliche Versuche und Vorarbeiten, Bd. 31), Berlin/New York, 1971.

Melmet Çetin Şahin, Die Entwicklung der griechischen Monumentaltäre, Bonn, 1972.

F. Studniczka, "Altäre mit Grabenkammern," Jahreshefte des Österreichischen archäologischen Institutes, 6, 1903, 123–186.

## NYMPHAEA

**O. Bernhard,** "Ueber Badeswesen und Hygienisches auf griechischen und römischen Münzen," Schweizerischen Numismatischen Rundschau, xxiv, 1928, 3–30.

**J. Des Gagniers, P. Devambez, L. Kahil, P. Ginouvès,** Laodicée du Lycos, Le Nymphée (Université Laval, Recherches Archeologiques, Series I, Fouilles, Campaignes, 1961–1963 Paris, 1969.

**Norman Neuerberg,** L'architettura delle fontane e dei ninfei nell' Italia antica (Reale Accademia di archeologia, lettere e belle arti di Napoli, Memorie, 5) Naples, 1965.

**Salvatore Settis,** "Esedra' e 'Ninfeo' nelle Terminologia architettoni del mundo romano dall'età repubblicana alla tarda antichità, Aufsteig und Niedergang der römischen Welt, Geschichte und Kultur Roms in Spiegel der neureren Forschung, hrsg. von Hildegard Temporini, I, Von Anfängen Roms bis zum Ausgang der Republic, 4 Bd., Berlin, 1973, 661–745.

## ARCHES, ETC.

**M. Bieranacka-Lubanska,** "Iconographie. Sources to the history of Roman aqueducts in Western Thrace," Archaeologia Polona, xiv, 1973, 315–329.

**A. Blanchet** "Les villes fortifiées de péninsule balkanique d'après les monnaies de l'époque romaine" Buletinul Societatii Numismatice Române 18, 1923, 1–14.

**F. Noack,** Triumph und Triumphbogen, Vorträge der Bibliothek Warburg, hrsg., von Fritz Saxl, 1925/6, Berlin, 1928, 147 ff.

**M. Stuart,** "The Denarius of M. Aemilius Lepidus and the Aqua Marcia," American Journal of Archaeology, 49, 1945, 222–251.

**D. Tudor,** Podurile Romane de la Dunărea de Jos, Bucharest, 1971, 53–153.

## ROME

**Marie R. Alföldi,** "Signum Deae, die Kaiserzeitlichen Vorgänger des Reichsapfels," Jahrbuch für Num. und Geld. 11, 1961, 19–32.
    Aufsteig und Niedergang der römischen Welt, Geschichte und Kultur Roms im Spiegel der neueren Forschung, hrsg. von Hildegard Temporini, I; Von Anfängen Roms bis zum Ausgang der Republik, Bd. IV, Berlin, 1973, 636–639.

**Alfonso Bartoli,** Curia Senatus, Lo Scavo ed il Restauro (Istituto de Studi Romani, I monumenti Romani, III) Roma, 1963.

**Alfonso Bartoli,** "Il monumento della perpetuità del Senato," Studii Romani, ii, 2, 1954, 127–137.

**Axel Boëthius,** "Veteris Capitoli humilia tecta," Acta ad archaeologia et artium historiam pertinentia, Inst. Rom. Norwegiae, Oslo Universitets-forlaget, 1962, 27–33; cf. Gjerstad's reply, Ibid., "A propositio della recostruzione del Tempio arcaico di Giove Capitolino in Roma," 35–40.

**Donald F. Brown,** Temples of Rome as Coin Types. Numismatic Notes and Monographs, 90, New York, 1940.

**Donald F. Brown,** Architectura Numismatica, Part 1: The Temples of Rome, New York University, unpublished diss., 1941.

**A.M. Colini,** "Meta Sudans," Rendiconti, Atti della Pontificia accademia Romana di archeologia, 13, 1937, 15–39.

**Donald R. Dudley,** Urbs Romana, a source book of classical texts on the city and its monuments selected and translated with a commentary, Phaidon, 1971 (Capitolum, 55–58, Curia 87–88).

**Günter Fuchs,** Architekturdarstellungen auf römischen Münzen der Republik und der frühen Kaiserzeit (Deutsches Archäologisches Institut, Antike Münzen und Geschnittene Steine, ed. Erich Boehringer, Bd. 1) Berlin, 1969, passim.

**Einar Gjerstad,** Early Rome, III, Fortifications, Domestic Architecture, Sanctuaries, Stratigraphic Excavations (Acta Instituti Romani, Regni Sueciae, xvii, 3) Lund, 1960, 168–204; Ibid., xvii, 4; Early Rome, IV, 2, Synthesis of the Archaeological Evidence, Lund, 1966, 388–398.

**Einar Gjerstad,** "Discussions Concerning Early Rome, 3," Historia, xvi, 1967, 257–278.

**Tony Hackens,** Histoire et iconographie du temple capitolin. Dissertation, Univ. Catholique Louvain, 1962, Unpublished.

**Tony Hackens,** "De Tempol en de Goden van het kapitool op de romeinse Minten," Exposition Numismatique, Brussels, 1966, 33–36.

**Per Gustaf Hamberg.** Studies in Roman Imperial Art with Special Reference to the State Reliefs of the Second Century, Uppsala, 1945, 96 (reprint, 1968).

**Hans Jucker,** "Capitolium restitutum," Jahrbuch des Bernischen Historischen Museums, 1959/60, 289–295.

**Steven Lattimore,** "A Greek Pediment on a Roman Temple," American Journal of Archaeology, 78, 1974, 55–61.

**Ernest Nash,** Pictorial Dictionary of Ancient Rome, London, 1968 (Capitolium, 530–533, Colosseum, 16–25; 268–269; Curia, 287–289).

**A. Palladio,** Le Terme dei Romani, 1797, Tavv. v, vi, (Royal Institute of British Architects, vol. ii fol. i).

**Romolo A. Staccioli,** Modelli di edifici etrusco-italici (Rome (City) Università. Instituto di etruscologia e antichità italiche. Studi e materiali, 6) Florence, 1968.

**Bluma L. Trell,** "Architectura Numismatica, Early Types, Greek, Roman, Oriental," Numismatic Chronicle, xii, 1972, Capitolium, 53–54; Curia, 55–57.

**Bluma L. Trell,** Num. Chron. xiii, 1973, 225.

**E. Voeral,** "Die Darstellung eines Keltentempels auf einem Denar von Kaisar Augustus," Jahrbuch der Schwiezerischen Gesellschaft für Urgeschichte, 1939, 150–157.

**A. Von Gerkan,** "Das Obergeschloss des flavischen Amphitheatres," Römische Mitteilungen, 40, 1925, 11–50.

## ATHENS

**J. Svoronos,** Les monnaies d'Athènes, Munich, 1923–1926.

**John Travlos,** Pictorial Dictionary of Ancient Athens, New York, 1971.

**Paulys Supp.** xiii, 1973, s.v. Athenai, 56–139.

## CORINTH

**Oscar Broneer,** "Hero Cults in the Corinthian Agora," Hesperia, ii, 1942, 128–161.

**Corinth,** Results of Excavations conducted by the American School of Classical Studies at Athens, vol. VI, 1, part 1³, H.N. Fowler, Introduction, Architecture, 1932; vol. V. 1, part 2, Richard Stillwell, Architecture, 1941; vol. I, part vi, Bert Hodge Hill, The Springs, Peirene, Sacred Spring, Glauke, 1964, Princeton.

**W.B. Dinsmoor,** "Note on a Circular Monument in the Corinthian Agora" Hesperia, 11, 1942, 314–315.

**Robert L. Hohlfelder,** "Pausanias I, 2,3, A Collection of Archaeological and Numismatic Evidence, "Hesperia, xxxix, 1970, 326–331.

**F.W. Imhoof-Blumer and P. Gardner,** A Numismatic Commentary on Pausanias, Supplement, 154–158, London, 1887 (reprint, 1964).

**Georges Roux,** Pausanias en Corinthie (Livre II, 1 a 15), texte, traduction, commentaire archéologique et topographique (Annales de l'Université de Lyons, sér. 3, Lettres, fasc. 31) Paris, 1958.

## DELPHI

**École Française d'Athènes,** Fouilles de Delphes, Tome II, F. Courby, Le sanctuaire d'Apollon, La Terrasse du temple, Paris, 1927.

**F.W. Imhoof-Blumer and P. Gardner,** A Numismatic Commentary on Pausanias, London, 1887, (reprint, 1964), 118–123.

## AMASEIA

**J.G.C. Anderson,** "A Journey of Exploration in Pontus," Studia Pontica, I, Bruxelles, 1903, 47–50.

**J.G.C. Anderson, Franz Cumont, Henri Grégoire,** Recueil des inscriptions grecques et latines du Pont, de l'Arménie, Studia Pontica, III, fasc. I., Bruxelles, 1910, 109–148.

**A.R. Bellinger,** "The Eighth and Ninth Dura Hoards," Numismatic Notes and Monographs 85, New York, 1939, 9–13.

**Franz Cumont et Eugene Cumont,** "Voyage d'exploration archéologique dans le Pont et la petite Arménie," Studia Pontica, II, Bruxelles, 1906, 138–184.

**Maximova, M.I.,** Cities of The Black Sea (Russian) Moscow/Leningrad, 1956.

**W.H. Waddington, E. Babelon, Th. Reinach,** Recueil général de monnaies d'Asie Mineure, vol. I, fasc. i, Paris, 1904, 26–42.


## NEOCAESAREA

**A.R. Bellinger,** The Coins; The Excavations at Dura-Europos, Final Report, VI, New Haven, 1949, pl. xl, figs, 1995–2023.

**Paulys. Suppl.** x (1965) s.v. Neocaesarea 485; xvi (1933), 2409–2413.

**Franz Cumont,** "Voyage d'exploration archéologique dans le Pont et la petite Arménie, (Studia Pontica, II) 1906, 267–273.

**Henri Seyrig,** "Une déesse Anatolienne," Antike Kunst, 13, 1971, 76–78.

**Rudolf Winks,** Clipeata Imago, Studien zu einer römischen Bildnisform, Bonn, 1969, 130.


## NICAEA

**Cevriye Artuk,** "Die Tempel von Nikaia nach Münzdarstellungen," Türk Tarih Kongresi, Ankara, 1961, 38–49.

**Alfons Maria Schneider,** "The City Walls of Nicaea," Antiquity, xii, 1938, 437–443.

**Alfons Maria Schneider,** Die römischen und Byzantinischen Denkmäler von Isnik-Nicaea (Istanbuler Forschungen des archäologischen Institutes des Deutschen Reiches, Abteilung Istanbul, Bd. 16) Berlin, 1943.

**Alfons Maria Schneider and Walter Karnapp,** Die Stadtmauer von Iznik (Niçaea) (Istanbuler Forschungen des archäologischen Institutes des Deutschen Reiches, Abteilung Istanbul, Bd. 9) Berlin, 1938.

**W.H. Waddington, E. Babelon, Th. Reinach,** Recueil générale des monnaies grecques d'Asie Mineure, Vol. 1, 3, 395–511.


## TROY

**Alfred R. Bellinger,** Troy, Excavations Conducted by the University of Cincinatti, 1932–1938, The Coins, Princeton, 1961; cf. review by L. Robert, Monnaies Antiques on Troade (Hautes Études Numismatiques, I) Paris, 1966.

**G.W. Blegen, C.G. Boulter, J.L. Casky, M. Mawson and J. Sperling,** Troy, Excavations conducted by the University of Cincinatti, Princeton, vol. ii, 1951; vol. iii, 1953; vol. iv, 1958.

**F.W. Goethart and H. Schleif,** Der Athena Tempel von Ilion, (Deutsch. Arch. Insti., Denkmäler antiker Architektur, x) Berlin, 1962. cf. review by H. Kähler, Gnomon xxxvi, 1964, 79–87.

**Heiner Knell,** "Der Athenatempel in Ilion, eine Korrektur zur Grundnissekonstruktion," Athenische Mitteilung, 88, 1973, 131–133.

**Anna Sadurska,** Les Tables Iliaques (Centre d'archéologie mediterranéenne de l'Academie Polonaises de Sciences) Warsaw, 1964, p.28.

## CYZICUS

**Bernard Ashmole,** "Cyriac of Ancona and the Temple of Hadrian at Cyzicus," Journal of the Warburg Institute, 19, 1956, 179–191.
**A. Boëthius and J. Ward-Perkins,** Etruscan and Roman Architecture, Hammondsworth 1970, 392, 478/9, 574(18)[15].
**Bernard Goldman,** The Sacred Portal, a Primary Symbol in Ancient Judaic Art, Detroit, 1966, passim.
**Hans Peter Laubscher,** "Zum Fries des Hadrianstempel in Kyzikos," Istanbuler Mitteilungen (Deutsches Archäologisches Institut, Abteilung Istanbul), Bd. 17, 1967, 211–217.
**Phyllis Williams Lehmann and Karl Lehmann,** Samothracian Reflections, Aspects of the Revival of the Antique (Bollingen Series, xcii) Princeton, 1973, 27–56.
**Fernand Robert,** Thyméle, recherches sur la signification et la destination des monuments circulaires dans l'architecture religieuse de la Grèce (Bibliothèque des écoles Françaises d'Athènes et Rome, Fasc. 147), Paris, 1939.
**G. Roux,** L'architecture de l'Argolide au IVe et IIIe siecles av. J.C., Paris, 1961, 131–200.

## PARIUM

**Bluma L. Trell.** "Tomb, Altar or Shrine? – The Numismatic Evidence," Transactions of the International Numismatic Congress, New York/Washington, D.C., September, 1973, (Basel, 1976), 163–169.
**Paulys Suppl.,** xii 1970, s.v. Parion, 982–986.

## PERGAMUM

**A. Boëthius and J. Ward-Perkins,** Etruscan and Roman Architecture, Harmondsworth, 1970, 476–479.
**Königliche Museen zu Berlin,** Altertümer von Pergamon, Berlin, 1885 – III[1] Jakob Schrammen, Der Grosse Altar. Der Obere Markt, 1906, III[2] Hermann Winnefeld, Der Friese des grossen Alters, 1910.
**Elisabeth Rohde,** Pergamon, Burgberg und Altar (Staatliche Museen zu Berlin, Antiken-Sammlung) Berlin, 1969, 99–102.
**Maria Floriani Squarciapino,** Leptis Magna, Basel, 1966.

## EPHESUS

**Anton Bammer,** Die Architektur des jüngeren Artemision von Ephesos, (Veroff. d. Deutsch. Arch. Inst.) Wiesbaden, 1972.
**Anton Bammer,** "Recent Excavations at the Altar of Artemis in Ephesos," Archaeology, 27, 1974, 202–205.
**Anton Bammer,** Istanbuler Mitteilungen, 25, 1975, 319–334.
**Robert Fleischer,** Artemis von Ephesos und verwandte Kultstatuen aus Anatolien und Syrien, Leiden, 1973.
**Hugh Plommer,** "St. John's Church, Ephesus," Anatolian Studies, 12, 1962, 119–129.
**Paulys Suppl.** xii (1970), s.v. Ephesos, 1654–1673; 1666–1673.
**Brunhilde Sesmondo Ridgway,** "A Story of Five Amazons," American Journal of Archaeology, 78, 1974, 1–17.
**Sabine Schultz,** Die Münzprägung von Magnesia am Mäander in der römischen Kaiserzeit, Berlin, 1975.
**Bluma L. Trell,** The Temple of Artemis at Ephesos, (Numismatic Notes and Monographs, No. 107), New York, 1945.

## SAMOS

**Helmut Berve and Gottfried Gruben,** Griechische Tempel und Heiligtümer, München, 1961, 236–243, 282.
**Thomas Drew-Bear,** "Representations of Temples on the Greek Imperial Coinage," American Numismatic Society Museum Notes, 19, 1974, 27–63.
**Oscar Reuther,** Der Heratempel von Samos seit der Zeit des Polykrates, Berlin, 1957.

234

**Rinate Tölle,** Die Antike Stadt Samos, ein Fuhrer. (Deutsches. Archäologishes Institut, Athens), Mainz, 1969, bibl., p. 120.

**Bluma L. Trell,** The Temple of Artemis at Ephesos, Numismatic Notes and Monographs, No. 107, New York, 1945, 33–35.

**Hans Walter,** Das griechische Heiligtum, Heraion von Samos, München, 1965.


## SARDIS


**Bulletin, American Schools of Oriental Research,** 154, 1959; 157, 1960; 158, 1960; 162, 1961; 166, 1962; 170, 1963; 191, 1968; 199, 1970, bibl. pp. 7–8; 203, 1971; 206, 1972; 211, 1973, bibl. pp. 14–15, note I. (Excavation Reports).

**K.S. Frazer, C.H. Greenwalt, Jr., G.M.A. Hanfmann,** Sardis, Report I, Harvard University Press, 1976.

**Gottfried Gruben und Peter Robert Franke,** "Beobachtungen zum Artemis-Tempel von Sardis," Mitteilungen des Deutschen Archäologischen Institutes, Athenischen Abteilung, bd. 76, 1961, 155–208.

**George M.A. Hanfmann,** "Greece and Lydia," 8ᵐᵉ Congrès internationale d'archéologie classique, le rayonnement des civilisations grecque et romain sur les cultures péripheriques, Paris, 1963, Paris, 1965, 490–500.

**George M.A. Hanfmann,** From Croesus to Constantine, the cities of Western Asia Minor and the Art in Greek and Roman times, Michigan University, Paris, 1975.

**George M.A. Hanfmann,** Letters from Sardis, Cambridge, 1973.

**F. Imhoof-Blumer,** "Die Lydische Kore", Nomisma, Untersuchungen auf dem Gebiete der Antiken Münzkunde, viii, 1913, 20–22.

**A.E.M. Johnston and T.V. Buttrey,** "Greek and Roman Coins Found at Sardis," Bulletin, American School of Oriental Research, 211, 1973, 34–36, A full publication of the coins found in the Sardis excavations, and a die study of the mint of Sardis is in press.

**P.R. Métraux.** "A New Head of Zeus from Sardis," American Journal of Archaeology, 75, 1971, 155–159.

**John Griffiths Pedley,** Sardis in the Age of Croesus, Oklahoma University Press, 1968, 9.

**John Griffiths Pedley,** Ancient Literary Sources of Sardis (Archaeological Exploration of Sardis, Monograph 2) Harvard University Press, 1972, nos 276–7.

**Bluma L. Trell,** The Temple of Artemis at Ephesos, Numismatic Notes and Monographs, no. 107, New York, 1945, 36–39.

**Bluma L. Trell,** "Tomb, Altar or Shrine? – The Numismatic Evidence," Transactions of the International Numismatic Congress, New York/Washington, D.C., September, 1973, (Basel, 1976), 163–169.


## SELGE


**Helène Danthine,** Le palmier-dattier et les arbres sacrées dans l'iconographie de l'asie occidentale ancienne, "Paris, 1937.

**Robert Fleischer,** "Selge", Jahrbuch Österreichisches Archäologisches Institut, Grabungen, 1968, 19–23.

**M. Leglay,** Saturne Africain, Histoire (Bibliothèque des Écoles Françaises d'Athènes et de Rome, fasc. 225), Paris, 1966, see especially pp. 288–9 for barriers.

**A.A. Mansel,** "Osttor und Waffenrelief von Side," Archäologischer Anzeiger, (Beiblatt zum Jahrbuch des Deutschen Archäologischen Institutes) Berlin, 1968, 260–261, 272.

**Bluma L. Trell,** "Tomb, Altar or Shrine? – The Numismatic Evidence," Transactions of the International Numismatic Congress, New York/Washington, D.C., September, 1973, (Basel, 1976), 163–169.


## PAPHOS


**Einar Gjerstadt,** The Cypro-Geometric, Cypro-archaic and Cypro-classical Periods (The Swedish Crypus Expedition, vol. iv, part 2) Stockholm, 1948, 428–453.

**Sir George Hill,** A History of Cyprus, Cambridge, vol. I, 1940.

235

V. **Karageorghis,** "A representation of a temple on an 8th century B.C. Cypriot Vase," Rivista di studi fenici, I, 1974, 9–13.

**F.G. Maier,** "Ausgrabungen in Alt Paphos" Archäologischer Anzeiger, Beiblatt zur Jehrbach, 1967, 303–330.

**F.G. Maier,** "Alt Paphos auf Zyperen," Antike Welt, II, 1971 (Zurich), 3–114.

**Bogdan Rutkowski,** Cult Places in the Aegean World (Polish Academy of Sciences, Institute of the History of Material Culture) Bibliotheca antiqua x, Warsaw, 1972, passim.

**Bluma L. Trell,** "Architectura Numismatica Orientalis, A Short Guide to the Numismatic Formulae of Roman Syrian Die-Makers," Numismatic Chronicle, x, 1970, 42–43.

**Olaf Vessberg and Alfred Westholm,** The Hellenistic and Roman Periods in Cyprus (The Swedish Cyprus Expedition, vol. iv, part 3) Stockholm, 1956, 1–8.

**Alfred Westholm,** "The Paphian Temple of Aphrodite and its relation to Oriental Architecture," Acta Archaeologica, iv, 1933, 201–236.

## BYBLOS

**Paul Collart,** "La tour de Qualaat Fakra," Syria, 1, 1973, 137–161.

**R. Donceel,** "Recherches archéologiques au Liban, 1962–1965", L'antiquité classique, xxxv, 1966, 232–237.

**Robert du Mesnil du Buisson,** Études sur les dieux phéniciens hérités par l'Empire Romain (Études préliminaires aux religions orientales dans l'Empire Romain, tome 14) Leiden, 1970, 56–72.

**Robert du Mesnil du Buisson,** Nouvelles études sur les dieux et les mythes de Canaan (Études préliminaires aux religions orientales dans l'Empire Romain, tome 33), Leiden, 1973, 88–89.

**Maurice Dunand,** Byblos, son histoire, ses ruines, see legends,[2] Beyrouth/Paris, 1968.

**H. Kalayan,** "Rapport préliminaire sur les travaux de reconnaissance du site de Maschnaka," Mathaf, Bulletin du musée de Beyrouth, xvii, 1964, 107–110.

**Henri Seyrig,** "La résurrection d'Adonis et le texte de Lucien," Syria, xlix, 1972, 97–100.

**Henri Seyrig,** "Intailles relatives à des cultes Syriens," Syria, 1972, 109–112.

**Bluma L. Trell,** "Architectura Numismatica Orientalis, A Short Guide to the Numismatic Formulae of Roman Syrian Die-Makers," Numismatic Chronicle, x, 1970, 31–32.

**Bluma L. Trell,** "Tomb, Altar or Shrine? – The Numismatic Evidence," Transactions of the International Numismatic Congress, New York/Washington, D.C., September, 1973, (Basel, 1976), 163–169.

## SIDON

**M. Jean Babelon,** "Le voile d'Europe," Revue archéologique, 1942/3, 125–140.

**Winifred Bühler,** Europa, ein Überblick über die Zeugnisse des Mythos in der antiken Literatur und Kunst, München, 1968.

**Robert du Mesnil du Buisson,** "L'ancien dieu Tyrien Ouoo sur des monnaies de Tyre," Mélanges de l'Université Saint-Joseph, Tome xli, fasc. 1, 1965, 1–27.

**Robert du Mesnil du Buisson,** Études sur les dieux phéniciens, hérités par l'Empire Romain (Études Prél. aux religions orientales dans l'Empire Romain, Tome 14). Leiden 1970, passim.

**Robert du Mesnil du Buisson,** Nouvelles études sur les dieux et les mythes de Canaan (Études préliminaires aux religions orientales dans l'Empire Romain, Tome 33) Leiden, 1973, 99–125.

**Adolf G. Horn,** "Canaan and the Aegean Sea; Greco-Phoenician, Origins Reviewed." Diogenes 58, 1967, 37–61.

**René Mouterde, S.J.** "Regards sur Beyrouth Phénicienne, Hellénistique et Romaine, Mélanges de l'Université Saint-Joseph, Tome xl, fasc. 2, 1964, 145–181.

**Bogdan Rutkowski,** Cult Places in the Aegean World (Polish Academy of Sciences, Institute of the History of Material Culture) Bibliothea antiqua, x, Warsaw, 1972, pp. 163–7, 197–203, p. 264. no. 17.

**S. Schaeffer,** "Marsyas et les Phrygiens en Syrie," Revue des Études Antiques, xxi, 1919, 239–248.

**Bluma L. Trell,** "Architectura Numismatica Orientalis, A Short Guide to the Numismatic Formulae of Roman Syrian Die-Makers," Numismatic Chronicle, x, 1970, 29–50.

## BAALBEK-HELIOPOLIS

Robert Amy, "Temples à escaliers," Syria, xxvi, 1950, 82–136.
Robert Amy, "La reconstruction de l'autel monumental de Baalbek," Rev. arch., 1953, 50–67.
A. Boëthius and J. Ward-Perkins, Etruscan and Roman Architecture, Harmondsworth, 1970, 417–426.
Donald F. Brown, "The Arcuated Lintel and the Symbolic Interpretation in Late Antique Art," American Journal of Archaeology, 46, 1942, 389–399.
Paul Collart and Pierre Coupel, L'autel monumental de Baalbek (Institut Francais d'Archéologie de Beyrouth. Bibliothèque Archéologique et Historicque, vol. lii) Paris, 1951; cf. review E. Bradford Wells in American Journal of Archaeology, 57, 1953, 155–156.
R. Donceel, "Recherches et travaux, archéologiques recents au Liban, 1962–1965," L'antiquité classique, xxxv, 1966, 224–254.
René Dussaud, "Jupiter Héliopolitanus, bronze de la collection Charles Sursock," Syria, I, 1920, 3–15.
René Dussaud, "Temples et cultes de la Triade Héliopolitaine à Baalbek," Syria, xxiii, 1942/3, 33–77.
Enciclopedia dell'arte antica, classica e orientale, (1960), s.v. Heliopolis, 1137–1140.
Kazimierz Michalowski, Art of Ancient Egypt, n. d. Edfu, 544–546, Denderah, 501–505.
Henri Seyrig, "Nouveau monuments de Baalbek et la Becque," Bulletin du Musée de Beyrouth, xvi, 1961, 109–135.
Henri Seyrig, "Le Culte du Soleil en Syria a l'époque romaine," Syria, xlviii, 1971, 345–349.
George Taylor, The Roman Temples of Lebanon, a Pictorial Guide," Beyrouth, 1967, 32–51.
Gustavo Traversari, Gli spettacoli in Acqua nel teatro tardo-antico, Roma, 1960, 98–103.
D. Winnefeld, "Zur Geschichte des Syrischen Heliopolis," Rheinisches Museum für Philologie 69, 1914, 139–159.


## EMISA

Hans Roland Baldus, Uranius Antoninus, Münzprägung und Geschichte (Antiquitas, Abhand, zur Vor-und Früh-Geschichte zur Klass. und prov. Röm. archäologie und zur Geschichte d. Altertums, Bd. 11) Bonn, 1971.
Henri Seyrig, "Antiquités Syriennes, 76, Caractères de l'histoire d'Émèse," Syria, xxxvi, 1959, 184–192.
Henri Seyrig, "Culte du Soleil on Syrie, II, Émèse," Syria, xlviii, 1971, 340–345.


## NEAPOLIS, SAMARIA

Biblical Archaeologist, xxvi, 1965; xxxi, 1968; 1969 (Excavation Reports).
R.J. Bull, "A Preliminary Excavation of an Hadrianic Temple at Tell-er-Ras on Mt. Gerizim," American Journal of Archaeology, 71, 1967, 387–393.
R.J. Bull, "The Two Temples at Tell er Ras on Mt Gerizim in Occupied Jordan." American Journal of Archaeology, 74, 1970, 189–190.
R.J. Bull, and G.E. Wright, "Newly Discovered Temples on Mt. Gerizim (Hadrianic)," Harvard Theological Review, lviii, 1965, 234–237.
Bulletin of the American Schools of Oriental Research, 190, 1968; 204, 1971; 205, 1972.


## JERUSALEM

M. Avi-Yonah, "The Facade of Herod's Temple, an Attempted Reconstruction," Essays in Memory of E.R. Goodenough, Leiden, 1968, 327–335.
F. Bickerman, "Une proclamation Seleucide relative au Temple de Jérusalem," Syria xxv, 1946–8, 67–85.
Le Compte du Mesnil du Buisson, "L'inscription de la niche central de la synagogue de Doura-Europos," Syria, 1963, 303–314.
Bernard Goldman, The Sacred Portal, A Primary Symbol in Ancient Judaic Art, Detroit, 1966, passim.
Carl H. Kraeling, The Synagogue (The Excavations at Dura Europos. Final Report viii, 1), New Haven, 1956, 54–66.

**A. Muehsam,** Coin and Temple, a Study of the Architectural Representation on Ancient Jewish Coins, (Near Eastern Research, I, Leeds University Oriental Society) Leiden, 1966.

**André Parrot,** Le Temple de Jérusalem (Cahier d'archéologie biblique, 5), New York, 1955.

## ALEXANDRIA

**M.L. Bernhard,** "Quelques remarques sur Alexandria," Revue archéologique, 1972, 317–320. Pharos lamp, see fig. 2.

**Danielle Bonneau,** Le Fisc et le Nil, incidences des irrégularités de la crue du Nil sur la fiscalité foncière dans l'Egypte grecque et romaine, Paris, n.d. (1971?).

**B.W. Deusser,** "A Numismatic Contribution to the Evidence for Dating the Building Program of the Alexandrian Serapis Temple," unpublished paper submitted to the American Numismatic Society Seminar, 1968.

**L. Fourcher,** "Les Mosaiques Nilotiques Africaines," Colloques Internationaux du Centre National de la recherche scientifique, sciences humaines, la mosaique Gréco-Romaine, Paris, Aout-Sept., 1963, Paris, 1968, 137–145.

**P.M. Frazer,** Ptolemaic Alexandria, Oxford, 1972.

**J. Hackin and J.R. Hackin,** Recherches Archéologiques à Begram, chantier 2 (Mémoires de la délégation archéologique française en Afghanistan, Tome IX) Paris, 1939, 42–44.

**J. Hackin, J. Auboyer, V. Elisséeff, O. Kurz, Ph. Stern,** Rencontre de Trois Civilisations, Inde-Grèce-Chine, Nouvelles recherches archéologiques à Begram (ancien Kapici), 1939–1940 (Mémoire de la délégation archéologique française en Afghanistan, Tome XI), Paris, 1954, 101–102.

**Susan Handler,** "Architecture on Roman Coins of Alexandria," American Journal of Archaeology, 75, 1971, 57–74.

**Susan Handler,** The Architecture of Alexandria in Egypt as depicted on the Alexandrian Bronze Coinage of the Roman Imperial Period, unpublished dissertation, Bryn Mawr, 1967/8.

**William Hornbostel,** "Sarapis, Studien zur Überlieferungsgeschichte den Erscheinungsformen und Wandlung der Gestalt eines Gottes," Leiden, 1973, see index, s.v. Serapeum.

**S. Loescheke,** Antike Lanternen und Lichthäuschen, Bonner Jahrbücher, Jahrbücher des Vereins von Altertums Freunden in Rheinlands, 118, 1909, 307–430.

**Kazimierz Michalowski,** Art of Ancient Egypt, New York, 1970, Alexandria, 501–505; Kom Omba, 547, fig. 936.

**P. Pfister,** "Nil, Nilomètre et l'orientalisation du paysage Hellénistique," Revue des Arts Asiatiques, vii, 1931, 120–140.

**Charles Picard,** "Sur quelques représentations nouvelles du Phare d'Alexandrie et sur l'origine alexandrine des paysages portuaires," Bulletin de Correspondence Hellénique, lxxvi, 1952, 61–95.

**M. Th. Picard-Schmitter,** "L'Allégorie de l'Egypte sur un relief provenant de Carthage," Revue archéologique, 1971, 29–56.

**Paulys Suppl.** xii, 1970, Nachträge, s.v. Ephesos, 1652–1654.

**Alan Rowe,** Discovery of the Famous Temple and Enclosure of Serapis at Alexandria with an explanation of the enigmatical inscriptions on the Serapeum placques of Ptolemy IV by Etienne Drioton (Supplément aux Annales due Services des Antiquités de l'Egypte, Cahier 2) Cairo, 1946.

**Alan Rowe, B.R. Rees,** "A Contribution to the Architecture of the Western Desert, IV, The Great Serapeum of Alexandria," Bulletin of the John Rylands Library, 1957, 484–520.

**R. von Salditt-Trappman,** Tempel der Ägyptischen Götter in Griechenland und an der Westküste Kleinasiens (Études préliminaires aux religions orientales dans l'Empire Romain, Tome 15, Leiden, 1970.

**John E. Stambaugh,** Sarapis under the Early Ptolemies (Études préliminaires aux religions orientales dans l'empire Romain, tome 25), Leiden, 1972, 79–84.

**Durk Wortman,** "Kosmogonie und Nil Flut," Bonner Jahrbücher des rheinisches Landesmuseums in Bonn und des Vereins von Altertums Freunden in Rheinlande, Bd. 166, 1966, 62–112.

# ABBREVIATIONS USED IN THE CATALOGUE

| | |
|---|---|
| AMNG | B. Pick et al., Die Antiken Münzen Nord-Griechenlands (Berlin, 1898). |
| Ann. Soc. Num. | Annuaire de la Société française de numismatique et d'archéologie (Paris). |
| ANS | The American Numismatic Society |
| Arch. Anz. | Archäologischer Anzeiger. |
| Arch. Polona | Archaeologia Polona (Warsaw). |
| Babelon, Perses | E. Babelon, Les Perses Achéménides (Paris, 1893). |
| Beltran | A. Beltran, Curso di Numismatica I, Numismatica antigua (Cartagena, 1950). |
| BM | The British Museum. |
| BMC | Catalogue of Greek Coins in the British Museum. |
| BMCRE | Coins of the Roman Empire in the British Museum. |
| CNP | Corpus Nummorum Palestinensium (Tel Aviv/Jerusalem, 1956–). |
| Dattari | G. Dattari, Monete imperiali greche, Num. Augg. Alexandrini Cairo, 1901). |
| De Saulcy | L.F.J.C. de Saulcy, Numismatique de la Terre Sainte (Paris, 1874). |
| Garrucci | P.R. Garrucci, Le Monete dell' Italia antica (Rome, 1885). |
| Grant FITA | M. Grant, From Imperium to Auctoritas: A historical study of the aes coinage in the Roman Empire 49 B.C.–A.D.14 (Cambridge, 1946) |
| Hunter | G. Macdonald, Catalogue of Greek Coins in the Hunterian Collection University of Glasgow (1899–1905). |
| Imh. Bl. Gr. u. Rom. | F. Imhoof Blumer, Zur griechischen und römischen Münzkunde (Geneva, 1908). |
| JEA | Journal of Egyptian Archaeology. |
| JNG | Jahrbuch für Numismatik und Geldeschichte |
| Jurukova | J. Jurukova, Die Münzprägung von Deultum (Berlin, 1973). |
| KIM | F. Imhoof Blumer, Kleinasiatische Münzen (Vienna, 1901–2). |
| Lyd. Stadtm. | F. Imhoof Blumer, Lydische Stadtmünzen (Geneva/Leipzig, 1897). |
| Mabbot | Hans F.C. Schulman (New York) Sale catalogue 6–11 June 1969. |
| Mazard | J. Mazard, Corpus Nummorum Numidiae Mauretaniaeque (Paris, 1955). |
| Meshorer | Y. Meshorer, Jewis Coins of the second Temple period (Tel Aviv, 1967). |
| Mouchmov | N.A. Mouchmov, Ancient Coins of the Balkan Peninsular (Sofia, 1967). |
| MundM | Münzen und Medaillen A.G., Basel. |
| NC | Numismatic Chronicle. |
| NCP | F. Imhoof Blumer and P. Gardner, A numismatic Commentary on Pausanias (London, 1887). |
| Oeconomidou | M. Oeconomidou, The Coinage of Nicopolis (Athens, 1975). |
| Pick, Bulgarien | B. Pick, Münzbilder aus Bulgariens (Gotha, 1931). |
| Receuil | W.H. Waddington et al. Receuil général des monnaies grecques d'Asie Mineure (Paris, 1904–1925). |
| Rhein. Mus. f. Philol. | Rheinisches Museum für Philologie. |
| Robert | A. Dupont Sommer and L. Robert, La déesse de Hierapolis Castabala (Paris, 1964). |
| Schonert | E. Schonert-Geiss, Die Münzprägung von Perinthos (Berlin, 1965). |
| SNG ANS | Sylloge Nummorum Graecorum, The American Numismatic Society. |
| SNG Cop | Sylloge Nummorum Graecorum, The Royal Collection of Coins and Medals, Danish National Museum. |
| SNG FW | Sylloge Nummorum Graecorum, Fitzwilliam Museum, Cambridge. |
| SNG vonA | Sylloge Nummorum Graecorum, Sammlung von Aulock. |
| Sydenham | E.A. Sydenham, The Coinage of Caesarea in Cappadocia (London, 1933). |
| vA MinL | H. von Aulock, Die Münzprägung der Gordian III und der Tranquillina in Lykiens (Tübingen, 1974). |

| | |
|---|---|
| Vives | A. Vives, La Moneda Hispanica (Madrid, 1924–26). |
| v.Fritze | H. von Fritze, Die antike Münzen Mysiens (Berlin, 1913). |
| Weber | L. Forrer, Descriptive Catalogue of the Collection of Greek Coins formed by Sir Hermann Weber (London 1926). |
| ZfN | Zeitschrift für Numismatik (Berlin). |

# The Architectural Coin Types of the Ancient World
## (Not including the coins of Rome)

This is a catalogue of the buildings in each city which appear on coins, not a catalogue of coin varieties. For ease of reference, different views of the same building — e.g. perspective views — are given separate entries; but all facades (for example) of the same building come under a single heading, with some note as to the varieties found in different examples. The appearance of the building at different times in a coin series is not distinguished, nor are coins of larger or smaller flans. Where the building forms part of the whole type — e.g. when held by a goddess — it is included only if it is not found as a separate type, or if it supplies a different view. Small altars, pillars, and other architectural fragments, are not included. Rome has been omitted because lists of building types can be easily found in such works as Roman Imperial Coinage and Coins of the Roman Empire in the British Museum. We have, however, illustrated several pieces.

The catalogue follows the normal numismatic order of geography, except that the cities of the province of Asia are listed alphabetically and not by ethnic areas. The provinces and geographical areas come in the order:

Hispania Citerior
Hispania Ulterior
Gaul
Italy
Sicily
Sardinia
Bosporus
Moesia
Thrace
Macedonia
Illyria
Epirus
Southern Greece
Aegean Islands
Pontus
Bithynia
Asia
Galatia
Pisidia
Lycia
Pamphylia
Cilicia
Cyprus
Commagene
Syria
Arabia
Mesopotamia

Parthia
Persia
India
Egypt


    Each entry gives the type of building, the number of columns on the facade, with varieties where relevant, the deity illustrated as cult image, or named in a dedication, and other notes of architectural interest. A reference to one of our illustrations, or to another published illustration, or to the museum where a specimen may be found, is also given. This can only hope to be the briefest guide to the main varieties found in national museums and in published sources. The authors have made every effort to sift out misattributions and wrong descriptions that plague all work such as this, and in the main there are included only such coins as they have seen. They are fully aware that the list may be far from complete, and would welcome information on types not apparently included. As explained elsewhere, certain details such as arched lintels and spiral fluted columns, may have meaning for the appearance of the edifice, but may also be attributed to the artists decorative approach to the subject. Each building series requires a separate study with all examples collected. In the meantime the list may act as a guide to the buildings found at different cities, and in particular it underlines the quantity and variety of buildings depicted on ancient coins of the eastern Medierranean.

| City and Building (Columns) | Cult or Image | Remarks | Reference |
|---|---|---|---|
| **Hispania Citerior** | | | |
| Caesaraugusta | | | |
| 1    Temple (4,6) | Augustus | Corinthian capitals | Vives pl.CL.3 |
| Carthago Nova | | | |
| 2    Temple (4) | Augustus | Pronounced door | Vives pl.CXXXI.13−6 |
| Ilici | | | |
| 3    Temple (4) | Juno | Pronounced door | Fig.37 |
| Tarraco | | | |
| 4    Temple (8) | Augustus | Corinthian capitals; sometimes with parotids | Vives pl.CLXX.3 |
| **Hispania Citerior** | | | |
| Abdera | | | |
| 5    Temple (4) | Solar cult | Pronounced doors | Vives pl.LXXXI.1−4 |
| 6    Temple (4) | | Two fish (columns) | Fig.335 |
| 7    Temple (4) | | Arched lintel | Paris |
| 8    Two temples | Imperial cult? | | Beltran p.50,Figs.10−13 |
| Emerita | | | |
| 9    Temple (4) | Augustus? | | Vives pl.CXLIV.9−10 |
| 10    Gate with walls above | | | Fig.521 |
| 11    Altar | | Ara Pacis type | Vives pl.CXLIV.17−10 |
| Gades | | | |
| 12    Temple (4) | | Pronounced doors | Vives pl.LXXVII.4−5 |
| Lascuta | | | |
| 13    Stepped altar | | | Vives pl.CXII.8 |

| City and Building (Columns) | Cult or Image | Remarks | Reference |
|---|---|---|---|
| Malaca | | | |
| 14  Temple (4) | Solar cult | | Vives pl. LXXXV. 4 |
| **Gaul** | | | |
| Vienne | | | |
| 15  Gate and harbour buildings | | | Fig. 62 |
| **Africa** | | | |
| Cirta | | | |
| 16  (Juba 1) Turreted gate | | Two lower arches | Mazard 523 |
| 17  (Juba 1) Temple or portico (8) | | Steps in front | Fig. 508 |
| 18  (Juba 1) Temple or portico (5) | | Three Atlas caryatids | Fig. 38 |
| 19  (Juba 11) Temple (2, 4, 6) | Augustus | | Fig. 128 |
| Sabratha | | | |
| 20  Temple (5) | | | Fig. 421 |
| **Italy** | | | |
| Paestum | | | |
| 21  Three storied building | | Pitched roof, sometimes domed | Fig. 475 |
| 22  Arcade (Basilica?) | | | SNG Cop. 1365 |
| 23  Temple (2) | Bona Mens | | SNG Cop. 1363 |
| 24  Temple (2) ¾ view | | | SNG ANS 782 |
| 25  Aedicula | | | Paris |
| Tarentum | | | |
| 26  Dovecot? | | | Garrucci pl. C. 33 |
| Terina | | | |
| 27  Fountain | | | Fig. 92 |
| **Sicily** | | | |
| Himera | | | |
| 28  Fountain in sanctuary | | | Fig. 91 |

| City and Building (Columns) | Cult or Image | Remarks | Reference |
|---|---|---|---|
| **Panormus** | | | |
| 29 Lighthouse or tower | | | Fig. 67 |
| 30 Temple (4) | | | ANS |
| **Selinus** | | | |
| 31 Altar in sanctuary | | | Fig. 437 |
| **Sardinia** | | | |
| Carallis | | | |
| 32 Temple (4) | Venus | Pronounced doors | Fig. 120 |
| Turris Libisonis? | | | |
| 33 Temple (6) | | | Grant FITA p. 205 |
| **Bosporus** | | | |
| Panticapaeum? | | | |
| 34 Gate | | | BM |
| 35 Gate and walling | | | NC 1971 pl. 24.1 |
| 36 Temple (5) | | Capitolium type | SNG Cop. 53 |
| **Moesia** | | | |
| Callatis | | | |
| 37 Gate | | Figure in niche | Fig. 88 |
| Dionysopolis | | | |
| 38 Temple (4) | | | Berlin |
| Marcianopolis | | | |
| 39 View of city and forum | | | Fig. 25 |
| 40 Temple (4) | Serapis | | AMNG pl. XX. 25 |
| 41 Temple (4) | Tyche | | SNG Cop. 261 |
| 42 Temple (4) | Apollo and Pytho | | AMNG pl. XX. 21 |
| 43 Arch | | Four figures above | Fig. 85 |
| 44 Gate | | One or three openings | Figs. 499, 501 |

245

| City and Building (Columns) | Cult or Image | Remarks | Reference |
|---|---|---|---|
| Nicopolis ad Istrum | | | |
| 45    Gate | | Palatial building above, and temple through gate | Fig. 26 (Colour p. 14) |
| 46    Gate with walls above | | | Berlin |
| 47    Temple ¾ view | Serapis ? | Among trees | Fig. 402 |
| 48    Nymphaeum | | | Fig. 70 (Colour p. 49) |
| 49    Temple (4) | Dionysus | | BM |
| 50    Temple (4) | Asclepius | | AMNG pl. XX |
| 51    Temple (4) | Zeus | | AMNG 1981 |
| 52    Temple (4) | Artemis | | Mabbott 663 |
| 53    Temple (4) | Tyche | | BM |
| 54    Temple (4) | Concordia | | SNG Cop. 290 |
| 55    Temple (4) | Serapis | Spiral flutes | AMNG pl. XX. 22 |
| 56    Temple (5) | | | AMNG pl. XX. 17 |
| 57    Gate | | Two towers | AMNG pl. XX. 13 |
| 58    Gate | | Three towers | Berlin. |
| Odessus | | | |
| 59    Temple (4) | Tyche | Parotids, spiral flutes | Fig. 5 (Colour p. 32) |
| Tomi | | | |
| 60    Temple (4) | Dionysus | | JNG 1949, 626 |
| 61    Temple (4) | Tyche | | AMNG pl. XX. 19 |
| 62    Temple (4) | Zeus | | BM |
| 63    Temple (4) | Imperial ? | | BM |
| 64    Temple (4) | | | Paris |
| 65    Temple with colonnade in front | | | Mouchmov pl. V. 23 |
| 66    Gate | | Three or four openings | Fig. 500 |
| **Thrace** | | | |
| Anchialus | | | |
| 67    Gate | | Surmounted by warrior | Fig. 87 |

| City and Building (Columns) | Cult or Image | Remarks | Reference |
|---|---|---|---|
| 68 Gate | | Two towers | AMNG pl. VI. 17 |
| 69 Gate | | Figure in niche | AMNG pl. VII. 10 |
| 70 Turreted wall | | | AMNG pl. VI. 34 |
| 71 Temple (4) | Concordia | Spiral flutes | AMNG pl. VIII. 28 |
| 72 Temple | Serapis | | AMNG pl. VI. 35 |
| | | | |
| Apollonia Pontica | | | |
| 73 Temple (4) | Apollo | | Pick, Bulgarien. Fig. 23 |
| 74 Altar | | | Fig. 441 |
| | | | |
| Augusta Trajana | | | |
| 75 Temple (4) | Serapis | | BM |
| 76 Temple (4) | Asclepius | | BM |
| 77 Aedicula (2) | Apollo | Barrel vault ? | Fig. 490 |
| 78 City walls on hill | | | Mouchmov pl. xxix. 9 |
| 79 Gate | | Two or three towers | Fig. 86 (Colour p. 14) |
| 80 Temple (4) | Artemis | On garlanded podium | Pick, Bulgarien, Fig. 11 |
| | | | |
| Bizya | | | |
| 81 City view | | | Fig. 24 (Colour p. 101) |
| 82 Gate with walls above | | | Mouchmov pl. XVIII. 8 |
| 83 Gate | | | Fig. 497 |
| | | | |
| Deultum | | | |
| 84 Temple (4) | Concordia | | Jurukova 136 |
| 85 Temple (4) | Zeus/Serapis | Spiral fluted | Jurukova 133 |
| 86 Temple (4) | Asclepius | Window in pediment | Jurukova 343 |
| 87 Temple (4,6) | Apollo | Corinthian capitals | Jurukova 134 |
| 88 Temple (4) | Tyche | | Jurukova 175 |
| 89 Temple (4) | Genius | | Jurukova 379 |
| 90 Temple ¾ view | Serapis | | Jurukova 262 |
| 91 Temple ¾ view | Aphrodite | | Jurukova 261 |

247

| City and Building (Columns) | Cult or Image | Remarks | Reference |
|---|---|---|---|
| 92 Temple ¾ view | Apollo | | Jurukova 263 |
| 93 Temple ¾ view | Asclopius ? | | Jurukova 266 |

### Hadrianopolis

| | | | |
|---|---|---|---|
| 94 Temple (4) | Tyche | Spiral flutes | SNG Cop590 |
| 95 Temple (4) | Zeus | Spiral flutes | BM |
| 97 Temple on podium | Artemis | Spiral flutes | Mouchmov pl. XIX.8 |
| 98 Gate | | | Fig. 504 |
| 99 Nymphaeum | | | Fig. 69 |

### Maronea

| | | | |
|---|---|---|---|
| 100 Temple (6) | Dionysus | Broken pediment | Fig. 383 |

### Pautalia

| | | | |
|---|---|---|---|
| 101 Mountain with five temples and nymphs | | | Fig. 29 |
| 102 Temple ¾ view | Asclepius | Among trees | Paris |
| 103 Temple and 2 altars | Asclepius | With tree | Fig. 434 |
| 104 Temple (4) | Asclepius | | SNGFW 1741 |

### Perinthus

| | | | |
|---|---|---|---|
| 105 Temple (6,8) | | Often with galley | Schonert 461 |
| 106 Two temples | Actia and Pythia | | Schonert 519 |
| 107 Two temples ¾ view | Actia and Pythia | Held by Tyche | Fig. 44 |

### Philippopolis

| | | | |
|---|---|---|---|
| 108 Temple (4,8) | Dionysus | | Mouchmov pl. XXXII.3 |
| 109 Temple ¾ view | | Often held by standing figures | Fig. 416 |
| 110 Temple (4) | Tyche | | BM |
| 111 Temple (6) | | | Paris |
| 111A City view with three hills | | | Arch. Polona 1973, 321 |
| 111B Temple and colonnade on hill | | | Arch. Polona 1973, 325 |

### Serdica

| | | | |
|---|---|---|---|
| 112 Temple (4) | Asclepius | Sometimes altar in front | BM |
| 112A Aedicula (4) | Asclepius | On podium; conical roof | Numismatika (Sofia) 3.1970, 41.5 |

| City and Building (Columns) | Cult or Image | Remarks | Reference |
|---|---|---|---|
| 113  Fountain ? | | | Arch. Polona 1973, 317. |

Sestus

| | | | |
|---|---|---|---|
| 114  Tower of Hero | | | BM |

Topirus

| | | | |
|---|---|---|---|
| 115  Round shrine | | Sometimes with horsemen | Figs. 471, 472. |

Coela

| | | | |
|---|---|---|---|
| 116  Temple (4) | Genius | | BM |

**Macedonia**

Beroea (including koinon issues)

| | | | |
|---|---|---|---|
| 117  Temple (4) on podium | | With figures | BM (cast) |
| 118  Temple ¾ view | | | AMNG III. 1. pl. V. 11 |
| 119  Aedicula (2) | Heracles (Farnese) | | AMNG pl. IV. 33 |
| 120  Two temples | | Sometimes with column between | Fig. 451 |
| 121  Two temples ¾ view | | | Paris |

Cassandrea

| | | | |
|---|---|---|---|
| 122  Temple (2) | Dionysus | | JNG 1949 pl. II. 22 |
| 123  Aedicula (2) | Zeus Ammon | | AMNG pl. XIII. 15 |

Dium

| | | | |
|---|---|---|---|
| 124  Temple (2) | Asclepius | | SNG Cop 159 |

Edessa

| | | | |
|---|---|---|---|
| 125  Temple (4) | Dionysus | Arcuated lintel | JNG 1949 pl. II. 25 |

Pella ?

| | | | |
|---|---|---|---|
| 126  City view | | | Fig. 522 |

Stobi

| | | | |
|---|---|---|---|
| 127  Temple (4) | Asclepius | | AMNG pl. XXI. 24 |
| 128  Temple (4) | Dionysus | | Paris |
| 129  Temple (4) round ? | | | AMNG pl. XXI. 25 |

| City and Buildings (Columns) | Cult or Image | Remarks | Reference |
|---|---|---|---|
| **Thessalonica** | | | |
| 130 Temple (2,4) | Apollo Pythios | Sometimes without architrave | AMNG pl. XXIV. 29 |
| 131 Temple ¾ view | Apollo Pythios | | SNG Cop 435 |
| 132 Temple (2) | Cabeirus | | AMNG pl. XXIV. 12 |
| 133 Four temples | Neocorate | | Fig. 458 |
| **Illyria** | | | |
| Apollonia | | | |
| 134 Temple | Zeus | Corinthian capitals; among trees | Fig. 436 |
| 135 Temple ¾ view | Apollo | Among trees | Fig. 398 |
| 136 Temple ¾ view | Heracles | Altar to r. | BM |
| **Epirus** | | | |
| Buthrotum | | | |
| 137 Aqueduct | | | Fig. 80 |
| 138 Temple (2) | Helios | | Ashmolean |
| Nicopolis | | | |
| 139 Temple ¾ view | Aktia ? | Porch of 2 columns | Oeconomidou pl. 27. 20 |
| 140 Temple (2,4) | Asclepius | | Oeconomidou pl. 42. 186 |
| 141 Aedicula (2) | Nemesis ? | | Oeconomidou pl. 20. 4 |
| 142 Aedicula (2) | Heracles Farnese | | Oeconomidou pl. 1. 5 |
| 143 Altar | | | Oeconomidou pl. 18. 56 |
| 144 Gate | | | Oeconomidou pl. 17. 51−5 |
| 145 Fountain | | Meta Sudans type | Fig. 76 |
| 146 Domed two-storey structure (Heroon ?) | | | Fig. 48 |
| Corcyra | | | |
| 147 Temple ¾ view | Apollo | Porch of two columns | Fig. 400 |
| 148 Temple (6) | | | ANS |
| 149 Aedicula (2) | Zeus Kasios | | BM |
| **South Greece** | | | |
| Delphi | | | |
| 150 Temple (2,4,6) | Apollo | | Fig. 156 |

| City and Buildings (Columns) | Cult or Image | Remarks | Reference |
|---|---|---|---|
| 151 Temple ¾ view | Apollo | | Fig. 155 |
| 152 Altar | | With pediment | Fig. 157 |
| **Tanagra** | | | |
| 153 Temple (2,4) | Artemis | | Fig. 427 |
| 154 Shrine (2) | Dionysus | 2 Caryatids | Fig. 341 |
| **Chalcis** | | | |
| 155 Temple (2) in which baetyl | | | Fig. 19 |
| **Athens** | | | |
| 156 Acropolis | | Impression often reversed | Figs. 130–1 (Colour p.68) |
| 157 Theatre of Dionysus | | | Fig. 133 (Colour p.68) |
| **Aegosthena** | | | |
| 158 Enclosure in which snake and tree | | | Athens |
| **Megara** | | | |
| 159 Shrine (2) in which herm | | Barrel vault ? | Fig. 495 |
| 160 Gate and harbour | | | Fig. 482 |
| 161 Temple ¾ view | Athena | | Berlin |
| 163 Processional shrine | | | Fig. 41 |
| **Pagae** | | | |
| 164 Shrine (2) | Artemis | Among trees | NCP pl. A.ii |
| 165 Temple (2) | Isis | | NCP pl. FF.iv |
| 166 Gate in which Heracles | | Two story | Fig. 512 |
| 167 Temple ¾ view | | | ANS |
| 168 Arch | | Three openings and figures | Fig. 498 |
| **Aegina** | | | |
| 169 Harbour | | | Fig. 59 |
| 170 Temple ¾ view | | No roof | Fig. 411 |

| City and Buildings (Columns) | Cult or Image | Remarks | Reference |
|---|---|---|---|
| **Corinth** | | | |
| 171 Acrocorinth and temple of Aphrodite | | | Fig.135—6 |
| 172 Temple (6) | Gens Julia | | Fig.143 |
| 173 Temple (6) | Tyche | | BM |
| 174 Temple (2,4,6) | Seated Hermes | | BM |
| 175 Temple (4) | Seated Apollo | | BM |
| 176 Temple (4) | Artemis, Huntress | Arcuated lintel | Fig.144 |
| 177 Temple (4) | Capitoline triad | | Fig.142 |
| 178 Temple (4) | Nero ? | | SNG Cop.235 |
| 179 Temple (2,4) | Aphrodite | | BM |
| 180 Temple (4) | Poseidon | | BM |
| 181 Temple ¾ view | Poseidon | | Fig.145 |
| 182 Arch | | Single opening | Fig.152 |
| 183 Arch | | Three openings | BM |
| 184 Conical monument on which statue | | | Fig.153 |
| 185 Lighthouse | | | Fig.147 |
| 186 Harbour | | | Fig.146 |
| 187 Agora | | | Fig.148 |
| 188 Peirene fountain | | | Figs.139,139A |
| 189 Fountain | | Meta Sudans type | Fig.113 |
| 190 Round shrine, domed Melicertes | | Among trees | Figs.150—1 |
| 191 Enclosure in which tree | | | Fig.479 |
| 192 Tomb of Lais | | | Fig.149 |
| **Sicyon** | | | |
| 193 Aedicula (2) | Artemis | | NCP pl.H.xix. |
| 194 Temple on podium | | Flanked by herms, sometimes among trees | Fig.425 |
| **Aegium** | | | |
| 195 Temple ¾ view | | With torches | BM |

| City and Buildings (Columns) | Cult or Image | Remarks | Reference |
|---|---|---|---|
| **Bura** | | | |
| 196 Hill with temple ¾ view and shrine of Heracles | | | Fig. 2 |
| 197 Arcade or portico (6) | | | Fig. 478 |
| **Cynaetha** | | | |
| 198 Hill and city | | | Fig. 1 |
| **Patras** | | | |
| 199 Temple (8) | Imperial | Tondo in pediment | Fig. 392 |
| 200 Temple (2) | Hermes | | SNG Cop. 205 |
| 201 Temple (2) | Athena | | SNG Cop. 200 |
| 202 Fountain | | | Fig. 74 |
| 203 Harbour from the sea | | | Fig. 60 |
| 204 Harbour from the land | | | Fig. 61 |
| **Zacynthus** | | | |
| 205 Temple (2) | Imperial | | Paris |
| 206 Aedicula (2) | Female and infant | | Paris |
| **Colone** | | | |
| 207 Temple (2) | | | NCP pl. GG. xxii |
| **Mothone** | | | |
| 208 Harbour | | | Fig. 484 |
| 209 Temple (2) | Asclepius and Hygieia | | Mabbott 959 (pl. 956) |
| **Gytheium** | | | |
| 210 Temple (4) | Asclepius | Half fluted columns | Fig. 4 |
| **Argos** | | | |
| 211 Round Shrine on podium | | | Fig. 45 |
| 212 Temple ¾ view | Asclepius | No architrave | NCP pl. GG. iii |
| 213 Temple on acropolis | Athena | | NCP pl. K. xliii |
| 214 Temple (2) | Leto and Choe | | Paris |
| 215 Temple ¾ view | | Possibly in antis | Fig. 404 |
| 216 Temple (2) | Hera ? | | Corinth Excavations |

253

| City and Buildings (Columns) | Cult or Image | Remarks | Reference |
|---|---|---|---|
| Epidaurus | | | |
| 217   Temple (4) | Asclepius | | Fig. 355 |
| 218   Round temple (Tholos ?) | Elpis | | Fig. 47 |
| Troezen | | | |
| 219   Round peristyle building with portico Corinthian | | | Fig. 46 |
| 220   Fountain of Heracles | | | Fig. 75 |
| 221   Temple (2) | Asclepius | | NCP pl. GG. xiv |
| 222   Acropolis | | | NCP pl. M. iii—iv |
| 223   Temple (2) | Female deity | | Paris |
| Phigaleia | | | |
| 224   Aedicula (2) in which herm | | | NCP pl. V. xi |
| **Islands** | | | |
| Tenos | | | |
| 225   Temple (2) | Poseidon and Dionysus | | JNG 1949 pl. VIII. 25 |
| Thera | | | |
| 226   Temple (4) | Apollo | Ionic capitals | Paris |
| Crete (Koinon): Gortyn? | | | |
| 227   Temple (2) | | | Svoronos pl. XXXII. 18 |
| Cnossus | | | |
| 228   Labyrinth | | | Fig. 21 |
| Cydonia | | | |
| 229   Temple (6) | | | Svoronos pl. X. 17 |
| **Pontus** | | | |
| Koinon | | | |
| 230   Temple (4) (at Amaseia ?) | | | Receuil 1 |
| 231   Temple ¾ view (at Neocaesarea ?) | | | Receuil 2a |

| City and Buildings (Columns) | Cult or Image | Remarks | Reference |
|---|---|---|---|
| **Amaseia** | | | |
| 232  View of city | | | Figs. 159,162 (Colour p.101) |
| 232A Construction of city tower | | | Fig. 159A |
| 233  Temple (4) | | Marked parotids | Fig. 164 |
| 234  Temple (4) | Serapis ? | No pediment | Receuil 41 |
| 235  Temple (2,4) | Tyche | Sometimes with arcuated lintel or without architrave | Fig. 6 |
| 236  Temple ¾ view | | | Paris |
| 237  Altar of Zeus Stratios | | | Fig. 163 |
| **Amisus** | | | |
| 238  Mountain, altar, and temple (4) | Zeus | Sometimes doors instead of temple image | Fig. 426 |
| 239  Temple (4) | Zeus ? | | Receuil 113 |
| 240  Temple (4) | Demeter | Corinthian capitals | Fig. 352 |
| 241  Temple (3) | Aphrodite | Spiral flutes | SNG von A 6749 |
| **Comana** | | | |
| 242  Temple (2,4) | Ma/Enyo | | Figs. 176,351 |
| 243  Portico (4) | | Broken pediment | Fig. 364 |
| **Neocaesarea** | | | |
| 244  Portico (5) | | | Fig. 173 |
| 245  Sanctuary gate | Ma/Zeus | Often walling between columns | Figs. 165–174 (Colour p.49) |
| 246  Temple ¾ view (4) | | Peripteral | Fig. 414 |
| 247  Temple ¾ view (4) | | Prostyle | Paris |
| 248  Temple (4) | Seated Zeus | | Fig. 175 |
| 249  Two temples | | | Fig. 178 |
| 250  Two temples ¾ view | | | Fig. 179 |
| 251  Gate (or nymphaeum) Tyche | | | Fig. 71 (Colour p.14) |
| **Sebastopolis-Heracleopolis** | | | |
| 252  Stoa | Heracles | Two tetrastyle wings and barrier | Figs. 8–9 |
| 253  Aedicula ¾ view | Heracles | | Fig. 443 |
| 254  Temple (4) | | | Receuil pl. XIV. 24 |

| City and Buildings (Columns) | Cult or Image | Remarks | Reference |
|---|---|---|---|
| **Zela** | | | |
| 255  Temple/portico (4,6) | | Sometimes with altar, trellis, broken pediment or arcuated lintel | Figs.263,330,362–3,384 (Colour p.102) |
| 256  High with walls and propylon | | | Fig.514 |
| 257  Temple (4) | Tyche | Corinthian, arcuated lintel | Berlin |
| 258  Hill with altar | | | Fig.304 |
| **Paphlagonia** | | | |
| Gangra-Germanicopolis | | | |
| 259  City buildings | | | Fig.517 |
| 260  Temple (4) | | | Receuil pl.XXII.I |
| Neoclaudiopolis | | | |
| 261  Temple (4) | | | Receuil pl.XXIII.II |
| 262  Temple (4) | Artemis Ephesia | | Receuil 13 |
| Sinope | | | |
| 263  Aedicula (2) | Apollo | | BM |
| 264  Aedicula (2) | Nemesis | | BM |
| 265  Temple (2) | Nemesis | | Receuil p..P.8 |
| **Bithynia** | | | |
| 266  Temple (4,6,8) | Rome and Augustus at Nicomedeia ? | | Fig.396 |
| 267  Temple (2) | Capitoline triad | | Receuil pl.XXXVI.7. |
| 268  Arch supporting capricorn | | | Receuil pl.XXXV.4 |
| 269  Altar (Nicaea) | Zeus | | Fig.188 |
| Bithynium | | | |
| 270  Temple (8) | Imperial | Sometimes without image | Receuil pl.XLIII.19 |
| 271  Temple ¾ view | | | Receuil pl.XLIII.10 |
| Caesareia Germanica | | | |
| 272  Temple (4) | Zeus | | SNG Cop.345 |
| 273  City walls and gate | | | Fig.513 |
| 274  Harbour | | | Fig.57 (Colour p.50) |

| City and Buildings (Columns) | Cult or Image | Remarks | Reference |
|---|---|---|---|
| **Calchedon** | | | |
| 275 Temple (4) | Apollo | Arcuated lintel | Receuil pl. XLVIII.11 |
| **Creteia Flaviopolis** | | | |
| 276 Temple (4) | Tyche | | Receuil 12 |
| 277 Temple (4) | Zeus | | Receuil pl. LIV.6 |
| 278 Temple ¾ view | Zeus | | SNG vonA 519 |
| 279 Temple (4) | | Between two statues | Receuil pl. LIII.24 |
| **Heraclea Pontica** | | | |
| 280 Temple (6) | Rome | | Fig. 7 |
| 281 Temple (4) | Zeus | Corinthian, with parotids | BM |
| 282 Lighthouse | | | Fig. 63 |
| 283 Stadium with temple of Heracles | | | Fig. 473 |
| **Juliopolis** | | | |
| 284 Temple (4) | Tyche | | Receuil pl. LXIII.24 |
| **Nicaea (cf. Koinon)** | | | |
| 285 Temple (4,6) | Tyche | | Fig. 186 |
| 286 Temple ¾ view | Tyche | | SNG vonA. 595 |
| 287 Temple ¾ view | | | Fig. 187 |
| 288 Temple (4) | Asclepius | | Receuil pl. LXXI.4 |
| 289 Temple (4) | Dionysus | | Receuil pl. LXXII.18 |
| 290 Temple (4, 6) | | | Receuil pl. LXXXIV.22 |
| 291 Two temples | | | Mabbott 1155 |
| 292 Building with pediment and statues | | 2 columns in antis | Fig. 189 |
| 293 City walls | | | Fig. 190 |
| 294 Colonnade (4,6) | | | Figs. 180–1 |
| 295 Gate or portico | | Sometimes on head of Tyche | Figs. 182–3, 496 (Colour p. 14) |
| **Nicomedia (cf. Koinon)** | | | |
| 296 Temple (6,8) | Neocorate | Corinthian | Figs. 390 |

| City and Buildings (Columns) | Cult or Image | Remarks | Reference |
|---|---|---|---|
| 297 Two temples | Neocorate | Sometimes held by Tyche or above ship | Fig. 446 |
| 298 Temple (6) | Demeter | | Receuil pl. XCI. 5 |
| 299 Temple (4) | Concordia | | Receuil pl. XCI. 28 |
| 300 Two temples and column on which Demeter | | | Receuil pl. XCV. 10 |
| 301 Three temples | | Sometimes above ship | Fig. 457 |
| 302 Three temples (one above of Demeter) | | | Fig. 456 |
| 303 Temple (4) and worshippers | | | SNG von A. 7120 |

Prusa

| | | | |
|---|---|---|---|
| 304 Temple (6) | Zeus | Corinthian | Receuil pl. CI. 35 |
| 305 Temple (6) | | Ionic | BM |
| 306 Temple (4) and two river gods | | Arcuated lintel | Receuil pl. CII. 10 |
| 307 Round temple with emperor and tree | Peripteral | | Fig. 49 (Colour p. 102) |

Prusias ad Hypium

| | | | |
|---|---|---|---|
| 308 Temple (4) | Zeus Capitolios | | NC 1967, pl. III. 1 |
| 309 Gate | | | Fig. 505 |

Tium

| | | | |
|---|---|---|---|
| 310 Temple (2) | Zeus | | Receuil pl. CX. 6 |

**Asia** (i.e. Mysia, Troas, Aeolis, Ionia, Caria, Lydia, Phrygia)

Ionian League (cf. Sardes)

| | | | |
|---|---|---|---|
| 311 Temple (6) | Imperial | | SNG von A. 7814 |

Abydus, Troas

| | | | |
|---|---|---|---|
| 312 Temple (8) | Artemis Ephesia | Sometimes without image | SNG von A. 7542 |
| 313 Temple ¾ view | | | SNG Cop. 62 |
| 314 Tower of Hero | | | Fig. 36 |
| 315 Tower | | With trumpeters and ship | Fig. 486 |

Acrasus, Lydia

| | | | |
|---|---|---|---|
| 316 Temple (6) | Artemis Ephesia | | Paris |

| City and Buildings (Columns) | Cult or Image | Remarks | Reference |
|---|---|---|---|
| **Aezani, Phrygia** | | | |
| 317 Temple (8) | | | SNG von A.3355 |
| 318 Temple (4) | Zeus | | SNG vonA.3357 |
| 319 Temple (4) | Artemis | | SNG vonA.3354 |
| **Alabanda, Caria** | | | |
| 320 Temple or large altar (4) Apollo | | | NC 1971, pl.26.21 |
| **Alexandria, Troas** | | | |
| 321 Temple (2,6) | Apollo Smintheus | | SNG vonA.1462 |
| 322 Temple ¾ view | | Prostyle | Fig.401 |
| 323 Bouleuterion | | | Fig.474 |
| 324 Top of arch | | Three openings | KlM.pl.XXX.13 |
| 325 Top of arch | | Single opening | KlM.pl.XIX.12 |
| **Alia, Phrygia** | | | |
| 326 Temple (4) | | | KlM.pl.XX.11 |
| **Amorium, Phrygia** | | | |
| 327 Temple (2,4) | Zeus | Sometimes arched lintel | BMC36 |
| 328 Temple (4) | Athena | Spiral flutes | BMC54 |
| 329 Temple (6) | | Spiral flutes | SNG vonA.3412 |
| 330 Gate in which altar (4) | | | SNG vonA.3402 |
| **Ancyra, Phrygia** | | | |
| 331 Temple (4) | Tyche | Arched lintel | SNG von A.3444 |
| **Antioch, Caria** | | | |
| 332 Bridge | | | Fig.82 (Colour p.50) |
| 333 Temple (4) | Tych | Arcuated lintel, spiral flutes | SNG Cop.37 |
| 334 Temple (4) | Athena | | SNG Cop.39 |
| 335 Temple (4) | Zeus Capitolios | Ionic | SNG vonA.2424 |
| **Apamea, Phrygia (cistophorus; cf. Ephesus and Laodicea)** | | | |
| 336 Round aedicula (4) | | With barrier | BMC 31 |

| City and Buildings (Columns) | Cult or Image | Remarks | Reference |
|---|---|---|---|
| **Aphrodisias, Caria** | | | |
| 337 Temple (2,4,8) | Aphrodite | Often arched lintel | BM |
| 338 Covered altar | Aphrodite | | Prowe Sale (1914)1173 |
| 330 Aedicula (2) | Artemis Ephesia | | SNG vonA.2435 |
| 340 Enclosure with tree | | | SNG vonA.2449 |
| **Apollonia ad Rhyndacum, Mysia** | | | |
| 341 Temple (4) | Apollo | Sometimes without cult image | Fig.350 |
| **Apollonia Salbace, Caria** | | | |
| 342 Temple (4) | Leto, Apollo, Artemis | Sometimes spiral flutes | Fig.27 |
| **Apollonis, Lydia** | | | |
| 343 Temple (4) | Dionysus | | JNG 1949,pl.II.31 |
| **Apollonos Hieron, Lydia** | | | |
| 344 Temple (6) | Apollo | Broken entablature | BM |
| **Attaea, Mysia** | | | |
| 345 Temple (4) | Zeus | | v.Fritze,pl.VI.23 |
| **Attuda, Caria** | | | |
| 346 Temple (4) | Cybele | Centre columns spiral fluted, side columns half fluted | Fig.366 |
| **Bargasa, Caria** | | | |
| 347 Temple (4) | Asclepius | Spiral flutes, arcuated lintel | SNG von A.2513 |
| **Blaundus, Lydia** | | | |
| 348 Temple (4) | Apollo | Ionic, spiral flutes | Fig.365 |
| **Bruzus, Phrygia** | | | |
| 349 Temple (4) | Zeus | Incomplete architrave | SNG vonA.3527 |
| **Cadi, Phrygia** | | | |
| 350 Temple (4) | Zeus | Spiral flutes, arched lintel | SNG von A.8390 |

| City and Building (Columns) | Cult or Image | Remarks | Reference |
|---|---|---|---|
| 351 Temple (4) | Artemis Ephesia | Sometimes with spiral flutes, arched lintel or with architrave | SNG von A. 3691 |
| **Ceramus, Caria** | | | |
| 352 Temple (4) | Zeus | | SNG von A. 2581 |
| **Ceretapa, Phrygia** | | | |
| 353 Temple (6) | | | Paris |
| **Cibyra, Phrygia** | | | |
| 354 Temple (6) | | Doric entablature, spiral flutes | Paris |
| 355 Temple (4) | | | KlM. pl. VII. 13 |
| 356 Temple (2) in which basket | | Spiral flutes | SNG von A. 3756 |
| **Cidramus, Caria** | | | |
| 357 Temple (2) | | in which veiled deity with snake | SNG von A. 2589 |
| **Cilbiani, Lydia** | | | |
| 358 Temple (6) | Artemis Ephesia | | SNG von A. 2995 |
| 359 Temple (4) | Apollo | With worshippers | Paris |
| **Colophon, Ionia** | | | |
| 360 Temple (4) | Apollo Clarios | Altar and worshippers in front | Fig. 440 |
| **Cos** | | | |
| 361 Temple (2) | Asclepius and Hygieia | | BM |
| 362 Temple (4) | Heracles Farnese | | Paris |
| **Cyme, Aeolis** | | | |
| 363 Gymnasium or sanctuary with athlete | | | Fig. 20 |
| 364 Temple (2,4) | Artemis Ephesia | Sometimes with caryatids | Fig. 13 |
| 365 Temple (6) | Isis | | Paris |
| **Cyzicus, Mysia** | | | |
| 366 Round masonry building and Persephone | | | Figs. 200–2 (Colour p. 102) |
| 367 Round aedicula | Demeter | | Fig. 208 |
| 368 Temple and round building | | | Figs. 198–9 |

| City and Building (Columns) | Cult or Image | Remarks | Reference |
|---|---|---|---|
| 369 Temple (8) | Neocorate | | SNG von A.1260 |
| 370 Temple (4) in which herm | | | Fig.210 |
| 371 Two temples | Neocorate | Sometimes held by emperor or Tyche | Fig.448 |

**Daldis, Lydia**

| | | | |
|---|---|---|---|
| 372 Temple (4) | Apollo | Arch in pediment, sometimes in rural scene | Fig.435 |

**Dardanus, Troas**

| | | | |
|---|---|---|---|
| 373 Temple (2) with sacrificial scene | | | Fig.405 |

**Dioshieron, Lydia**

| | | | |
|---|---|---|---|
| 374 Temple (4) | Zeus | Sometimes arcuated lintel | SNGFW 4856 |

**Docimeum, Phrygia**

| | | | |
|---|---|---|---|
| 375 Temple (6) | Sometimes standing figure in pediment | | SNG Cop.352 |
| 376 Temple ¾ view | | Corinthian | Fig.410 |
| 377 Two storey colonnade with equestrian statues | | | Fig.28 |

**Dorylaeum, Phrygia**

| | | | |
|---|---|---|---|
| 378 Aqueduct | | | Fig.78 |

**Ephesus, Ionia (See also Philadelphia)**

| | | | |
|---|---|---|---|
| 379 Temple (2,4,6,8) | Artemis Ephesia | | Figs.221,224,229 (Colour p.120) |
| 380 Temple ¾ view (4) | Neocorate | Corinthian | Fig.412 |
| 381 Temple (4) | Neocorate | With altar and worshippers | Fig.438 |
| 382 Two temples | | | BM |
| 383 Three temples | | | BM |
| 384 Four temples around | | Sometimes on single podium | Fig.243 |
| 385 Beacoa shrine ? | | | Fig.53 |
| 386 Round aedicula | | With barrier | BMC pl.XII.11 (See Apamea and Laodicea) |
| 387 View of City above which Jupiter Pluvius | | | Fig.518 |
| 388 View of City above which galley and Artemis Ephesia | | | Fig.520 |

| City and Building (Columns) | Cult or Image | Remarks | Reference |
|---|---|---|---|
| 389 Portable shrine drawn by horses | | | Fig. 459 |
| **Ephesus—Magnesia** | | | |
| 390 Two temples | Artemis Ephesia and Artemis Leukophryene | | BM |
| **Eresus, Lesbos** | | | |
| 391 Temple (8,11) | | | Fig. 397 |
| **Erythrae, Ionia** | | | |
| 392 Temple (4) | Heracles | | SNG Cop. 771 |
| 393 Temple (4) | Tyche | | Paris |
| **Eucarpeia, Phrygia** | | | |
| 394 Temple (4) | Tyche | | BMC. 3 |
| **Eumeneia, Phrygia** | | | |
| 395 Temple (4,6) | Artemis Ephesia | Sometimes with conical roof and spiral flutes | Figs. 32,423 (Colour p. 120) |
| 396 Temple (4) | Tyche | Spiral flutes | BMC 61 |
| 397 Temple (6) | Emperor | Spiral flutes | Paris |
| **Germe, Mysia** | | | |
| 398 Temple (4) | Apollo Citharoedus | Spiral flutes | SNG von A. 7228 |
| **Hadrianopolis, Phrygia** | | | |
| 399 Temple (4) in which oil basin | | | Fig. 342 |
| 400 Portico (4) with steps leading to altar | | | Fig. 15 |
| **Halicarnassus, Caria** | | | |
| 401 Temple (2,4) | Tyche | | SNG von A. 2535 |
| **Harpasa, Caria** | | | |
| 402 Temple (6) | Athena | Arcuated lintel | SNG von A. 2540 |
| **Heraclea ad Latmum, Ionia** (cf. Heraclea Salbace) | | | |
| 403 Temple (2) | Artemis | In antis | Fig. 343 |

| City and Building (Columns) | Cult or Image | Remarks | Reference |
|---|---|---|---|
| Heraclea Salbace, Caria | | | |
| 404 Temple (2,4) | Artemis Ephesia | | SNG Cop.405 |
| Hierapolis, Phrygia | | | |
| 405 Temple 4,6) | Apollo Citharoedus | Spiral flutes, arcuated lintel | Fig.371 |
| 406 Temple (6) | | Ionic; standing figure in pediment | Paris |
| 407 Three temples, one of emperor | | | KlM.p.241.32 |
| 408 Temple (6) | Emperor | Bust of 'Men' in pediment | Fig.389 |
| 409 Temple ¾ view | Emperor ? | | Fig.403 |
| Hierocaesarea, Lydia | | | |
| 410 Temple (4) | Artemis | | BM |
| Hypaepa, Lydia | | | |
| 411 Temple (4,6) | Artemis Anaitis | Often spiral flutes; sometimes arched lintel | Fig.382 |
| 412 Temple (4) | Tyche | | BM |
| 413 Gate in which flaming altar | | | Lyd.Stadtm.pl.IV.10 |
| Iasus, Caria | | | |
| 414 Temple (8) | | Corinthian | Munich |
| Ilium, Troas | | | |
| 415 Temple (6) | Athena | | Fig.195 |
| Julia Ipsus, Phrygia | | | |
| 416 Temple (2) | Men | | SNG von A.3680 |
| Lampsacus, Mysia | | | |
| 417 Temple (6) | Priapus | Arcuated lintel | Fig.372 |
| 418 Temple (4) | Zeus | Arcuated lintel | Vienna |
| Laodicea, Phrygia | | | |
| 419 Temple (2) in forum scene | | | Fig.23 (Colour p.31) |
| 420 Temple (8) in front of which sacrifice | | Windows in pediment | Fig.226 |
| 421 Temple (2,4,6,8) | Emperor | | Cop.SNG 573 |

| City and Building (Columns) | Cult or Image | Remarks | Reference |
|---|---|---|---|
| 422 Temple (4,6,8) | | | SNG von A.3846 |
| 423 Temple (4) | Zeus and Domitian | | BM |
| 424 Three temples | Zeus, emperor, ? Asclepius | | SNG von A.3858 |
| 425 Two temples on posia | | | SNG von A.2864 |
| 426 Aedicula (2) | Athena/Roma | Held by Tyche | SNG von A.8418 |
| 427 Round temple (6) with barrier | | | KIM 264.7 (cf. Apamea and Ephesus) |

Lesbos (Koinon) Cf. Mytilene

| | | | |
|---|---|---|---|
| 428 Temple (8) | | | SNG von A.7743 |

Maeonia, Lydia

| | | | |
|---|---|---|---|
| 429 Temple (4) | Hestia | | SNG von A.8235 |

Magnesia ad Maeandrum, Ionia (cf. Ephesus)

| | | | |
|---|---|---|---|
| 430 Temple (4) | Artemis Leukophryene | | Fig. 225 |
| 431 Shrine (2) | Leto ? | | BM |
| 432 Shrine (2) | Dionysus | | JNG 1949 pl. IX.19 |
| 433 Beacon-shrine ? | | | BM |

Magnesia ad Sipylum, Lydia

| | | | |
|---|---|---|---|
| 434 Temple (4) | Tyche | Sometimes spiral flutes or without architrave | SNG von A.3006 |
| 435 Temple (2,4) | Cybele | | Cop. SNG 272 |

Metropolis, Ionia

| | | | |
|---|---|---|---|
| 436 Temple (2,4) | Ares | Arcuated lintel | Fig. 370 |

Metropolis, Phrygia

| | | | |
|---|---|---|---|
| 437 Temple (4) | Cybele | | Paris |
| 438 Temple (4) | Zeus | Arcuated lintel | SNG von A.8424 |

Midaeum, Phrygia

| | | | |
|---|---|---|---|
| 439 Temple (4) | | | SNG von A.3890 |

Miletus, Ionia

| | | | |
|---|---|---|---|
| 440 Aedicula (4) | Apollo of Didyma | Arcuated lintel, spiral flutes | Fig. 239 |

| City and Building (Columns) | Cult or Image | Remarks | Reference |
|---|---|---|---|
| 441 Temple (6) | | | SNG Cop.1007 |
| **Mylasa, Cria** | | | |
| 442 Temple (2,4) | Zeus Labraundus | | Fig.353 |
| 443 Temple (4) | Zeus Osogoas | | Fig.332 |
| **Myrina, Aeolis** | | | |
| 444 Temple (6) | Apollo of Grynium | | Fig.386 |
| **Mytilene, Lesbos** | | | |
| 445 Temple (2,4) | Hera | | SNG Cop.416 |
| **Nacrasa, Lydia** | | | |
| 446 Temple (4) | Artemis huntress | | SNG von A.3035 |
| **Neapolis, Ionia** | | | |
| 447 Temple (4) | Apollo | | BM |
| 448 Temple (4) | Artemis Leukophryene | | ZfN 1887,44 |
| **Nysa, Lydia** | | | |
| 449 Temple (4,6) | Men Kamareites | Somtimes with arched lintel | Fig.388 |
| 450 Temple (6) | Dionysus | | Lyd.Stadtm.p.110.17 |
| 451 Colonnade (9) on which figures | | | Fig.476 |
| **Parium, Mysia** | | | |
| 452 Altar in sanctuary | Parius | | Figs.214−5 |
| 453 Altar ¾ view | | | Fig.98 |
| 454 Gate | | | Figs.211,213 |
| **Peltae, Phrygia** | | | |
| 455 Temple (2,4) | Artemis Ephesia | | BMC 23 |
| **Pergamum, Mysia** | | | |
| 456 Portico to altar court | | | Fig.217 (Colour p.119) |
| 457 Temple (2,4,6) | Rome and Augustus | | Fig.349 |
| 458 Temple (4) | Trajan and Zeus | | Fig.3 |

266

| City and Building (Columns) | Cult or Image | Remarks | Reference |
|---|---|---|---|
| 459 Temple (6) | | | Weber 5207 |
| 460 Two temples and column | | | Fig.450 |
| 461 Temple and courtyard Aphrodite Paphia | | | Fig.268 |
| 462 Temple (6) | Asclepius | | Fig.327 (Colour p.32) |
| 463 Temple (2) on high podium | Telesphoros | | Fig.337 |
| 464 Temple (4) | Seated Caracalla | | Fig.439 |
| 465 Three temples | Augustus, Caracalla, Trajan | | Fig.30 |
| 466 Three temples one above | | | Fig.454 |

**Philadelphia, Lydia**

| | | | |
|---|---|---|---|
| 467 Temple (6) | Artemis Anaitis | | BM |
| 468 Temple (2,4) | Helios | | SNG von A.3081 |
| 469 Temple (4) | Dionysus | | Paris |
| 470 Temple (10) with emperor sacrificing | | | Prague |
| 471 Temple (4) | Artemis Ephesia | Arched lintel | SNG von A.3077 |
| 472 Temple ¾ view with worshippers and Artemis Ephesia | | | Paris |
| 473 Temple (2,4) | Zeus | | SNGFW4873 |
| 474 Temple (4) | Aphrodite ? Arcuated lintel | | Paris |
| 475 Aedicula (2) | Aphrodite | Spiral flutes | Lyd.Stadtm.pl.V.14 |

**Philadelphia-Ephesus**

| | | | |
|---|---|---|---|
| 476 Temple ¾ view on high stepped podium | | | Fig.408 |

**Philomelium, Phrygia**

| | | | |
|---|---|---|---|
| 477 Temple (round?) with hexagonal court | Dionysus | | Fig.19 |
| 478 Temple (6) | Snake | Corinthian | Fig.387 |

**Pionia, Mysia**

| | | | |
|---|---|---|---|
| 479 Temple (4) | Standing Artemis ? | | SNG von A.1566 |

**Prymnessus, Phrygia**

| | | | |
|---|---|---|---|
| 480 Temple (4) | Dikaiosyne ? | | BMC 37 |

| City and Building (Columns) | Cult or Image | Remarks | Reference |
|---|---|---|---|
| **Saitta, Lydia** | | | |
| 481 Temple (4) | Aphrodite | Arcuated lintel, spiral flutes | MundM 18:vi:70,433 |
| **Samos** | | | |
| 482 Naiskos (4) | Hera | Arcuated lintel, sometimes with altar | Figs. 324,236 |
| 483 Temple (3) | Hera | Ionic | Fig. 235 |
| **Sardis, Lydia** | | | |
| 484 Temple (4,6) | Kore | | Fig. 241 |
| 485 Temple (4,6) | | | SNG von A.3137 |
| 486 Temple (6) | Emperor ? | | Fig. 380 |
| 487 Two temples ¾ view | Neocorate | | Fig. 328 (colour p.49) |
| 488 Three temples | Neocorate | | Fig. 242 |
| 489 Four temples around | Neocorate | | BM |
| 490 Four temples in a row | Neocorate | | MundM 6.vi.51,132 |
| 491 Temple and court-yard | Aphrodite Paphia | | Fig. 31 |
| 492 Altar | Zeus Lydios | | Figs. 244−5 (Colour p.49) |
| 493 City walls | | Lion in front | Fig. 519 |
| **Sibidunda, Phrygia** | | | |
| 494 Temple (2) in which baetyl | | | Lewis coll., Cambridge |
| 495 Temple (2) in which altar etc. | | | Hirsch Sale XIII,4157 |
| **Silandus, Lydia** | | | |
| 496 Temple (4) | Dionysus | | Fig. 354 |
| 497 Temple (4,6) | | | BM |
| **Smyrna, Ionia** | | | |
| 498 Temple (8) | | Parotids and statues | Fig. 326 (Colour p.32) |
| 499 Temple (4) | Tiberius | | SNG Cop. 1338 |
| 500 Two temples | Tiberius and Hadrian | | SNG von A.2248 |
| 502 Three temples | Tiberius, Roma, Hadrian | | Fig. 455 |
| 502 Three temples, two in ¾ view, in central, Roma | | | SNG von A.2224 |
| 503 Temple (4) | Tyche | | SNG von A.2190 |

| City and Building (Columns) | Cult or Image | Remarks | Reference |
|---|---|---|---|
| 504  Temples (4) | Nemesis | | BMCRE III pl.74.7 (Cistophorus) |
| 505  Temple (6) | | Held by Roma or Amazon | SNG von.A.8009 |

**Synnada, Phrygia**

| | | | |
|---|---|---|---|
| 507  Temple (8) | Dionysus | | SNG Cop.732 |
| 508  Temple (6,8) | Zeus | | SNG von A.3995 |
| 509  Temple (2) | Amaltheia | | SNG von A.3994 |
| 510  Aedicula (2), in which cippus | | Domed roof | SNG von A.3992 |
| 511  Temple (2) in which cippus | | Arched lintel | KIM pl.IX.19 |

**Teos, Ionia**

| | | | |
|---|---|---|---|
| 511A  Temple (4) | Augustus | | Fig.356 |

**Thyateira, Lydia**

| | | | |
|---|---|---|---|
| 512  Temple (4) | Apollo Tyrimnaeus | | Lyd. Stadtm. pl.VI.15 |
| 513  Temple (4) | Athena/Roma | Arched lintel | Fig.368 |

**Tiberiopolis, Phrygia**

| | | | |
|---|---|---|---|
| 514  Temple (4) | Artemis Ephesia | | BMC 19 |
| 515  Temple (4) | Tyche | | SNG von A.4031 |

**Tralles, Lydia**

| | | | |
|---|---|---|---|
| 516  Temple (4) | Zeus | Arched lintel | Fig.377 |
| 517  Temple (8,10) | | Eagle in pediment | Fig.391 |
| 518  Two temples | Emperor or Zeus | | Fig.447 |
| 519  Shrine in cave | | | BM |

**Tripolis, Lydia**

| | | | |
|---|---|---|---|
| 520  Temple (4) | Leto | | SNG von A.3327 |

**Galatia**

Ancyra (including Koinon)

| | | | |
|---|---|---|---|
| 521  Temple (8) | | | SNG von A.6142 |
| 522  Temple (4,6) | | Sometimes on stepped podium | Fig.379 |
| 523  Temple ¾ view | | Peripteral | SNG von A.6149 |

269

| City and Building (Columns) | Cult or Image | Remarks | Reference |
|---|---|---|---|
| 524 Temple ¾ view | Men | Prostyle or in antis with arched lintel | Fig. 399 |
| 525 Two temples ¾ view in which thymiateria | | No roof line | Fig. 449 |
| 526 Temple held by goddess | | | Paris |
| 527 Temple (4) | Athena | | ANS |

**Germa**

| | | | |
|---|---|---|---|
| 528 Temple (2) | Imperial | | Fig. 336 |

**Pessinus**

| | | | |
|---|---|---|---|
| 529 Temple (6) | | | ₣ SNG von A. 6208 |

**Tavium**

| | | | |
|---|---|---|---|
| 530 Temple (6) on podium | | | SNG von A. 6238 |

**Caesarea, Cappadocia (Eusebeia)**

| | | | |
|---|---|---|---|
| 531 Two towers, sanctuary and Mt. Argaeus | | | Imh. Bl. Gr. u. Rom. pl. VIII. 18 |
| 532 Temple (4) at foot of Mt Argaeus | | | SNG von A. 6498 |
| 533 Temple (2,4) | Mt. Argaeus | | Fig. 54 |
| 534 Temple (4) | | On podium | Sydenham p. 29 fig. 2 |
| 535 Temple (4) | Athena/Roma | Eagle in pediment | Paris |
| 536 Temple (6) | Neocorate | Decorated architrave, eagle in pediment | Fig. 378 |
| 537 Temple (2) | Artemis Pergaia | Sometimes with inner naiskos | Fig. 346 |
| 538 Temple (4) | Tyche | | Sydenham p. 78. 275 |
| 539 Pyramid ? | | | SNG von A. 6340 |

**Pisidia**

**Adada**

| | | | |
|---|---|---|---|
| 540 Temple (6) | Trajan | Prominent column bases | NC 1964, pl. XII. 16 |
| 541 Altar on platform | | | Arch. Anz. 1931. pl. 15. 5 |

**Andeda**

| | | | |
|---|---|---|---|
| 542 Temple (2) | Artemis Pergaia | | SNG von A. 4908 |

| City and Building (Columns) | Cult or Image | Remarks | Reference |
|---|---|---|---|
| **Antioch** | | | |
| 543 Temple (6) | Men | Barrier in front | Fig. 265 |
| 544 Aedicula (round ?) (4) | Tyche/Fortuna | | BM |
| **Apollonia Mordiacum** | | | |
| 545 Temple (8) | Emperor | | Fig. 393 |
| 546 Temple (2) | | | Paris |
| **Ariassus** | | | |
| 547 Temple (2) | Artemis Pergaia | | Fig. 331 |
| **Baris** | | | |
| 548 Temple (2) | Tyche | Scalloped design in pediment | SNG von A. 5013 |
| **Codrula** | | | |
| 549 Temple (2) | 'Dios Kotanous' | | NC 1969, 31.11 |
| **Comama** | | | |
| 550 Temple (2) | Veiled female | | Paris |
| 551 Temple (2) | Two veiled females seated | | Paris |
| **Conana** | | | |
| 552 Temple (4) | Tyche | Arched lintel | SNG von A. 5074 |
| **Cremna** | | | |
| 553 Temple and inner shrine | Luna | | Fig. 345 |
| 554 Temple (2) | Cybele | | SNG von A. 8602 |
| **Etenna** | | | |
| 555 Monument with cadueeus | | | Fig. 52 |
| **Isinda** | | | |
| 556 Aedicula (2) | Roma | | BMC 22 |
| **Lysinia** | | | |
| 557 Temple (2) | Artemis Leukophryene ? | | Vienna |

| City and Building (Columns) | Cult or Image | Remarks | Reference |
|---|---|---|---|
| **Olbasa** | | | |
| 558 Temple (2,4) | Aphrodite | | JNG 1971,pl.2,15 |
| 559 Temple in which altar or inner shrine | | | JNG 1971,pl.I.4 |
| **Pednelissus** | | | |
| 560 Temple (2) | Baetyl | | BMC 3 |
| **Pogla** | | | |
| 561 Aedicula (2) | Artemis Pergala | | SNG von A.5142 |
| **Prostanna** | | | |
| 562 Temple (2) | Men | Decorated lower columns | Paris |
| **Sagalassus** | | | |
| 563 Temple (8) in which herm | | | Fig.394 |
| 564 Sanctuary (3) with altars | Dioscuri | | Fig.256 |
| 565 Temple (2,4) | Tyche | Sometimes with arched lintel or with figure and mountain on architrave | Fig.360 |
| **Claudioseleuceia** | | | |
| 566 Temple (2) | Snake on base | Altar outside | Fig.428 |
| **Selge** | | | |
| 567 Sanctuary on platform with two trees and altars | | | Figs.252—3,261—2,(Colour p.154) |
| 568 Temple in which round object | | | Fig.259 |
| 569 Temple (2) | Artemis Pergaia | | SNGFW5199 |
| **Termessus** | | | |
| 570 Temple (2) | | | SNG von A.5344 |
| 571 Aedicula (2) | Emperor | Spiral flutes, Ionic | SNG von A.5357 |
| **Timbriada** | | | |
| 572 Temples (2.4) | Tyche | BM | |
| **Tityassus** | | | |
| 573 Temple (4) | Cybele | Grills between outer columns Ionic, often snake in pediment | SNG von A.5375 |

272

| City and Building (Columns) | Cult or Image | Remarks | Reference |
|---|---|---|---|
| **Isaura** | | | |
| 574 Gate in which Tyche seated | | | Fig. 502 |
| 575 Temple (4) | Tyche | | Paris |
| 576 Temple in which bust on column (4) | | Spiral flutes | SNG von A. 5412 |
| 577 Temple (4) | | | Paris |
| **Lycia** | | | |
| **Acalissus** | | | |
| 578 Temple (2) | Female deity | | vA MinL. pl. I. 3 |
| **Aperlae** | | | |
| 579 Altar in court | | | Fig. 18, 18A |
| 580 Portico (4) in which altar | | | Fig. 17 |
| **Gagae** | | | |
| 581 Temple (2) | Two images, one holding Nike | | vA MinL pl. 4. 56 |
| **Myra (including Koinon)** | | | |
| 582 Temple (2,4) | Aretmis | Sometimes spiral flutes | Fig. 333 |
| 583 Enclosure with column | | | vA Min L pl. 10. 169 |
| **Patara** | | | |
| 584 Temple (2) | Zeus | | vA MinL pl. 13. 217 |
| 585 Aedicula (4) | Tyche | Canopy supported by figures | Fig. 424 |
| 586 Two columns on which statues supporting arch | | | vA MinL pl. 13. 233 |
| **Patara-Myra** | | | |
| 587 Temple (2) | Zeus and Artemis | | vA MinL pl. 14. 258 |
| **Pamphylia** | | | |
| **Aspendus** | | | |
| 588 Temple (4) | Serapis ? | | Fig. 381 |
| 589 Temple (4) | Two images | Spiral flutes | BMC pl. XXII. 1 |
| 590 Two aediculae | | | BMC 79 |
| 591 Temple (4) | Cybelc | | ANS |

| City and Building (Columns) | Cult or Image | Remarks | Reference |
|---|---|---|---|
| **Attalea** | | | |
| 592 Temple (2,4,6) | Athena | | SNG von A.4618 |
| 593 Temple (2) | Artemis Pergaia | | SNG von A.4627 |
| **Perga** | | | |
| 594 Temple (2,4) | Artemis Pergaia | Sometimes with inner columns | Fig. 334, 344 |
| 595 Temple (2) | Tyche | | SNG von A.4750 |
| 596 Temple (2) in which eagle, with standards | | | Fig. 338 |
| **Side** | | | |
| 597 Temple (4,6) | Apollo | Sometimes held by Tyche | BM |
| 598 Temple ¾ view | Apollo | Arched lintel | Fig. 407 |
| 599 Temple (2,4) | Athena/Roma | Sometiems held by Tyche | BMC 87 |
| 600 Temple (2) | Eagle and standards | | SNG Cop. 432 |
| 601 Temple (2) | Three images | Inner shrine | Naville Sale XVII.1542 |
| 602 Gate in which victory crowning standards | | | Fig. 503 |
| 603 Aedicula (round ?) | Tyche | Arched lintel, conical roof | Fig. 470 |
| 604 Harbour | | | Fig. 481 |
| 605 Three temples | | | Fig. 453 |
| **Cilicia** | | | |
| **Adana** | | | |
| 606 Aedicula (2) | Seated Tyche | | BM |
| **Aegeae** | | | |
| 607 Temple (4,6,8) | Asclepius | Corinthian, sometimes arched lintel | Fig. 395 |
| 608 Temple (4) | | Eagle in pediment | Ann. Soc. Num. VIII.1884,149–51 |
| 609 Temple (2) | Seated Tyche | | ANS |
| 610 Temple ¾ view | | Arched lintel | Fig. 406 |
| 611 Aedicula (2) | Eagle | | BM |
| 612 Walls and gate of Thebe with Cadmus | | | Fig. 35 |
| 613 Lighthouse | | | Fig. 66,485 |
| **Anazarbus** | | | |
| 614 Temple (7,8,10) | | | SNG von A.5499 |

| City and Building (Columns) | Cult or Image | Remarks | Reference |
|---|---|---|---|
| 615 Shrine drawn by elephants | | | Fig. 461 |
| 616 Temple (6) | Emperor | | SNG von A. 5495 |
| 617 Temple ¾ view | | | Paris |
| 618 Tripartite shrine | | Sometimes central part only | Figs. 429–32 |
| 619 Two temples | | | SNG FW 5227 |
| 620 Temple (2) | | Spiral flutes | Paris |
| 621 Acropolis and buildings | | Head of Zeus in front | Fig. 516 |
| 622 Aqueduct | | | Fig. 81 (Colour p. 50) |
| 623 Temple (2,4) | Seated Tyche | Arched lintel | Fig. 339 |

Anemurium

| | | | |
|---|---|---|---|
| 624 Temple (2,4) | Tyche | Sometimes spiral flutes or arched lintel | SNG von A. 5529 |

Antioch

| | | | |
|---|---|---|---|
| 625 Temple (4) | Tyche | Arched lintel | SNG Cop. 67 |

Carallia

| | | | |
|---|---|---|---|
| 626 Temple (2) | Tyche | | SNG von A. 5608 |

Colybrassus

| | | | |
|---|---|---|---|
| 627 Temple (4) | Zeus | | BMC14 |
| 628 Temple (4) | Oil Basin | 'Gymnasiarchia' | Fig. 357 |
| 629 Temple (4) | Roma | | SNG von A. 5664 |

Coropissus

| | | | |
|---|---|---|---|
| 630 Temple (2,4) | Seated Tyche | | SNG von A. 5675 |

Diocaesarea

| | | | |
|---|---|---|---|
| 631 Temple (6) | Zeus | Altar sometimes to left | Fig. 385 |
| 632 Gate | | | Fig. 507 |

Germanicopolis

| | | | |
|---|---|---|---|
| 633 Temple | Seated Tyche | | Paris |

| City and Building (Columns) | Cult or Image | Remarks | Reference |
|---|---|---|---|
| **Hierapolis Castabala** | | | |
| 634    Temple (4) | | | Robert pl. XXIX. 105 |
| 635    Aedicula (2) | Tyche | | Robert pl. XIX. 108 |
| **Lamus** | | | |
| 636    Temple (4) | | | Paris |
| **Lyrbe** | | | |
| 637    Enclosure, baetyl, and tree | | | SNG von A. 5697 |
| **Mallus** | | | |
| 638    Temple (4) | Nemesis | | BM |
| **Mopsus** | | | |
| 639    Bridge | | | Fig. 83 |
| **Ninica** | | | |
| 640    Temple (4) | Emperor | | BMC 9 |
| 641    Temple ¾ view | | | Paris |
| **Olba** | | | |
| 642    Tower | | | Fig. 487 |
| **Philadelphia** | | | |
| 643    Temple (2) | Eagle | | SNG von A. 5800 |
| **Seleuceia ad Calycadnum** | | | |
| 644    Temple (4) | Artemis Pergaia | | Paris |
| 645    Aedicula (2) | Seated Tyche | | KlM pl. XX. 24 |
| 646    Altar and two standards | | | Imh. Bl., Gr. u Rom. pl. VIII. 8 |
| **Selinus** | | | |
| 647    Temple (4) | Trajan | | BMC 1 |
| **Soli-Pompeiopolis** | | | |
| 648    Harbour | | | Fig. 483 |

| City and Building (Columns) | Cult or Image | Remarks | Reference |
|---|---|---|---|
| **Tarsus** | | | |
| 649 City walls | | | Fig. 94 |
| 650 Shrine of Ana | | | Fig. 96 |
| 651 Temple (10) | Neocorate | | SNG von A. 5981 |
| 652 Two temples | Neocorate | Sometimes held by Tyche | SNG von A. 5996 |
| 653 Two temples ¾ view | Neocorate | Tyche steated between | NC 1925, 315, 18 |
| 654 Temple (4) | | Tyche seated to right; no lintel | Paris |
| 655 Temple (4) | Seated Tyche | No architrave | SNG von. A. 6055 |
| 656 Temple (6) | Heracles and Asclepius? | | Hunter |
| 657 Temple (4) | Aphrodite | | Mabbott Sale 2236 |
| 658 Temple (4) | Vase | Grills between outer columns | BMC 139 |
| 659 Temple (4) | Perseus | | Paris |
| 660 Temple (4) | Apollp Pythios | | BM |
| 661 Temple ¾ view | Apollo Lykios | | BM |
| 662 Temple ¾ view and emperor | | | Paris |
| 663 Monument of Sandan | | | Fig. 97 |
| 664 Aedieula (2) | Sandan | | BM |
| 665 Aedicula (2) | Julia Domna | | Paris |
| 666 Gate | | | Fig. 511 |
| | | | |
| **Titiopolis** | | | |
| 667 Aedicula (2) | Tyche | | BMC 1 |
| | | | |
| **Elaeusa-Sebaste** | | | |
| 668 Aedicula (2) | Figure on globe | | KlM pl. XVII. 4 |
| | | | |
| | | | |
| **Cyprus** | | | |
| **Koinon** | | | |
| 669 Temple (4) | Tyche | Stairs in front; arcuated lintel | Fig. 369 |
| | | | |
| **(Paphos)** | | | |
| 670 Temple and colonnades | Aphrodite | Courtyard in front | Fig. 266 (Colour p. 154) |

| City and Buildings (Columns) | Cult or Image | Remarks | Reference |
|---|---|---|---|
| **Commagene** | | | |
| Samosata | | | |
| 671 Temple | Seated Tyche | | Vienna |
| Zeugma | | | |
| 672 Temple on hill | Zeus Katabaites | | Fig. 22 |
| **Syria** | | | |
| **Cyrrhestica** – Cyrrhus | | | |
| 673 Temple (6) | Zeus | | SNG Cop. 49 |
| Hierapolis Bambyce | | | |
| 674 Temple (2) | Hadad ? | | Fig. 95 |
| 675 Temple (2) | Standard | Figures of Hadad and Atargatis | Fig. 293 |
| **Chalcidice** – Chalcis | | | |
| 676 Aedicula ¾ view | Helios | | Fig. 444 |
| **Pieria** – Antioch | | | |
| 677 Portable shrine (4) | Seated Tyche | | Fig. 42 |
| Balanea (Leucas) | | | |
| 678 Aedicula (4) | Astarte/Tyche | Domed | ANS |
| Emisa | | | |
| 679 Temple (6) | Elagabal | | Figs. 296–8 |
| 680 Temple ¾ view | Elagabal | | Fig. 299 |
| 681 Altar | | | Fig. 301 |
| Gabala | | | |
| 682 Aedicula (2) | Roma | | BMC 10 |
| 683 Aedicula (2) | Astarte/Tyche | | ANS |
| 684 Aedicula (2) | Julia Domna | | Paris |
| Laodicea ad Mare | | | |
| 685 Lighthouse | | | Fig. 65 |

| City and Building (Columns) | Cult or Image | Remarks | Reference |
|---|---|---|---|
| 686 Aedicula (2) | Eagle | | BMC 95 |
| 687 Aedicula (2,4) | Astarte/Tyche | Spiral flutes | SNG Cop.358 |
| 688 Aedicula (2) | Julia Domna | | Fig.469 |

Nicopolis

| | | | |
|---|---|---|---|
| 689 Aedicula (2) | Nemesis ? | Spiral flutes | BMC 2 |

Paltus

| | | | |
|---|---|---|---|
| 690 Portable shrine | | | Fig.462 |
| 691 Temple (2) | Athena | | Paris |
| 692 Temple (4) | Astarte/Tyche | | BM |

Seleucia

| | | | |
|---|---|---|---|
| 693 Temple (2) | Astarte/Tyche | | Paris |
| 694 Temple (4) | Zeus Kasios | | BM |
| 695 Aedicula ¾ view | Zeus Kasios | | Fig.445 |

**Coele Syria** – Damascus

| | | | |
|---|---|---|---|
| 696 Three temples in lower of which Tyche | | | Fig.452 |
| 697 Temple (4) and river grotto  Marsyas (sometimes Hadad ?) | | | Fig.433 |
| 698 Temple ¾ view and river | | | Fig.413 |
| 699 Temple (4) | Astarte/Tyche | Arched lintel, sometimes with shell in pediment | Fig.43 |
| 700 Aedicula (2,4) | Astarte/Tyche | Sometimes with ram on plinth with carry bars | Fig.467 |

Heliopolis

| | | | |
|---|---|---|---|
| 701 Temple (10) | Hadad/Zeus | | Fig.280 |
| 702 Temple ¾ view | Hadad/Zeus | | Figs. 279,290 (Colour p.171) |
| 703 Temple and sanctuary ¾ view | Simios/Hermes | | Fig.282 (Colour p.171) |
| 704 Two temples | | | Fig.281 |
| 705 Portico with towers | | | Fig.284 |
| 706 Temple (4) | Astarte/Venus | | Rhein.Mus.f.Philol.1914 p.144 fig.6 |

| City and Building (Columns) | Cult or Image | Remarks | Reference |
|---|---|---|---|
| **Phoenicia** – Aradus | | | |
| 707    Aedicula (2) | Astarte/Tyche | | Fig. 340 |
| Berytus | | | |
| 708    Temple (4,6) | Poseidon | | SNG Cop. 113 |
| 709    Temple (4) | Astarte/Tyche | | Fig. 275 |
| 710    Gate in which Marsyas | | | Fig. 276 |
| 711    Lighthouse | | | Fig. 64 |
| Botrys | | | |
| 712    Temple (6,8) | Astarte/Tyche | | SNG Cop. 131 |
| Byblos | | | |
| 713 Sanctuary with baetyl | | | Fig. 271 (Colour p. 153) |
| 714    Temple (6) | Astarte/Tyche | Sometimes with flat roof actuated lintel | Fig. 375 |
| 715    Aedicula (round ?) (2,4) | Astarte/Tyche | Sometimes conical roof | SNG Cop. 147 |
| Caesarea ad Libanum | | | |
| 716    Temple (4) | Astarte/Tyche | | BMC 8 |
| 717    Aedicula (2) | Astarte/Tyche | Caryatids | Fig. 14 |
| Dora | | | |
| 718    Temple (4) | Astarte/Tyche | | BM |
| Orthosia | | | |
| 719    Temple (4) | Astarte/Tyche | Sometimes arched lintel | Fig. 376 |
| Ptolemais | | | |
| 720    Acropolis and buildings | | | Fig. 515 |
| 721    Temple (4,6,8) | Astarte/Tyche | | SN Cop. 184 |
| 722    Temple (4) | Serapis, Isis, Astarte/Tyche | | |
| 723    Portable Shrine (2) | Hadad/Zeus | | Fig. 463 |
| 724    Portable shrine ¾ view | Hadad/Zeus | | de Saulcy pl. VIII. 10 |
| 725    Aedicula (2) | Aphrodite | | BM |
| 726    Two tower/altars and tree | | | CNP IV pl. XVI. 226 |
| 727    Sanctuary with portico and temple (nymphaeum) | | | Fig. 73 |
| 728    Harbour | | | Fig. 480 |

| City and Building (Columns) | Cult or Image | Remarks | Reference |
|---|---|---|---|
| **Sidon** | | | |
| 729 City walls and slipway | | | Fig. 93 |
| 729A Stepped pyramid ? | | | ANS MN 1976,13. |
| 730 Temple and sanctuary | Astarte | | Fig. 277 (Colour p.13) |
| 731 Temple (4,6) | Astarte/Tyche | | Fig. 361 |
| 732 Temple, altar, and columns | | | Fig. 359 |
| 733 Temple (4) | Dionysus (probably Astarte) | | JNG 1949,96,648 |
| **Tripolis** | | | |
| 734 Tripartite temple | Astarte/Tyche | Central aedicula and 4 columns on each wing | Fig. 420 |
| 735 Tripartite temple and facade (4) | Astarte/Tyche | | Ashmolean |
| 736 Aedicula (2) | Astarte/Tyche | | SNG Cop. 286 |
| 737 Flat roofed shrine | Astarte/Tyche | | BMC 139 |
| 738 Gate to Sanctuary (4) | Zeus Hagios | | SNG Cop. 288 |
| 739 Temple and gate | Zeus Hagios | | Fig. 238 (Colour p. 32) |
| 740 Temple (4) | Emperor | With parotids | Paris |
| **Tyre** | | | |
| 741 Temple (8) | | | BMC 361 |
| 742 Temple ¾ view | Melkart | | Fig. 415 |
| 743 Temple (4,6) | Astarte/Tyche | Sometimes with altar and palm tree in front | Fig. 237,373 |
| 744 Temple (2) and worshippers | Astarte/Tyche and Marsyas | | ANS |
| 745 Aedicula (4) | With smaller aedicula and statues on pedestals within, caryatids support canopy | | Fig. 329 (Colour p.102) |
| 746 Portable shrine (2) ¾ view in which celestial images | | | Figs. 40,464−5 |
| 747 Portable aedicula (2) Astarte/Tyche | | | Fig. 468 |
| 748 Walls and gate of Carthage, and Dido | | | Fig. 34 |
| 749 Walls and gate of Thebes, and Cadmus | | | Babelon, Perses 2341 |
| 750 Fountain house | Oceanus | | ANS |
| **Trachonitis** − Caesarea Panias | | | |
| 751 Sanctuary of Pan | | | Figs. 10−12 |
| 752 Temple (4) | Astarte/Tyche | | BM |

| City and Building (Columns) | Cult or Image | Remarks | Reference |
|---|---|---|---|
| 753 Temple (6) | Athena | | de Saulcy pl.XVIII.4 |
| 754 Temple (4) | Zeus | | ANS |
| 755 (Herod Philip II) Temple (4) | Sun Disc | Unusual inset podium | Fig.358 |
| 756 (Herod Agrippa I) Temple (2) | Female deities | | Meshorer pl.XII.89 |
| 757 Temple (6) on podium | Claudius ? | | de Saulcy pl.XVIII.3 |
| 758 Temple (2) on podium | Agrippina ? | | de Saulcy pl.XVIII.3 |

**Decapolis — Abila**

| | | | |
|---|---|---|---|
| 759 Gate and towers in which altar | | | Fig.258 |
| 760 Temple (2,4) | Astarte/Tyche | | de Saulcy pl.XVI.5 |

Antiochia ad Hippum

| | | | |
|---|---|---|---|
| 761 Temple (4) | Zeus Arotesios | | BM |

Capetolias

| | | | |
|---|---|---|---|
| 762 Temple (8,10) | Zeus | | BM |
| 763 Gate and towers in which temple of Zeus | | | Fig.285 (Colour p.13) |
| 764 Temple (4,6) | Astarte/Tyche | | de Saulcy pl.XVI.9 |

Dium

| | | | |
|---|---|---|---|
| 765 Gate (6) in which altar | | Arched lintel | Fig.374 |

Gadara

| | | | |
|---|---|---|---|
| 766 Temple (2,4) | Zeus | Corinthian | de Saulcy pl.XV.4 |
| 767 Aedicula (2) | Astarte/Tyche | | Paris |

Pella

| | | | |
|---|---|---|---|
| 768 Town and temple on mountain | | | Fig.56 (Colour p.172) |
| 769 Temple (4) | Asclepius ? | | de Saulcy pl. XVI.8 |
| 770 Nymphaeum | | | Fig.72 |

| City and Building (Columns) | Cult or Image | Remarks | Reference |
|---|---|---|---|
| **Galilee** – Gaba | | | |
| 771  Temple (4) | Astarte/Tyche | Domed roof | BM |
| | | | |
| Diocaesareia (Sepphoris) | | | |
| 772  Temple (4) | Zeus | | BMC 26 |
| 773  Temple, tripartie | Zeus | | de Saulcy pl. XVII.5 |
| 774  Temple (4) | Astarte/Tyche | | de Saulcy pl. XVII.6 |
| 775  Two temples | | | Vienna |
| | | | |
| Tiberias | | | |
| 776  Temple (4) | Zeus/Hadrian ? | | de Saulcy pl. XVII.12 |
| | | | |
| **Samaria** – Antipatris | | | |
| 777  Temple (4) | Astarte/Tyche | | ANS |
| | | | |
| Caesarea Maritima | | | |
| 778  Temple (4) | Astarte/Tyche | Sometimes colonnade and altar in front | Fig. 367 |
| 779  Temple (6) in which altar | | | CNP. II pl. VIII.93 |
| 780  Altar | | (Sometimes like Cyzicus no. 366) | CNP. II pl. VIII. 229–230 |
| | | | |
| Diospolis | | | |
| 781  Aedicula (4) | Astarte/Tyche | | BM |
| | | | |
| Neapolis | | | |
| 782  Temple and buildings on Mt. Gerizim | | | Figs. 302–3 (Colour p.172) |
| 783  Two temples and Mt. Gerizim | | | BMC 159 |
| 784  Temple (2,4) | Astarte/Tyche | Arched lintel | Fig. 422 |
| | | | |
| Nysa-Skythopolis | | | |
| 785  Temple  (4) | Astarte/Tyche | Corinthian | ANS |
| | | | |
| Sebaste | | | |
| 786  Temple (4) | Capitoline  triad | | BMC 12 |
| 787  Temple (4) | Astarte/Tyche | | ANS |

| City and Building (Columns) | Cult or Image | Remarks | Reference |
|---|---|---|---|
| **Judaea — Jerusalem** (Aelia Capitolina) | | | |
| 788   Temple (4,6) | Astarte/Tyche | | Fig.311 |
| 789   Temple (4,2) | Capitoline triad (sometimes Zeus alone) | | Fig.312 |
| 790   Temple (4) | Jehovah | Flat roof | Fig.306 |
| Agrippias (Anthedon) | | | |
| 791   Temple (4) | Astarte/Tyche | Domed roof | Paris |
| Ascalon | | | |
| 792   Temple (2) | | Flat roof, inner shrine | Fig.465 |
| Eleutheropolis | | | |
| 793   Temple (4) | Astarte/Tyche | Arched lintel | BM |
| Gaza | | | |
| 794   Gate in which owl (AR) | | | BM |
| 794A  City walls (copied from Sidon) | | | BM |
| 795   Temple (2) or gate | Marnas and Io | | BM |
| 796   Temple (4,6) | Astarte/Tyche | | BM |
| Nicopolis | | | |
| 797   Temple (4) | Astarte/Tyche | | ANS |
| **Arabia** | | | |
| Adraa | | | |
| 798   Aedicula (2,4) | Astarte/Tyche | | ANS |
| 799   Altar of Dusares | | | Fig.442 |
| Bostra | | | |
| 800   Temple (2,4) | Astarte/Tyche | | BM |
| 801   Temple (2) | Athena/Roma | | BM |
| 802   Temple (2) | Dusares/Dionysus | | BM |
| 803   Altar of piled stones (Dusares) | | | BM |
| 804   Altar of Dusares on terrace ¾ view | | | Fig.257 |

284

| City and Building (Columns) | Cult or Image | Remarks | Reference |
|---|---|---|---|
| Charachmoba | | | |
| 805 Altar on terrace | | | BMC 3 |
| Esbous | | | |
| 806 Temple (4) | Astarte/Tyche | | BM |
| Petra | | | |
| 807 Temple (2,4) | Tyche | | Berytus 1947, pl.XIV.1−4 |
| Philadelphia | | | |
| 808 Processional shrine drawn by horses | | | BM |
| **Mesopotamia** | | | |
| Carrhae | | | |
| 809 Temple (4) in which baetyl and standards in inner shrine | | | Fig.418 |
| 810 Altar with steps | | | ANS |
| Edessa | | | |
| 811 Temple (2) or altar with pediment | | | Paris |
| 812 Temple ¾ view in which baetyl | | | BM |
| 813 Temple (2) in which shrine | | | Fig.347 |
| 814 Podium on which two figures | | | Paris |
| Nesibis | | | |
| 815 Temple (4) | Tyche | Head of Helios in pediment, and windowed pilasters | Fig.417 |
| 816 Aedicula (2) | Tyche | Spiral flutes | BM |
| 817 Temple ¾ view | | | Paris |
| Rhesaena | | | |
| 818 Temple ¾ view | Eagle | Sometimes without roof | SNG Cop.245−6 |
| Rabathmoda | | | |
| 819 Temple (4) as statue base of Hadad/Ares | | | Fig.419 |
| **Parthia** | | | |
| 820 City walls | | | BM |

| City and Buildings (Columns) | Cult or Image | Remarks | Reference |
|---|---|---|---|
| 821 Aedicula (2) | Zeus seated | | BM |
| 822 Aedicula (2) | Zeus standing | | BM |

**Persis**

| | | | |
|---|---|---|---|
| 823 Altar shrine | | | Figs. 50–51 |

**India**

Bactra ?

| | | | |
|---|---|---|---|
| 824 Enclosure with tree | | | BM |
| 825 Stupa ¾ view with colonnade | | | Fig. 99 |
| 826 Shrine (2) | Female deity | | BM |
| 827 Shrine with three figures | | | BM |

**Taxila**

| | | | |
|---|---|---|---|
| 828 Enclosure with tree | | | BM |

**Egypt**

Alexandria

| | | | |
|---|---|---|---|
| 829 Pharos | | | Fig. 313 |
| 830 Temple (2,4) | Serapis (Sometimes with Isis and other figures) | | Dattari pl. XXX. 1154 |
| 831 Temple with 3 doors | Serapis | | Fig. 318 |
| 832 Temple (2) | Serapis | One or two inner shrines or stelai | Fig. 348 |
| 833 Temple (2) | Harpocrates | | Fig. 492 |
| 834 Temple (2) | Canopi | | Fig. 493 |
| 835 Temple (2,4) | Zeus/Serapis | | Dattari pl. XXX. 1157 |
| 836 Temple (2) | Tyche reclining | | Dattari pl. XXX. 3062 |
| 837 Altar gate | Tyche (sometimes with snake) | | Fig. 16 |
| 838 Single arch | | | Fig. 33 |
| 839 Triple arch | | With pediment and sometimes with windows | Fig. 89 |
| 840 Temple (2) | Sacred boat | | Dattari pl. XXX. 1158 |
| 841 Shrine carried by sacred boat, in which xoanon | | | Dattari pl. XXVII. 3557 |
| 842 Temple (2) | Nemesis (griffin) | Barrel vault ? | Fig. 494 |

| City and Building (Columns) | Cult or Image | Remarks | Reference |
|---|---|---|---|
| 843 Temple (2) | Tyche | | Dattari pl. XXX. 3061 |
| 844 Temple (2,4) | Nile | | Dattari pl. XXIX. 3801 |
| 845 Temple (2) | Hermanubis | | Dattari pl. XXXIX. 1138 |
| 846 Temple (2) | 'Demeter' | | Dattari pl. XXIX. 1133 |
| 847 Kiosk | Heracles | | Dattari pl. XXIX. 1136 |
| 848 Temple (2) | Elpis | | Dattari pl. XXIX. 3030 |
| 349 Temple (2,4) | Athena/Roma | | Dattari pl. XXIX. 1131 |
| 850 Fountain with statues on high podium | | | Fig. 488 |
| 851 Fountain with Heracles | | | Fig. 77 |
| 852 Pylon | Isis | | Fig. 509 |
| 853 Pylon | Canopus | | Dattari pl. XXX. 1167 |
| 854 Portable shrine | Canopi | | Dattari pl. XXIX. 1132 |
| 855 Round temple | Mars Ultor (copied from Cistophorus) | | Dattari pl. XXIX. 14 |
| 856 Nilometer | | Domed top | Figs. 321−2 |
| 857 Gate ? | | Possibly a couch | JEA 1961. 119−133 |

Aphroditepolite Nome

| | | | |
|---|---|---|---|
| 858 Temple (2) | Isis (between cats or birds on pedestals) | Barrel vault ? | Fig. 489, 491 |

Heracleopolite Nome

| | | | |
|---|---|---|---|
| 859 Temple (2) | Heracles | Flat roof decorated with Uraei | Fig. 510 |

Hermopolite Nome

| | | | |
|---|---|---|---|
| 860 Aedicula (2) | Thoth | | Dattari pl. XXIV. 6269 |

Menelaite Nome

| | | | |
|---|---|---|---|
| 861 Columned altar ? with uraei | Harpocrates | | Dattari pl. XXXIV. 6309 |

**Cyrene**

| | | | |
|---|---|---|---|
| 862 Tomb of Batus | | Pyramid surmounted by column | BM. |

The index incorporates references both to the text and to the illustrations. It does not list details of all buildings given in the catalogue (pp.241–287); but page references are given to cities to be found in the bibliography (Bibl.) and Catalogue (Cat.).

291

295

297

298